GENERAL LEGISLATION
IN THE
NEW CODE OF CANON LAW

GENERAL NORMS. (Can. 1-86.)
ECCLESIASTICAL PERSONS IN GENERAL.
(Can. 87-214.)

BY

VERY REV. H. A. AYRINHAC, S.S., D.D., D.C.L.
President of St. Patrick's Seminary, Menlo Park, Cal.
Professor of Moral Theology and Canon Law

NEW YORK
BLASE BENZIGER & CO., INC.
1923

Nihil Obstat.

ARTHUR J. SCANLAN, S.T.D.,
Censor Librorum

Imprimatur.

PATRICK J. HAYES, D.D.,
Archbishop of New York

NEW YORK, JULY 12, 1922.

GENERAL LEGISLATION IN THE NEW CODE OF CANON LAW

BY THE SAME AUTHOR

MARRIAGE LEGISLATION IN THE NEW CODE OF CANON LAW. *Net* $2.50.

PENAL LEGISLATION IN THE NEW CODE OF CANON LAW. *Net* $3.00.

TO

THE MOST REVEREND

EDWARD JOSEPH HANNA, D.D.

ARCHBISHOP OF SAN FRANCISCO

PROMOTER OF CLERICAL SCHOLARSHIP AND

CANONICAL DISCIPLINE

FOREWORD

This volume includes, after a general introduction to the study of canon law, a brief explanation of the first book of the Code and of the first section of the second book. The first book contains what the Code calls "General Norms"; to it is added here the first section of the second, which treats of Ecclesiastical Persons in general, partly because of its character and partly for the sake of convenience.

At the very outset of his work the legislator gives us certain rules for its interpretation, and he lays down the principles which govern the application of its various provisions; a careful study of these fundamental notions is clearly indispensable for the correct understanding of what follows.

Of the first six canons of the Code it was said that they stretch their tentacles to the other twenty-four hundred, changing many of them beyond recognition, and that any one who would master thoroughly these preliminary enactments would have overcome half of the difficulty of interpreting the new legislation. But it was stated at the same time that canonists would need a long time to assimilate them and apply them with a fair amount of accuracy to individual cases. In fact, several of the first applications made even by experienced canonists were rejected soon after by the Roman authorities. (Holy Office, March 20-22, 1918; Cong. of Religious, July 15, 1919; Cong. of the Council, Jan. 10, 1920.)

There still remain, no doubt, not a few obscure points, but many have been cleared up already by decisions of Congregations or of the Pontifical Commission for the Interpretation of the Code and by the Commentaries of canonists, some of whom had an important share in the framing of the law.

With these guides to show the way it may, perhaps, not be rash to hope that pitfalls into which others have fallen will be avoided and that these explanations will prove reliable and helpful. They follow strictly the order of the Code and, in conformity with instructions of the Congregation of Seminaries and Universities (Aug. 7, 1917), they endeavor to combine, in some measure at least, the historical with the positive method, to point out in a few words the origin and chief developments of the discipline, and to give a full exposition of all the prescriptions now in force, whether considered in themselves or in their mutual relations.

CONTENTS

BOOK I

GENERAL NORMS

(Can. 1-86)

PRELIMINARY CANONS

(Can. 1-7)

TITLE I

OF ECCLESIASTICAL LAWS

(Can. 8-24)

TITLE II

OF CUSTOM

(Can. 25-30)

TITLE III
OF THE COMPUTATION OF TIME
(Can. 31-35)

TITLE IV
ON RESCRIPTS
(Can. 36-62)

TITLE V

ON PRIVILEGES

(Can. 63-79)

TITLE VI

ON DISPENSATIONS

(Can. 80-86)

PART I

THE CLERGY

Section I.

ON THE CLERGY IN GENERAL

(Can. 108-214)

TITLE I

AFFILIATION OF CLERICS WITH, OR INCARDINATION IN, A DIOCESE

(Can. 111-117)

TITLE II

RIGHTS AND PRIVILEGES OF CLERICS

(Can. 118-123)

TITLE III
ON THE OBLIGATIONS OF CLERICS
(Can. 124-144)

TITLE IV
ON ECCLESIASTICAL OFFICES
(Can. 145-195)

CHAPTER I.
APPOINTMENT TO ECCLESIASTICAL OFFICES
(Can. 147-182)

ARTICLE I

ON FREE APPOINTMENT OR COLLATION

ARTICLE II

ON ELECTION

ARTICLE III

ON POSTULATION

CHAPTER II

LOSS OF ECCLESIASTICAL OFFICES

(Can. 183-195)

TITLE V

ORDINARY AND DELEGATED POWER

(Can. 196-210)

TITLE VI

RETURN OF CLERICS TO THE LAY STATE

(Can. 211-214)

GENERAL LEGISLATION IN THE NEW CODE OF CANON LAW

INTRODUCTION

I. NAME, DEFINITION, DIVISIONS OF CANON LAW

1. *Name.* The body of laws which constitute the Church's legislation is designated by various names: ecclesiastical law, pontifical law, decretal law, and principally canon law. (F. X. Wernz, Jus Decretalium, I, n. 49, Romae, 1905.)

The word *canon,* which in classical Greek had several meanings, acquired at a very early date an exclusive ecclesiastical significance, and was used in the sense of *rule.* (Gal. vi. 16.) At first it was applied to the general rule designed to control the whole Christian life, including faith, morals, and discipline; but the Council of Nicaea used the word to designate particularly the *disciplinary* regulations, and it is in this sense that it was used thereafter till the Council of Trent. This Council, on the contrary, called canons the *dogmatic* definitions.

The expression *canon law, jus canonicum,* as opposed to *jus civile,* seems to have become current about the middle of the twelfth century; but long before that the expressions, canons, canonical order, canonical law, are often met with referring to the ecclesiastical legislation. (Catholic Encyclopedia, Canons; Dictionnaire d'Archéologie par Dom F. Cabrol, Paris, 1909, Canons Apostoliques.)

2. *Definition.* Canon law may be defined as the body of laws enacted, adopted, or proposed by the ecclesiastical authority for the government of the Christian people.

In every society there must be an authority to guide its members towards the end for which the society was established; this is done by means of rules, commands, or prohibitions, which constitute the law of that society.

In the Church, which is a complete, perfect society, there is an authority and it is the exercise of its power which gives rise to canon law. That authority resides in the Supreme Pontiff and, under him, in the Bishops acting collectively, in Councils, or individually, in their respective dioceses. These are the immediate, formal sources of canon law.

The ecclesiastical authority may enact rules of its own, or it may, at times, adopt and confirm laws enacted by another authority, for instance, by the civil power, thus giving them a new binding force and making them its own; or, again, it may promulgate anew divine laws, which thus become, in some sense, ecclesiastical, because of the sanction they receive from the ecclesiastical authority. Thus, reception of the Holy Eucharist commanded by Christ in a general manner becomes, by ecclesiastical precept, binding once a year at Easter.

3. *Divisions.* Ecclesiastical laws are variously classified, according as we consider their source, mediate or immediate, the extent of their obligation, their form, their object, their chronological development.

(*a*) In the *Corpus Juris,* or in the *Codex Juris Canonici,* are included precepts of the natural law, ordinances that come from Christ Himself, principally regarding the constitution of the Church and the sacraments, and purely ecclesiastical laws.

(*b*) There are the general laws, binding on all the faithful, and the singular laws, intended only for certain classes of persons; universal laws, promulgated for the whole Church, and particular laws, which affect only certain territories; the common law, which is to be observed with regard to a certain matter unless an exception is made, and the special laws, which are more like exceptions and constitute a departure from common law.

(*c*) The law may be written, that is, formulated and promulgated by the legislator himself; or unwritten, as when it is handed down by tradition or introduced by custom, without being promulgated by the legislator or committed to writing.

(*d*) By reason of the object, law is divided into public and private. Some authors call public law that which is concerned, directly and chiefly, with the welfare of society as such, and defines the rights and duties of those in authority; and private law that which is concerned with the welfare of the individual, his rights also and duties.

Others define public law as that system of divine laws which determine the rights and duties of the Church as a perfect society; and private law as that body of laws which the ecclesiastical authority enacts or proposes for the government of Christian society. (Cavagnis: Institutiones Juris Publici Ecclesiastici, vol. I, n. 29, 30; Wernz: Jus Decretalium, vol. I, n. 50.)

(*e*) From the chronological point of view, canon law has been divided into ancient law, *jus antiquum,* recent or new law, *jus novum,* and most recent law, *jus novissimum;* corresponding to the three periods of its development.

The first period extends from the beginning of

Church History to the Decree of Gratian, in the twelfth century; the second from the Decree of Gratian to the Council of Trent; the third from the Council of Trent to the present day.

A fourth period might be said to have begun with the promulgation of the *Codex Juris Canonici* in 1917 or its going into effect in 1918.

II. RELATION OF CANON LAW TO DOGMA, MORAL AND CIVIL LAW

4. 1. Dogma is an object of belief, canon law a rule of action. One pertains to faith, the other to discipline, but faith supplies a foundation for discipline, and discipline, in turn, protects faith.

2. The moral law is also a rule of action, but it regulates human acts, whether internal or external, in their relation to man's last end, to the moral order and conscience; it is concerned primarily with the personal sanctification of the individual.

Canon law regulates man's activity in its relation to the social organism; it is concerned directly with the external order, with the spiritual welfare of Christian society, and with the good of the individual as a member of that society. As, however, the internal and the external order, the good of the individual and the good of society, are intimately connected, and as, moreover, what is commanded by canon law becomes binding in conscience, thus affecting the moral order, there exists a close relation between the moral and the canonical law; so close that it is often difficult to fix the limits of their respective provinces. Much of the matter contained in modern works of moral theology belongs in reality to canon law, as, for example, the greater part of the treatise on matrimony. Hence the axiom received in the schools: *nemo bonus moralista nisi bonus canonista.*

5. 3. Like the civil law, canon law is a positive ordinance destined to direct man to a certain end: but it proceeds from a different source, the ecclesiastical authority, which is independent and supreme in its own sphere; it has a special object, which is, to promote the spiritual welfare of men; a special subject, Christian society, which is not coextensive with any other society; a special subject-matter corresponding to the end to be attained. There are, however, several points of contact between the canonical and the civil law. Often they affect the same persons and deal with the same matter, for example, matrimony, contracts, property rights, etc.

Canon law has borrowed various ordinances from the civil, particularly Roman, law. It was an axiom received among canonists and afterwards inserted in the *Corpus Juris Canonici* that, when canon law is silent on a certain point, the Church follows the Roman law. The *Codex Juris Canonici* adopts the provisions of the civil legislation of each country on prescription, legal adoption and its effect on marriage, etc. (1, X, V, 32; Can. 1508, 1059, 1080.)

On the other hand, there was a time when canon law enjoyed the greatest authority in the civil courts themselves, and modern civil codes are indebted to it for numerous beneficial prescriptions. (Catholic Encyclopedia, Law, civil, p. 66.) "It is when we turn to the indirect influence of canon law upon the procedure of the secular courts, and even upon the substance of the secular law . . . that we must recognize in canon law one of the great civilizing and humanizing influences of the Middle Ages. It was chiefly through canon law that civil law transformed the jurisprudence of nearly the whole continent of Europe." (Rashdall: Universities of Europe in the Middle Ages, vol. I, p. 142.)

III. FORMATION OF CANON LAW

The Code of ecclesiastical laws is the result of a slow, gradual development.

6. 1. In the beginning, the Christian community was governed by the precepts of the natural law, by such ordinances of the Mosaic law as had not been abrogated at the coming of Christ, and by the laws given by Christ Himself to His Church.

That Christian divine law, which is found in the Gospels, in the writings of the Apostles, and in the living tradition, contained the essential elements of the Church's constitution and the fundamental principles of her legislation. It was for the legislative power instituted by Christ to draw the conclusions and make the applications called for by circumstances. The Apostles, to whom that power had been committed, exercised it from the beginning, as we see in the Acts and the Epistles. Their successors followed their example, and the Church's legislation grew with the Church herself.

2. The Bishops of Rome, beginning with St. Clement about the year 97, decide cases submitted to them or settle points of general discipline, carrying on ecclesiastical government by means of a correspondence which becomes more and more active as the Church spreads and the administration becomes more centralized. (Dictionnaire d'Archéologie et de Liturgie, Chancellerie, Canons Apostoliques, p. 1911.)

The other Bishops, either individually or united in Council, enact, for their dioceses or provinces, such regulations as local conditions require. Those decisions form the first nucleus of local canon law; then often they spread from one country to another, gradually obtain universal recognition, and thus become part of general canon law.

Provincial Councils are held as early as the end of the second century, and in the fourth begins the series of General Councils which, besides deciding the great questions of dogma, enact numerous disciplinary laws for the whole Church.

Custom also was an important factor in fixing various points of ecclesiastical discipline, particularly in those early days when the Church lived so largely on tradition.

7. 3. As must be expected, that legislation was at first incomplete and fragmentary. The laws were made as circumstances demanded, without any formal system or preconceived plan. There existed a certain uniformity of practice, based on the prescriptions of the divine law, in regard to the liturgy, the sacraments, the organization of the Church and of the clergy; but as long as the period of persecutions endures, the written canon law must necessarily remain very meagre, and unity of legislation in purely disciplinary matters is not possible. The tendency to unification and centralization is, however, apparent even in those early days, and it becomes more manifest as the Church grows.

4. The progress is particularly rapid when, after the Edict of Constantine, the Church is free to develop her own organization. The letters of the Popes and the decisions of the Councils continue to be the principal sources of ecclesiastical legislation, but they are now more frequent.

It is from that time chiefly that the Church borrows from the Roman law, sometimes adopting its provisions as they stand and making them her own; sometimes adapting them or simply imitating them. (La Premiére Ebauche du Droit Chrétien dans le Droit Romain; Charles Boucaud, Paris, Tralin.) As late as the twelfth century, canonists who undertook to systematize the ecclesiastical legislation did not hesitate to supply what was wanting by taking it from the Roman Code. Still great as was the influence of the Roman law on the development of the ecclesiastical legislation, the latter always retained its independence and individual character. Most of its prescriptions are of purely ecclesiastical origin, and as for those which are borrowed from the civil codes a new spirit is infused into them and they receive their binding force from the ecclesiastical authority. (Etudes, 20 Avril 1914, p. 143, 146.)

When all these elements were gathered together in a systematic manner, by the end of the twelfth century and the beginning of the thirteenth, the Church found herself in possession of an almost complete code of laws, the most perfect then in existence and one never surpassed for prudence, moderation, absolute fairness, and sound practical sense.

8. 5. The growth, however, did not stop here. As new needs were felt and new situations arose, new laws were made and new decisions given. Councils enacted new disciplinary decrees, but the legislative power was exercised particularly by the Popes, to whom legal difficulties and practical cases were referred for solution from all parts of Christendom. Their answers or Decretals, which fill large volumes, contain not only the solution of the proposed difficulty, but often also a general principle or rule applicable to all similar cases and constituting a real law.

6. The same work of legislation has continued to the present day and must continue, each Pope meeting new situations as they arise. In a living society there is constant need of a further adaptation of its laws.

In modern times, Papal Constitutions or decrees on various points of doctrine or discipline have been issued from time to time; the Roman Congregations authoritatively interpret and apply laws, and their decisions, even when they do not constitute new laws, tend to fix the jurisprudence which, by custom or papal sanction, often obtains in the course of time the force of law.

The *Codex Juris Canonici,* compiled by order of Pope Pius X and promulgated by authority of Pope Benedict XV, is a work principally of codification, as its name implies, but it is also one of reform and progress. Ancient laws have been better adapted to present conditions and new ones enacted in answer to the desiderata of the Catholic Episcopate and after consulting them. It marks an important step in the development of the Church's legislation but not the end of legislative activity; it contains the whole general law now in vigor but does not preclude the possibility of further legislation.

IV. COLLECTIONS OF ECCLESIASTICAL LAWS

(Ballerini, De Antiquis Collectionibus et Collectoribus Canonum, in Patrologia Latina, vol. LVI; Wernz, Jus Decretalium, t. I, n. 200 ff.; Catholic Encyclopedia, Canons, Collections; Philips, Histoire du Droit Canonique dans ses Sources, Paris, 1852; A. Tardif, Histoire des Sources du Droit Canonique, Paris, 1887.)

9. Laws enacted at different times and in different places would soon have been forgotten or have lost their efficacy if they had not been gathered together in Collections which could be consulted when needed. This became more and more necessary with the increase of legislation; and as legislation continued to grow new Collections had to be added to the old ones. Only the principal ones will be mentioned here, following the chronological order and the division into three periods referred to above. These old Collections have lost some of their legal value, but they retain all their historical interest.

First Period: From the Beginning to the Decree of Gratian.

1. *Collections which are called Apostolic.*—The Apostles issued some disciplinary regulations as inspired authors: they pertain to the immutable deposit of faith, are contained in the books of the New Testament (Epistles to Timothy and Titus, Acts of the Apostles, xv. 29) or in the living tradition of the Church, and form the Divine Apostolic Law.

Other regulations were issued by them simply as ecclesiastical legislators; they form what is called the Human Apostolic Law. They were preserved only by tradition and soon became fused with the rest of ecclesiastical legislation.

But the desire of preserving apostolic texts, and, in some cases, of giving an apostolic sanction to later legislation led to the forming of Collections of so-called Apostolic Canons. These Collections are mainly apocryphal, although in some of them there may be regulations of really apostolic origin. They are interesting, partly because of the vestiges they offer of the early Christian life, partly because many of these laws were for a long time considered as truly apostolic and, as such, seriously influenced the formation of later canon law.

10. The principal writings of this kind are: the Teaching of the Twelve Apostles, of the end of the first century or beginning of the second; the *Didascalia,* or Catholic Doctrine of the Twelve Apostles, written in Palestine or Syria, towards the middle of the third century, "the earliest attempt to compile a *Corpus Juris Canonici*" (Didascalia et Constitutiones Apostolorum, edidit F. X. Funk, 1906; Nau, La Didascalie); the Apostolic Constitutions, made out of older materials about the year 400 by a Syrian, a repertory of texts dating from the fourth and third centuries, and of the highest value for canon law, liturgy, and Christian life; the Apostolic Canons, a collection of eighty-five Greek canons derived, in great measure, from Councils of the fourth century. (Dictionnaire d'Archéologie Chrétienne et de Liturgie, Canons Apostoliques; Hefele: Histoire des Conciles, traduction par Dom H. Leclercq, T. I. P. II, Appendice IX.)

Other ancient texts that pretend to apostolic or very early origin are: the Apostolic Church Ordinance, the Canons of Antioch, the Canons of St. Peter, the Testament of Our Lord, the Octateuch of Clement, the Canons of Hippolytus, etc. (Lagarde, Reliquiae Juris Ecclesiastici Ant. Graecé.)

11. 1. All these writings, closely related to one another, form short treatises on ecclesiastical administration, liturgy, the duties of the clergy and the faithful. What was the exact date of their composition and the real nature of their mutual dependence, which of them borrowed from the others, are questions often difficult to answer and remain a matter of controversy among critics. The multiplication of such compilations is an evidence of the legislative activity of the Church in those early days, of the need that was felt of some authoritative code of laws, and of the respect for tradition and for the early ecclesiastical rulers that prevailed in the Christian community.

The authority which they enjoyed was mostly local. The Apostolic Constitutions were, for a time, accepted throughout the Orient and included in the canonical Collections of the Greek Church, but the Council in Trullo, in 692, rejected them and declared them apocryphal, as having been interpolated by heretics. They were never received as ecclesiastical laws in the Latin Church. The same Council in Trullo, on the contrary, accepted the eighty-five Apostolic Canons, and they have occupied since the first place in the Greek Collections. Dionysius Exiguus, a Western canonist, translated them into Latin and admitted the first fifty of them into the Collection which he published about the year 500. They thus passed into various Western Collections and afterwards into the *Corpus Juris*.

12. 2.—*Greek Collections.* (*a*) At the Council of Chalcedon, 451, several references were made to a Collection of previous Councils then in common use. Compiled by an unknown author, probably in Pontus early in the fourth century, it contains originally the canons of the Councils of Ancyra, 314, and Neo-Caesarea, 314-325. To these had been added successively the Canons of Gangra, 360-370, Nicaea, 325, and Antioch. The General Council of Chalcedon gave them an official sanction, so that all might have force of law throughout the whole Church. The Collection was increased by the addition of the decrees of Laodicea, 344, Constantinople, 381, Ephesus, 431, Chalcedon, 451 and later, Sardica, 343, and Carthage, 419; together with the canonical letters of some of the great Bishops. This constituted the ecclesiastical law of the East. (Hefele-Leclercq, Histoire des Conciles, T. II. p. 770; Wernz, p. 315.)

(*b*) The above Collections followed a merely chronological order. About the year 535 an unknown author attempted to classify the texts under sixty titles. His work has been lost, but it was used and perfected by John the Scholastic, a priest of Antioch, later on Patriarch of Constantinople, who brought out a more complete and more orderly Collection about the year 550.

(*c*) It is in the sixth century also that those Collections began to be compiled which are called Nomocanons, because they contained, together with the ecclesiastical laws, the imperial ordinances pertaining to the matter.

13. 3. *Latin Collections.* (*a*) Italy. In the West the first canonical Collections do not commence to appear till the beginning of the fifth century; they are all local and borrow nearly everything from the Greek Collections. Their compilers had a twofold work to do, to gather their materials and to translate them into Latin. There still remain two of those early versions of the Greek Councils; one is called the *Itala* or *Prisca;* the other the *Hispana* or *Isidoriana,* because it was inserted in the Spanish Collection ascribed to Isidore of Seville. Neither was very satisfactory.

A notable progress was achieved in the sixth century; it was due mainly to the work of the monk known as Dionysius Exiguus or the Little, a Scythian by birth but a Roman by adoption.

The Church of Rome had by this time completed her organization and was governed by the canons of her Synods and the decrees of her Bishops. Of these, however, there existed no Collection. About the year 500, Dionysius, who was well skilled in both Latin and Greek, brought out a new, more exact, and more intelligible translation of the Greek Councils, adding to them several African Councils, particularly those of Carthage; then he collected the letters or Decretals of the Popes from Siricius, 384-389, to Anastasius, 496-498. A little later he combined these two Collections into one, and it is in that form that his work has reached us.

Although not perfect, that Collection was far superior to the Collections then in existence and soon superseded them all. It became, if not officially, at least practically, the canonical code of the Roman Church. It was much used in Spain and Africa and even found its way into Gaul and Britain.

The new Decretals published by the successors of Anastasius were incorporated into it in due time. Thus enlarged, the *Collectio Dionysiana,* as it was called, was sent in 774 by Pope Adrian I (hence also the name of *Adriana*) to the emperor Charlemagne as the law of the Roman Church. The emperor caused it to be adopted by the Bishops of his whole empire at the Diet of Aix-la-Chapelle, in 802.

14. The *Adriana* did not, however, acquire thereby a universally obligatory and exclusive authority nor render useless all other Collections. One of them, known as the *Avellana,* which dates probably from the middle of the sixth century, contains many texts, nearly two hundred, which are not found in any other. (Migne, Patrologia Latina, vol. 67; Ballerini, 1, c. 818; C. H. Turner, Ecclesiae Occidentalis Monumenta Juris Antiquissima, vol. II, p. 11.)

(*b*) In Africa. The African Church, strongly organized with Carthage as a center, received its domestic code of discipline from the numerous Councils which, beginning at the end of the second century, 198, were held at different intervals. There were no less than twenty-two at Carthage, under Bishop Aurelius, 393-427. Important also were those of Hippo, in 393, 426, 427.

As it was customary in every Council to read and insert in the acts the decrees of the previous ones, an official Collection of canons thus gradually grew up. Its binding force could be only local, but its moral influence extended far beyond the limits of the province of Africa. Its canons were incorporated into the *Dionysiana* and the *Hispana,* thus becoming part of Western canon law; and through these channels they even made their way into the Greek Collections.

15. Other Collections due to private initiative are: the *Breviatio Canonum* of Fulgentius Ferrandus, a deacon of Carthage, compiled about the year 546; it contained two hundred and thirty abridged canons of Greek and African Councils disposed methodically under seven titles (Migne, Patrologia Latina, vol. 67); the *Concordia* of Cresconius, probably an African Bishop of the end of the seventh century. He uses the Decretals and canons of Dionysius, but classifies them under three hundred headings and, instead of reproducing the full text, gives only what pertains to the special subject. (Ballerini, P. IV, c. 3, p. 282; Patrologia Latina, 88.) The *Statuta Ecclesiae Antiqua,* one hundred and four canons, which have often been ascribed to a supposed Council of Carthage in 398, more probably belong to the Church of Arles, in Gaul.

16. (*c*) Spanish Collections. The series of Spanish Councils begins with the Council of Elvira, about the year 300, the first one whose disciplinary decrees have come down to us.

Others were held in the course of the fourth and fifth centuries, and they became particularly numerous at the end of the sixth and during the seventh, from the conversion of King Reccared in 587 to the end of the Visigothic kingdom and the Saracene invasion in 711. Between 400 and 700 eighteen Councils were held at Toledo, which occupied in Spain a position similar to that of Carthage in Africa. Here, too, it was the custom in each Council to read the canons enacted by the previous ones; canonical Collections, therefore, were necessary. The Fourth Council of Toledo speaks of the *Codex Canonum* from which the deacon reads what concerns the holding of a Council. This *Codex Canonum* became through successive additions the great Spanish Collection, the *Hispana,* attributed in the ninth century to St. Isidore of Seville, but without sufficient evidence. Like the *Dionysiana,* of which it is an imitation, it contained in a first part canons of Greek, African, Spanish, and Gallic Councils; in a second part the Decretals of Popes given by Dionysius, with the addition of a few others which concerned principally the Spanish Church.

The first compiler of the *Hispana* had followed the chronological order; towards the end of the seventh century another one recast the same materials in logical order and gave a methodical *Hispana* divided into ten books which were subdivided into titles and chapters.

The *Hispana* was approved as authentic by Pope Alexander III and enjoyed a great authority in Spain till the thirteenth century. (Text in Migne's Patrologia Latina, vol. 94.)

Among other Spanish Collections may be mentioned: the *Capitula Martini,* a translation and adaptation of Greek canons with a few Latin ones, by Martin, Archbishop of Braga, in the sixth century; the Spanish *Epitome,* which gives a summary of conciliary canons and papal Decretals from Siricius to Vigilius, 384-555.

17. (*d*) Gallican Collections. The Church in Gaul was governed by the decrees of the Eastern and African Synods, to which were added disciplinary laws enacted by local Councils beginning in the fourth century. Several Collections of them were made for the use of Bishops principally, but none of them had an official character or enjoyed universal recognition. In Gaul, except for the temporary primacy of the See of Arles, there was no central power and therefore no centralized legislation or universally accepted Collection.

The *Quesnelliana,* thus named from its editor, the Jansenist Paschasius Quesnel, was very extensively used from the sixth to the eighth century, when it gave way to the *Hadriana* or *Dionysiana,* which had been sent to Charlemagne by Pope Adrian. (Ballerini, l.c., P. II, c. X, Pat. Lat. vol. 56, p. 947.)

(*e*) English and Irish Collections. We meet with no Collection particular to the English or Irish Church till the seventh century. In the early part of the eighth century was published the *Collectio Hibernensis* or *Synodus Patritii.* Its influence extended far beyond the limits of the country in which it was compiled, for it was brought to France and Italy and till the twelfth century enjoyed great authority in both countries. It was a summary of previous legislation distributed into chapters and arranged in a systematic order, although not without some confusion. (Paul Fournier, De l'Influence de la Collection Irlandaise sur les Collections Canoniques, 1899; Ballerini, l.c., P. IV, c. VI.)

18. 4. *Apocryphal Collections.* They were particularly numerous in the ninth century. The most celebrated of them are: the *Capitula* of Benedict Levita, the *Capitula Angilramni,* the canons of Isaac of Langres, and above all the False Decretals of Isidore Mercator.

Pseudo-Isidorian Collection. (Hinschius, Decretales Pseudo-Isorianae, Leipzig, 1863; L. Saltet, False Decretals, in Catholic Encyclopedia; R. F. Clarke, S.J., False Decretals, Catholic Truth Society; E. H. Davenport, The False Decretals, 1914; P. Fournier, Etude sur les Fausses Décrétales, Louvain, 1906; Dictionnaire de Théologie; Dictionary of Christian Antiquities, etc.)

(*a*) Date, Place of Composition, Author. The so-called Isidorian Collection was published about the middle of the ninth century; it uses the Capitularies of Benedict Levita, a work which was completed only in 847 and the first reference to it is met with in 852.

The theory that the False Decretals were forged in Italy and in Rome has long since been abandoned; critics practically agree in placing their origin in France, at Rheims, or at Le Mans, in the province of Tours. The former place is favored by the majority of the German and a few French historians; the latter by such authorities as Langen, Döllinger, Viollet, Havet, P. Fournier, L. Duchesne.

The author of the compilation and forgery has remained unknown; Isidore Mercator or, as some manuscripts have it, Peccator, is a mere pseudonym.

19. (*b*) Contents. The work is divided into three parts: the first part contains sixty letters attributed to early Popes from St. Clement, 88-97, to St. Melchiades, 311-314; fifty-eight of them are forged. The second part contains the canons of Councils since Nicaea given in the *Hispana*. The third part reproduces the letters of the Popes which form the second part of the *Hispana* and adds about thirty more which are forged.

(*c*) Success of the Forgery. From France the False Decretals passed into Germany, where we find them quoted by the Council of Worms, in 868, and into Italy, where Popes Nicholas I, 838-867, and Adrian II, 867-872, seem to be acquainted with them. They did not, however, receive any real official recognition till the middle of the eleventh century, when the Bishop of Toul, in France, became Pope under the name of Leo IX, 1048-1052.

No one doubted, then, the authenticity of Isidore's Collection. Anselm of Lucca and Cardinal Deusdedit borrowed largely from it for their compilations and many of its texts found their way into the Decree of Gratian.

It is not till the fifteenth century that some of the scholars of the Renaissance period commenced to have their suspicions aroused. Two Cardinals were among the first to question the authenticity of the letters attributed to the early Popes.

After years of controversy, the apocryphal character of Isidore's Decretals was definitely established by the Protestant writer Blondel, in 1628, and more completely by two Catholic priests, the brothers Ballerini, in the eighteenth century. It was shown that the work is full of anachronisms; Popes of the first centuries quote documents of the fifth or fourth century, and Popes of the fifth century documents of the sixth, eighth, and even of the beginning of the ninth.

20. (*d*) Purpose of the Work and its Influences. The purpose of the Pseudo-Isidore can easily be gathered from the texts he forged. It was not, as Protestants and Jansenists used to contend, to increase the power of the Popes and support claims which they were not able to enforce otherwise; his principal aim was to strengthen the authority of Bishops, to win respect for them and safeguard their independence against the encroachments of civil rulers. He strongly emphasizes the supremacy of the spiritual over the temporal authority, the immunity of Bishops from the jurisdiction of the secular courts, their complete independence in their dioceses.

The rights of the Papacy are also insisted on, but this is because the Popes were made the defenders of the Bishops. It is false, then, to say, and independent critics now freely admit it, that these forgeries caused a revolution in Church discipline and became the foundation of the Popes' largest pretensions. In the sphere of history, for example, they exercised, it is true, an unfortunate influence; but in the domain of theology or canon law their action was without any serious consequences. They introduced nothing really new in the Church. They were very little used, if at all, by the Popes till the middle of the eleventh century and never as the sole or main foundation of any of their claims. Nicholas I used them to support his teaching on appeals to Rome, but he would have found the same support in other texts of undoubted authenticity. (Horace Mann, Lives of the Popes, vol. II, P. II, p. 135.)

21. 5. *Collections from the Latter Part of the Ninth Century to the Decree of Gratian.* About forty of them are known to us. They manifest a growing tendency to abandon the chronological for the logical order; and to the legal texts begin to be added the explanations of the compilers.

The *Collectio Anselmo Dedicata* is divided into twelve books, which treat of the hierarchy, judgments, ecclesiastical persons, rule of faith, precepts, sacraments, liturgies, and persons outside of the Church.

The Collection of Regino of Prüm, compiled about the year 906, treats, in two books, first of the clergy and ecclesiastical property, then of the laity.

The *Collectarium Canonum* or *Libri Decretorum* of Burchard of Worms, composed between 1013 and 1023, is divided into twenty books, dealing successively with the hierarchy, liturgy, the sacraments, delinquencies, sanctions, and criminal trials. Besides giving the texts, it tries to harmonize them and thus prepares the way for the *Decretum Gratiani.* (P. Fournier, Etudes Critiques sur le Décret de Burchard de Worms, Paris, Larose et Tranin; P.L., 140.)

The Collections of St. Anselm of Lucca, of Cardinal Deusdedit, of Bonizo, of Cardinal Gregory, insist in a particular manner on the rights of the spiritual power; it was the time of the Investiture struggle and the Gregorian reform.

To Yvo of Chartres are attributed three Collections: the *Tripartita,* a repertory, in three parts, of decretals of Popes, decrees of Councils and texts of the Fathers, and of Roman laws, all disposed chronologically; the *Panormia,* in which the materials of the *Tripartita* are arranged methodically; the *Decretum,* which, according to some, is an enlargement of the *Panormia,* and, according to others would have preceded it. (P. Fournier, Les Collections Canoniques attribuées á Yves de Chartres, Paris, 1897; A. Clerval, Les Ecoles de Chartres au Moyen-Age, L. III, c. I, sect. II, Chartres, 1895.)

The *Tripartita* and *Decretum* enjoyed great popularity until Gratian's work took their place.

Second Period: From the Decree of Gratian to the Council of Trent.

22. 1. *Decree of Gratian.* The Collection published about the year 1150 by the Camoldolese monk Gratian, professor of theology in the University of Bologna, was destined to supersede all the Collections which had preceded it and to become the classical text studied and commented upon in the schools.

The cause of its great success was the real progress it marked over previous similar works. It contained all the important texts given in the ancient Collections, and, as in the more recent ones, those texts were disposed in a logical order; there was added, besides, a brief explanation by Gratian himself in which he endeavored to reconcile apparently contradictory canons, discussed questions to which they gave rise, and solved difficulties. This is what is called the *dicta Gratiani,* maxims of Gratian. In the sixteenth century the Roman revisers inserted critical notes, which are designated by the words *Correctores Romani.*

Gratian's compilation was known as the *Concordia Discordantium Canonum, Decreta, Corpus Decretorum, Liber Canonum,* but principally as the *Decretum.* It is divided into three parts. The first contains one hundred and one "Distinctions" subdivided into chapters. The first twenty "Distinctions" constitute a general treatise on the nature and written sources of canon law; the other eighty-one treat of ecclesiastical persons and functions.

The second part is divided into thirty-six "Causes," each cause into questions, and each question into chapters. It treats of ecclesiastical administration and marriage. The third question of the thirty-third cause forms a treatise on penance in seven "Distinctions."

The third part is divided into five "Distinctions" and treats of the sacraments and sacramentals.

The texts of the first part are quoted by indicating the number of the canon or chapter and that of the distinction. Thus, c. 24, D.L., means canon or chapter 24 of the fiftieth distinction. The texts of the second part are quoted by indicating the number of the chapter, that of the cause and of the question; thus, c. 4, C. III, q. 2, means chapter fourth in the second question of the third cause, in the second part of the Decree. The special section, *De Poenitentia* in that part is quoted by adding the words, *de poen.;* thus, c. 24, D. IV, will suffice to indicate the twenty-fourth chapter of the fourth distinction in the treatise on penance which forms the third question of cause thirty-third in the second part of the Decree.

The texts of the third part are quoted like those of the first, adding the words *de Consecratione,* to show that the reference is to the third part.

At times, in the case of well known texts, only the first words are given, without any further indication; those who are not very familiar with the *Corpus Juris* may be obliged in searching for them to consult the alphabetical tables containing the first words of every chapter, printed in all the editions of the *Decretum.*

Although it enjoyed great authority, the work of Gratian never received official approbation and remained a private compilation.

23. 2. *From the Decree of Gratian to the Decretals of Gregory IX.* The Lateran Councils held in 1179 and 1215 enacted important disciplinary decrees; the Popes were appealed to and called upon to exercise their authority more and more frequently. Alexander III is said to have issued thirty-nine hundred and thirty-nine decrees and Innocent III over five thousand. The *Decretum,* therefore, soon became insufficient and other Collections were necessary.

One of the first to be made was the *Appendix Concilii Lateranensis,* divided into fifty parts and five hundred and thirty-seven chapters. It was followed by the *Collectio Bambergensis,* the *Collectio Lipsiensis,* the *Collectio Caselana,* the *Collectio Halensis* and *Lucensis,* all named from the libraries in which they were preserved.

But a more important one is that of the celebrated canonist Bernard of Pavia, called first *Breviarium Extravagantium, Libellus Extravagantium, Decretales et Extravagantia, i.e. vagantia extra Decretum;* and more commonly known as the *Compilatio prima,* 1187-1191. It is divided into five books and each book into titles and chapters. The order of the books is indicated in the well known verse: *Judex, judicium, clerus, connubia, crimen.* They treat successively of persons possessing jurisdiction, of civil trials of clerics, of marriage, of crimes and criminal trials.

The same order was followed in compilations made to continue the work of Bernard, which received the name of *Compilatio 2a, 3a, 4a, 5a.* The five of them are known as the *Quinque Compilationes Antiquae Decretalium.* Two of them had an official character: the *Compilatio 3a,* composed by order of Innocent III, approved by him in the Bull *Devotioni Vestrae* of Dec. 28, 1210, and sent to the University of Bologna to serve as a text for the lectures; and the *Compilatio Quinta,* approved by Honorius III, in the Bull *Novae Causarum,* 1227, and sent to the great canonist Tancred, that he might use it and cause it to be received both in courts and schools.

24. 3. *Decretals of Gregory IX.* Each one of the Collections made so far was incomplete in itself and insufficient for the use of canonists. Their frequent repetitions, and even at times contradictions, rendered it very difficult, in many cases, to find out what the law really was.

To remedy this, Gregory IX directed his chaplain, Raymond of Pennafort, a Dominican, to prepare a new Collection of Decretals which would replace all the others.

The work of Raymond consisted, principally, in combining together the *Quinque Compilationes Antiquae;* he adopted their division into five books, followed their method, and used most of their material, adding only five new titles.

The new Compilation, finished in four years, was approved by Gregory IX in the Bull *Rex Pacificus* of September 5, 1234, and published as the official Code of the Church. All the texts contained in it had force of law from the moment they were in the Collection, whatever their juridical value originally.

All the other Collections made since the *Decretum* were abrogated, and it was forbidden to make any new ones without the permission of the Holy See.

25. 4. *Later Collections of Decretals.* After

Gregory IX, Popes continued to issue new decisions and the canonists to gather them. Hence new Collections arose, some of which had an official character, notably those which were made by order of Innocent IV, Gregory X, and Nicholas III. Soon the need of greater unity was felt again; Boniface VIII, following the example of Gregory IX, abrogated all those fragmentary Collections and, to replace them, had one made which he called *Liber Sextus Decretalium.*

Continuing the work of his predecessor, Clement V collected his own Decretals, together with the decrees of the Council of Vienna; they formed the *Liber Septimus Decretalium,* more commonly called *Clementinae,* which was published and approved by John XXII. This was the last Collection of Decretals to receive official approbation.

The Constitutions of John XXII were collected by private authority and included in the *Corpus Juris* under the name of *Extravagantes Joannis XXII,* that is to say, *vagantes* outside of the official Collections. A few more belonging to other Popes formed the Collection of the *Extravagantes Communes.*

The Decree of Gratian, the five books of Decretals of Gregory IX, the sixth book of Decretals of Boniface VIII, the *Clementinae,* the *Extravagantes* of John XXII, and the *Extravagantes Communes* form the *Corpus Juris Canonici.* All these Collections had an official character except the *Decretum* and the *Extravagantes.*

The Decretals are quoted by indicating the chapter, the name of the Collection, the number of the book and of the title.

The Decretals of Gregory IX are designated by the letter X, that is, *extra Decretum;* those of Boniface VIII by the words "In Sexto," the others thus, "In Clem.," "Extrav. Joan. XXII," "Extrav. Commun." For example, c. 2, X de Translatione Episcopi, I, 7, refers to the second chapter of the Decretals of Gregory IX, book I, title 7. Often the heading of the title is given, as in the example, although this is not necessary; and at times the first words of the chapter are quoted instead of the number, when it is a chapter well known to canonists. The number may be found, if necessary, by consulting the index tables.

Third Period: From the Council of Trent to the Present Day; "Jus Novissimum."

26. The *Corpus Juris* is said to have been closed after the insertion into it of the *Extravagantes Communes;* not that it was forbidden then to make any further additions to it, but because, in reality, none was made.

Several attempts to obtain new official Collections proved unsuccessful. There was no longer the same need of them. The general principles of law were sufficiently well established by the texts on hand; the addition of new specific decisions, whilst helpful to fix the jurisprudence, would have served principally to increase the already numerous and massive legal Collections.

After the closing of the *Corpus Juris,* then, the ecclesiastical laws are scattered through various publications, and each canonist has to gather his texts from the documents accessible to him.

The sources of law during that period are the decrees of Councils, particularly the Council of Trent, the Constitutions of the Popes, the Rules of the

Apostolic Chancery and, in a certain sense, the decisions of the Roman Congregations.

27. 1. The disciplinary ordinances of the Council of Trent form of themselves a small code. (Canones et Decreta Sacrosancti Oecumenici Concilii Tridentini, Romae, 1564; Acta Genuina ss. Oecumenici Con. Tridentini, Theiner, 2 vols., Zagrab, 1874; Concil. Trid. Diariorum, Actorum, Epistularum, Tractatuum nova Collectio, ed. soc. Goerresiana, Freiburg, 1901; Pallavicino, Istoria del ss. Conc. di Trento, Roma, 1646-1657, French trans. Migne, 1844.)

The Acts of the Councils held from 1682 to 1870, including the Vatican Council, which, however, had no time to treat the questions of discipline, are found in the *Collectio Lacensis, Acta et Decreta Sacrorum Conciliorum Recentiorum,* 7 vol. in-4, Freiburg, 1869-1890.

28. 2. Of the Constitutions or Bulls of the Popes there exist several Collections called *Bullaria.*

The *Bullarium* of Laertius Cherubini, the first Collection to bear that name, a large folio volume, published in 1586, contained nine hundred and twenty-two Papal Constitutions from Gregory VII to Sixtus V. A second edition in three volumes was published in 1617; a third one in four volumes, extending from Leo I to Urban VIII, was printed in 1631, and in 1672 a fifth one in six volumes.

The so-called *Luxemburg Bullarium* is an enlarged reprint of the above, which, with the supplements added at intervals, comes down to Benedict XIV, 1752-57. The nineteenth and last volume bears the date of 1758.

The *Bullarium Romanum,* published by Girolamo Mainardi, 1739-1762, had thirty-two folio volumes and extended from St. Leo I in 450 to the death of Benedict XIV in 1758. A supplement in nine volumes, containing the Bulls of Clement XIII and his successors down to 1834, was published by A. Barberi, 1835-1857. That *Bullarium* is considered as the most accurate and the most practically useful.

The Turin *Bullarium* is less complete, less accurate, and contains documents the authenticity of which is very doubtful. It has twenty-seven quarto volumes and comes down to the death of Benedict XIV, 1758. The first twenty-two volumes were published at Turin, 1857-1872, the other five at Naples, 1867-85. (Catholic Encyclopedia, Bullarium; Dictionnaire de Théologie Catholique, Bullarium.)

It is to be noted that none of these Collections is really complete, and that none has an official character, except, in Mainardi's Collection, the first volume of the Constitutions of Benedict XIV, which appeared with that Pope's personal sanction and was sent by him to the University of Bologna to be used as an authentic source of law, *fons juris*.

29. 3. The Rules of the Apostolic Chancery are certain regulations which Popes for several centuries have been in the habit of promulgating in the beginning of their pontificate. They were formulated first by John XXII and increased or modified by subsequent Pontiffs, particularly Nicholas V and Clement XII. Regularly they cease to be in force at the death of the Pope; therefore each new Pope, the day after his election, confirms them, adding to, or taking from, those of his predecessors.

They have remained substantially the same since Nicholas V, and Urban VIII decreed that, whether confirmed or not, they would be in force the day following the creation of the new Pope.

Those rules are, generally, seventy-two in number, and concern the expedition of bulls, the reservation of benefices, and certain judicial causes.

30. 4. Some of the Roman Congregations had their decrees published in official Collections, but not all. There exist official Collections of the decrees of the Congregation of Rites and Indulgences.

For the Congregation of the Propaganda, the Collection published under the title: *Jus Pontificium de Propaganda Fide SS. D. N. Leonis XIII P. M. jussu recognitum,* possesses great legal and historical authority, still it is not official in the canonical sense of the term.

The *Thesaurus Resolutionum Sacrae Congregationis Concilii,* containing the decrees of that Congregation since 1700, is compiled by its secretary and has, in that sense, an official character; but it is not the same as a legal code, all parts of which would have the force of universal law. (Wernz, n. 270.)

The other Congregations have not published Collections of their decisions. The periodical *Acta S. Sedis* has published from 1865 to 1908 the principal Roman documents. Since 1909, under the name of *Acta Apostolicae Sedis* it has become the official organ of the Holy See, through which are promulgated the Pontifical Constitutions, laws, and decrees, and the decrees of the Roman Congregations and Offices. (Apost. Const. *Sapienti Consilio,* Sept. 28, 1908.)

V. PARTICULAR OR NATIONAL CANON LAW

31. Besides the general or common law, there is, as said before, a special law for certain parts of the Church. It is found in the decrees of Particular Councils, Constitutions addressed to particular Churches, concordats between the Holy See and civil governments, and customs legitimately established. The canon law peculiar to the Church in the United States has its origin in custom, the Provincial and National or Plenary Councils, and Decrees of the Congregation de Propaganda Fide. It was intended to meet exceptional and transitory conditions, and destined to be modified gradually, as conditions would change, so as to be brought more and more into harmony with the common law.

The first Synod was held in Baltimore in 1791, under Bishop Carroll. Provincial Councils were held likewise in Baltimore in 1829, 1833, 1837, 1840, 1843, 1846, 1849. (Concilia Provincialia; Baltimori habita 1829-1849, Murphy & Co., 1851.)

All the Bishops of the United States were called to these Councils, but as only one ecclesiastical province existed at the time, they are only Provincial Councils. When Oregon had been erected into an Archiepiscopal See, in 1846, St. Louis in 1847, New Orleans, Cincinnati and New York in 1850, it was possible to have National or Plenary Councils. The first one was held in Baltimore, in 1852, under the presidency of the Archbishop of that city, the Most Rev. Francis Patrick Kenrick, as Delegate of the Apostolic See. (Concilium Plenarium totius Americae Septentrionalis Foederatae, Baltimori habitum, anno 1852. Baltimori, apud Joannem Murphy et Socios, MDCCCLIII.) The second and third Plenary Councils were held also in Baltimore, in 1866 and in 1884, under the presidency of Archbishops Spalding and Gibbons, respectively. (Concilii Plenarii Baltimorensis II Acta et Decreta, Murphy & Co., Baltimore, 1868; Concilii Plenarii Baltimorensis III Acta et Decreta, Murphy & Co., Baltimore, 1886.)

Their Decrees were published after revision in Rome and became law for the whole country. As, however, they do not seem to have been approved in *forma specifica,* individual Bishops can, by virtue of custom, dispense in particular cases. (Wernz, Jus Decretalium, vol. I, n. 122; S. B. Smith, Counter-points in Canon Law, Art. 1, Newark, 1879.)

VI. THE SCIENCE OF CANON LAW

32. 1. *Its Development.* (Wernz, I, n. 284; Catholic Encyclopedia, Law, p. 62.) The legislative power existed and was exercised in the Church from the beginning; ecclesiastical laws were observed long before there was a science of canon law, just as the Christian dogmas were an object of belief long before they were expounded in complete theological treatises.

As long as there were no Collections of canons, or as long as these were gathered in a merely chronological order, there could not be any canonical science.

1°. A first and timid attempt at grouping the legal texts according to subjects was made, in the East, towards the end of the fifth century. In the West we meet with Collections following a more or less logical order, in the ninth and more frequently in the eleventh century. But the first scientific treatise on canon law is the Decree of Gratian, in the middle of the twelfth century. For the *Decretum* is not a code or a mere Collection of canons, it is a treatise, in which the texts are inserted to help establishing the law.

The study of Roman law had then been revived, in the University of Bologna, through the influence principally of the great jurist Inernius; Gratian sought to inaugurate a similar movement in favor of ecclesiastical law. From all the materials on hand he tried to build up a general system of canonical legislation and to give it a coordinated and methodical exposition.

33. It could not be expected that his work would be perfect; some of his conclusions are based on texts the spurious character of which is now universally recognized; several of his theories had to be modified or were rejected altogether. But he had shown the way, and thereby merited the title of "father of canon law," as Eusebius was called the father of ecclesiastical history.

The commentators of the *Decretum,* or Decretists, completed it on some points, elucidated obscure passages, and even attempted constructions of their own, in their separate treatises known as *Summae, Apparatus.* (Dictionnaire de Théologie Catholique, Gratien, p. 1732; J. de Ghellink, Le Mouvement Théologique au XIIe Siécle.)

Some of the most celebrated among the early Decretists are:

Paucapalea, Pocapaglia, disciple of Gratian, professor of canon law at Bologna, author of a Summa, Glosses, and Commentaries, d. 1150.

Roland Bandinelli, who became Pope under the name of Alexander III.

Omnibonus, Ognibene, also a disciple of Gratian and professor at Bologna. He published an *Abbreviatio Decreti* about the year 1156.

Rufinus, who taught canon law in the school of Paris and published a *Summa Decreti,* probably in 1165, not later than 1175.

Stephen of Tournai, born at Orleans; he studied at Paris and Bologna and published a *Summa*

Decreti in three parts before he became Bishop of Tournai in 1203.

John of Faenza, one of the best interpreters of the *Decretum.* His *Summa,* compiled from the works of Rufinus and Stephen, is said to have been so superior to them in arrangement of matter that it caused them to be almost forgotten. He died Bishop of Faenza in 1190. (Wernz n. 286.)

34. So far the Decretists had confined their attention, almost exclusively, to the materials contained in the *Decretum.* Simon of Bisiniano was the first to make an extensive use of the legislation enacted since Gratian's time by the Roman Pontiffs, particularly Alexander III.

His example was followed by Sicard of Cremona who, besides, instead of following strictly the divisions of the Decree and explaining each chapter one after the other, as had been done before him, adopted an order of his own, more logical and more systematic. He may be considered as the first author of *"Institutiones Canonicae."* He had no imitators till much later.

But probably the greatest of the ancient Decretists is Hugoccio of Pisa, a student and professor in the University of Bologna, where he had among his pupils the future Innocent III. His *Summa in Decretum* surpasses all those that had preceded it by its completeness, its thoroughness, and its originality. He died in 1210.

35. 2°. Another important step in the evolution of canon law is marked by the publication in the thirteenth century of the Collections of Papal Decretals. For, besides supplying new materials for the purpose of teaching, they represented a more advanced state of legislation and had, some of them at least, an official value. With them begins a period of great legal activity.

Like the *Decretum,* they immediately had their Commentators, the Decretalists. Among the most illustrious of these, previous to the sixteenth century, may be mentioned Bernard of Pavia, who, besides compiling the first collection of *Extravagantes,* wrote a *Summa Decretalium* and *Casus Decretalium* and other less extensive works on some special subjects. He died in 1213.

Tancred of Bologna, the greatest Decretalist of his time after Bernard. His *Summa de Matrimonio* and *Ordo Judiciarius* are consulted with profit even at the present day.

Raymond of Pennafort deserves a special mention as the compiler of the Collection of Gregory IX.

36. The first "Glosses" and "Lectures" on the new Collection were by Innocent of Spain, William Naso, and Philip. Others followed soon.

Sinibaldo Fieschi, afterwards Innocent IV, wrote a complete exposition of the five books of Decretals. John of God, a Portuguese by birth, for a number of years professor of canon law at Bologna, has left a *Liber Dispensationum, Liber Judicum, Liber Distinctionum,* and several other works of the same kind.

Bernard of Parma is the author of an *Apparatus ad Decretales Gregorii IX,* which was accepted as the *Glossa Ordinaria.*

William Durand, better known as Durand of Mende, from the name of the Diocese of which he was Bishop, occupied several important positions in the Roman Curia and played a prominent part in the Council of Lyons in 1274. His principal canonical work is the *Speculum Judiciale.*

Henry of Susa, Cardinal Bishop of Ostia,

whence the name of *Hostiensis,* was surnamed *"Monarcha Juris"* because of his eminent science. His *Summa* and *Lecturae* were frequently quoted by later canonists.

Joannes Andreae, a layman, who taught canon law at Bologna, wrote a *Glossa in Sextum,* an *Apparatus in Clementinas,* and other works. He was noted principally for his erudition, his knowledge of the sources of civil as well as of canonical law. He died in 1348.

He is the last of the great canonists of this period, the golden age of canon law. Then comes the decadence, brought on by various causes, chief amongst which are the Western Schism and the disorders of which it was the source. For about a hundred years canonical science remains stationary; it is still represented by some illustrious men, but they are few in number and they do not equal their predecessors. John Calderino, John de Lignano, Henry de Bohic, Baldus de Ubaldis, are among the best known.

37. 3°. Towards the middle of the fifteenth century a happy change took place: the printing press made legal texts more accessible to students; the canonists learned from the humanists to clothe their teachings in a less repelling form, the former subtle and useless discussions were gradually eliminated and greater attention began to be given to historical and critical investigations.

(*a*) More reliable editions of the sources were brought out, spurious texts, which had found their way even into the *Corpus Juris,* were discarded. Much credit for that work is due amongst others to: J. Quintin, 1500-1561; A. de Mouchy, d. 1574; A. Le Conte, 1517-1586; J. Sirmond, 1559-1651; P. Coustant, 1654-1721.

(*b*) The great promoter of the historical study of canon law in the sixteenth century was the learned Antonio Augustin, Archbishop of Tarragona. His principal work is the *De Emendatione Gratiani Dialogorum Libri Duo,* Tarragona, 1587.

In the seventeenth century the Oratorian Louis Thomassin, born at Aix in Provence, Aug. 28, 1619, compiled a history of Church discipline which has not been surpassed since for abundance of information and which constitutes one of the best commentaries on ecclesiastical legislation: *Ancienne et Nouvelle Discipline de l'Eglise,* 3 vol. in folio, Paris, 1679-1684. A Latin translation by the author himself was published soon after at the request of Pope Innocent XI, with some additions and modifications in the arrangement of the matter. These changes were embodied in another French edition, 1725, and also in a third one which appeared in 1864, 7 vol. in 8°, Paris, with corrections and further additions bringing it up to date, by Dr. André.

Peter and Jerome Ballerini have left, besides other works, an excellent edition of St. Leo the Great and learned Dissertations on the ancient Collections of Canons down to the time of Gratian. (Migne, Patrologia Latina, T. 56.) J. D. Mansi's name is attached to the Collection of Councils, the first volume of which appeared at Florence in 1759.

F. Zaccaria, S. J., 1714-1795, known principally as the champion of the true Constitution of the Church in his day, deserves also a mention for his work on the sources and history of canon law.

To the names already quoted may be added those of Maurus Sarti, 1709-1766, and José Pons, S.J., 1730-1816.

38. (*c*) After the Council of Trent the questions

of Introduction to canonical studies are treated by numerous authors: B. Epo, 1529-1599, *Antiquitatum Ecclesiasticarum Syntagma,* Duaci, 1578; Jean Doujat, 1609-1688, *Praenotionum Canon. Libri Quinque,* Paris, 1687; H. Plettenberg, S.J., *Introductio ad Jus Canonicum,* Hildesh. 1692; J. Zallinger, S.J., 1735-1813, and many others.

(*d*) It is also in the sixteenth century, about the time of the Council of Trent, that Giovanni Paolo Lancelotti published his famous *Institutiones Juris Canonici,* Perugia, 1563, a manual of law for students, modelled after the "Institutes" of Justinian, in which a vast system of legislation was reduced to a short, very simple, and didactic treatise, which could serve as an introduction to the more complicated study of the text. Although undertaken at the express request of Pope Paul IV, the work never received official approbation. It met, however, with very great success; it is inserted in most editions of the *Corpus Juris* and had its own commentators. The example of Lancelotti was imitated, in modern times, by very many canonists.

39. (*e*) As canonical science developed it became more and more difficult for one author to cover the whole ground: hence, from the sixteenth century on, the multiplication of particular treatises. In these, special points of law could be discussed more thoroughly and under their multiple aspects. An exposition of the variations of the discipline in the course of centuries, of its adaptation to the changing circumstances of times and places, would often help to elucidate obscure questions, settle old controversies, ascertain the real meaning of the law and its spirit, so as to make a sound application of it to existing conditions.

To draw up a complete list of particular treatises and their authors would be impossible; a few may be mentioned by way of example:

J. Morin, Commentarius Historicus de Disciplina in Administratione Poenitentiae, Paris, 1651; Commentarius Historicus et Dogmaticus de Sacris Ecclesiae Ordinationibus, Paris, 1665.

Navarrus, Consilia et Responsa, Lyons, 1591.

Covarrubias, Epitome de Sponsalibus et Matrimonio, 1545.

F. Sanchez, De Sancto Matrimonii Sacramento, Madrid, 1605.

J. Viviani, Praxis Jurispatronatus Acquirendi, Conservandi . . . Rome, 1620.

F. Delbene, De Immunitate et Jurisdictione Ecclesiastica, Lyons, 1650.

De Luca, Relatio Curiae Romanae, Cologne, 1683.

J. Riganti, Commentaria in Regulas Constitutiones et Ordinationes Cancellariæ Apostolicae, Romae, 1744.

Prosper Lambertini, afterwards Benedict XIV, De Servorum Dei Beatificatione et Beatorum Canonizatione, Bologna, 1734; De Synodo Diaecesana, Rome, 1748. D. Bouix, 1808-1871, De Papa, De Curia Romana, De Episcopis, De Parochis, etc.

Petrus Card. Gasparri, Tractatus Canonicus de Matrimonio, 2 vol., Paris, 1891; De Sacra Ordinatione, 2 vol., Paris, 1893; De SS. Eucharistia, 2 vol., Paris, 1897.

Michael Card. Lega, De Judiciis Ecclesiasticis, Romae, 1896, 1905.

S. Many, S.S., Praelectiones De Missa, Paris, 1903; De Locis Sacris, 1904; De Sacra Ordinatione, 1905.

Piatus Montensis, Praelectiones Juris Regularis, Tournai, 1906.

F. M. Capello, De Curia Romana, 2 vol., Rome, 1911, 1912; De Visitatione SS. Liminum et Dioeceseon, 2 vol., Rome, 1912, 1913.

(Hurter, S. J., Nomenclator Literarius . . . Oenipontae, 1892-1903; A Tardif, Histoire des Sources du Droit Canonique, Paris, 1887.)

40. (*f*) There were also, during this period, particularly during the second part of the seventeenth and the first part of the eighteenth century, general treatises on the whole canon law, which contributed not a little to the progress of the science and remain to this day standard works and most reliable sources of information. Almost every detail of the ecclesiastical legislation is discussed therein from the scientific as well as the practical point of view. Usually the general divisions of the *Corpus Juris* are adhered to, but the order of the chapters or canons is not followed strictly, to make it possible to give a more logical exposition of the matter and to bring out more clearly the principles underlying the individual enactments.

Some of the most illustrious in that series of great canonists and their principal works are:

Prospero Fagnani, Jus Canonicum seu Commentaria Absolutissima in Quinque Libros Decretalium, Rome, 1661.

Agostino Barbosa, 1589-1649, a Portuguese by birth, whose works fill more than thirty volumes.

J. B. De Luca, 1614-1683, Theatrum Veritatis et Justitiae, Rome, 1671.

Manuel González Téllez, Commentaria Perpetua in Singulos Textus Juris Canonici, Lyons, 1673.

Louis Engel, O.S.B., Universum Jus Canonicum

secundum Titulos Librorum Decretalium, Salzburg, 1671-1674.

Ehrenreich Pirhing, S.J., Jus Canonicum, Dillingen, 1674-1678.

Anaclet Reiffenstuel, O.S.F., Jus Canonicum Universum, Freising, 1700.

Peter Leuren, S.J., Forum Ecclesiasticum, Mainz, 1717.

Francis Schmalzgrueber, S.J., Jus Ecclesiasticum Universum, Dillingen, 1717.

In the nineteenth century a special mention is due to the important work of Franz Xaver Wernz, S.J., Jus Decretalium, Rome, 1898-1911.

41. 2. *Method in Canon Law.* 1°. The early canonists followed in their teaching and in their books, which differed little from their oral teaching, the method which is called exegetical; they would comment on the text of the law, that is, of the *Decretum* and afterwards of the Decretals, explaining the more difficult passages and drawing conclusions. It was the method universally in vogue at the time in the Universities, particularly in the law schools.

A jurist of Bologna, Odofredus, thus describes the manner in which he intends to give his *Lecturae:* "First I shall give you summaries of each title before I pass to the text; secondly , I shall give you as clear and explicit a statement as I can of the purport of each law included in the title; thirdly, I shall read the text with a view to correcting it; fourthly, I shall briefly repeat the contents of the law; fifthly, I shall solve apparent contradictions, adding any general principles of law, to be extracted from the passage, commonly called *Brocardica,* and any distinctions or subtle and useful problems, *Quaestiones,* arising out of the law with their solutions, as far as Divine Providence shall enable me. And if any law shall seem deserving, by reason of its celebrity or difficulty, of a Repetition, I shall reserve it for an evening Repetition." (H. Rashdall, The Universities of Europe in the Middle Ages, vol. I, p. 219.)

The summaries of the titles became the general summaries, *Summae,* of the *Decretum* or of the Decretals, some of which contained much more than a mere enumeration of questions and formed important works. Such were the *Summa* or rather the *Stroma* of Master Roland, the *Summa Coloniensis,* the *Summa Hostiensis.*

Odofredus, in the passage just quoted, does not mention the "Gloss" which the lecturer used to read after the text. It was a concise explanation which had come to be accepted as representing the teaching of the schools and which, although without official character, was treated as a sort of secondary legal document.

42. The first masters wrote down in their copies of the *Decretum,* between the lines or on the margins, the substance of their lecture, in a few words. These brief notes, carefully gathered by the pupils, grew little by little. Each master added his own gloss. In the schools it was found necessary to adopt one which would be followed uniformly. This was the *"Glossa Ordinaria,"* which served as an authoritative guide to both pupils and teachers.

The Ordinary Gloss of the *Decretum* was the work of John Zimeke, called the Teutonic. It was compiled from the notes of former Glossarists, about the year 1214; remodelled and completed by Bartholomew of Brescia in 1245.

The Ordinary Gloss of the Decretals of Gregory

IX, composed by Bernard of Parma, about 1263, received many additions afterwards from Joannes Andreae, who wrote also the Gloss of the *Liber Sextus* and of the *Clementinae.*

Some of the glosses were regular commentaries and contained on each chapter or canon copious explanations of unequal value: statement of the case which gave occasion to the decree, or of the problem to be solved; detailed analysis of the contents of the chapter; examples, real or fictitious, illustrating the various applications of the law; conclusions that may be drawn from it; discussions on opinions of previous canonists; references to parallel texts or to different readings of the same text. (A. Boudinhon, Glosses, in Catholic Encyclopedia; Laurin, Introductio in Corpus Juris Canonici, Freiburg, 1889.)

In particular treatises, which become more and more numerous after the middle of the fifteenth century, canonists allow themselves greater freedom, but in general treatises, for a long time, the order of the legal texts is strictly adhered to. Gonzalez Tellez, Fagnani, and Laymann still continue faithful to the exegetical method in the seventeenth century, and explain each chapter as it comes in the *Corpus Juris.*

43. 2°. Many of the canonists of that period, however, like Engel, Pirhing, Reiffenstuel, Schmalzgrueber, whilst conforming to the general divisions of the Decretals, did not take up each chapter in particular, but treated the matter of each title according to a logical and scientific plan, without regard to the disposition of the texts. It was found that the chapters followed one another without special connection.

Other canonists, like Barbosa, Luca, Pignatelli, Benedict XIV, went further and adopted an order of their own. For the exegetical was thus substituted the scholastic or, as it has been called, the juridico-dogmatic method. The laws actually in force were reduced to a system forming an organic body of doctrine; then each part of it was expounded scientifically by way of definition, division, and demonstration, as theologians did for dogmatic truths.

44. 3°. The plan and method followed by Lancelotti in his *Institutes* are simpler, as demanded by the nature of that work, which was intended to give only a brief summary of the principles of canon law and to serve as an introduction to the study of the legal texts themselves. It is divided into four books, which treat successively of persons, things, judgments, and crimes. Each book contains several titles, which are subdivided in turn into short paragraphs.

The general divisions, imitated from the Institutes of Justinian, have been followed, in modern times, by the authors of elementary treatises on canon law. They are substantially those of the new Code.

45. 4°. To the study of the law itself has been added, mainly since the time of the Renaissance and the Reformation, the study of its history. It was realized that to understand fully any point of legislation it was very useful and often necessary to go back to its origin, know the occasion of its enactment, the conditions it was meant to meet, the manner in which it was interpreted and enforced, the obstacles it encountered, the changes it underwent in the course of time, under the pressure of what circumstances it was perhaps revoked or allowed to fall into desuetude for a while and then put into force again. All this helps to ascertain the real mind of the legislator, to appreciate the true spirit of the law, and thus make of it a prudent application. It brings out also the continuity in discipline which we are to expect in so traditional a society as the Catholic Church; we see better the reason and opportuneness of measures which may have appeared arbitrary.

The legislative action of the Church in the past has been misunderstood and misrepresented by ill-informed or ill-disposed historians; the best defence we can offer for it is to put it in its true light.

Often, before settling a controversy, the Roman Congregations give a brief history of the discipline on the matter.

In the recent Instructions of the Congregation of Seminaries and Universities on the teaching of canon law, it is recommended, before proceeding to the discussion of a special point of legislation, to describe its origin, its gradual development, its modification in the course of time, so that the students may obtain a fuller understanding of it. (August 7, 1917.)

46. 5°. Each one of the methods here mentioned has its advantages and its deficiencies; perfection would, no doubt, consist in a happy combination of all of them. (Wernz, Jus Decretalium, vol. I, n. 59.)

Formerly it was difficult to reconcile the respective claims of the legal and of the systematic method; to follow a logical order, which is a necessary condition for scientific treatment, without losing sight of the legal texts and sources which ought to remain the foundation of all legal studies. That difficulty does not exist any more, since in the new Code the legal is also the logical order. Henceforth it will be possible to combine a literal interpretation of the texts with a scientific presentation of the principles, completed by historical exposition.

In the Roman Universities the course of canon law

is usually divided into two parts: a first year is devoted to the "Institutes," that is, to the questions of introduction and a general survey of the whole ecclesiastical legislation, according to the method of Lancelotti. Then comes the study of the text and the law in its details. Till the publication of the Code, the *Corpus Juris Canonici* served as a basis for this work, and here arose the difficulty referred to above, of following an order which would be sufficiently scientific without too much drawing away from the text. Some found the task an impossible one and adopted a plan of their own, entirely different from that of the Decretals. This was never without serious inconveniences and would now be without excuse.

47. The Congregation of Seminaries and Universities, in the decree already quoted, ordains that, in future, the new Code be used in schools as the only authentic source of canon law; that its contents be exposed to students not only in a synthetic but also in an analytic manner, explaining thoroughly each canon in particular and following strictly the order of the titles and of the chapters as they are found in the Code. Other works may be used, but their order must be adapted to that of the Code, not vice versa.

These prescriptions concern directly the Universities and the courses on the text; but they may serve as general directions in any exposition of ecclesiastical law, whether in the form of elementary treatises, for the use of beginners, or in more complete works. The best order to follow is that of the Code itself, if not in all its details, at least in its main lines; much confusion will thus be avoided and more unity in teaching secured. There will be less danger of wasting time in useless discussions. Pope Benedict XV declared that he would not approve teachers who, too fond of their own conceptions, would turn away from the clear and direct path marked out for them by the legislator and lose themselves and their pupils in subtle and intricate disquisitions. (Letter to the Patriarch of Venice and to the professors of canon law in the pontifical school of that city, July 16, 1917; A.A.S. Aug., 1917, p. 365.) What is demanded, then, is, after a brief history of the previous discipline, a clear, concise, practical explanation of the present law, leaving aside all merely theoretical or subtle questions. The Code is primarily a rule of action.

48. 3. *Utility and Necessity of the Canonical Science.* 1°. As laws remain useless unless they are known, the common as well as private good demands that the members of a society be acquainted with the legislation which has been enacted to govern it; all Catholics, then, must have some knowledge of the Church's disciplinary canons. In the so-called "Precepts of the Church" given in the books of catechetical instruction, the faithful have a summary of the laws of the Church which concern them more directly and which are of more frequent application. There are others, however, which they have to observe and in which they should be instructed, those, for example, about the sacraments, indulgences, confraternities, etc.; and there are many more still of which a Catholic should have at least some idea, if he is interested in his Church, its internal organization, its life and action.

49. 2°. As teacher of the law the priest must thoroughly understand that portion of the ecclesiastical legislation which he is to explain and enforce.

As a representative and minister of the Church he is under special obligation not to remain a stranger to anything that concerns her.

There exist, moreover, numerous ordinances which regard himself, his professional duties, his ministerial and professional life; with these he must evidently be familiar in all their details. "The life of a priest is of such importance that the Church has been always busy about it. In a long series of enactments, many of them going back to the early ages of Christianity, she has taken up and regulated every part and aspect of it. She has determined the dress he shall wear, and the prayers he shall say, the pursuits he may follow, and the recreations he must not indulge in as unsuited to his character. She has special prescriptions for each position he may hold, for almost every duty he has to perform. At the same time she watches over his dignity, and secures him in his rights, placing strong barriers to preserve him from the violence of the crowd, or from the arbitrary action of those above him. In a word, the priest lives and moves by rule; he is guarded by rule on all sides; to the ordinances of the Church he must turn, in every emergency and at every step, for protection and guidance, so that here again, in a new and wider shape, a knowledge of Church law becomes one of the essential requirements of his calling." (Clerical Studies, by Very Rev. J. B. Hogan, S.S., D.D., Boston, 1898, p. 307.)

50. A still wider knowledge of canon law is necessary to ecclesiastics who occupy a position of special authority or share in the responsibilities of Church administration, such as Vicars-General, Chancellors, officials of diocesan courts, without speaking of members of Roman Congregations or Tribunals. Arbitrary methods are always distasteful to the Church; she has carefully defined the limits within which the action of each one of her representatives ought to be exercised and the manner in which they are to proceed. They should ever be directed by her ordinances and should judiciously apply them. To do this it is not enough to have a superficial knowledge of them; it is necessary to get a good grasp of the general spirit of the canonical legislation, and this is acquired only by serious and prolonged study.

51. Hence it is that, after the study of the Scriptures, none was more frequently recommended to clerics, more strongly insisted upon by Fathers and Councils, almost from the beginning, than the study of the canons. The Second Council of Vaison, held in 529, directs pastors to prepare young clerics for their future functions, teaching them the psalter and the ecclesiastical laws (Can. 1); the Council of Macon, 581, can. 9, prescribes three days of fasting, every week, from the feast of St. Martin to Christmas, and those days are to be devoted, in a particular manner, to the reading of the sacred canons. Let priests, says the Fourth Council of Toledo, know the Scriptures and the canons (c. 25). The same recommendation is found in numerous other Councils and Decretals of Popes and frequently in the same terms. (Cf. Council of Lavaur, 1368, c. 3; Lateran, 1513, Sess. VIII.) Pope Innocent III refused to confirm a Bishop of Hungary because of his ignorance of theology and canon law. The Fourth Council of Milan, Part III, c. 1, ordains that Bishops devote some time every day to the study of the Scriptures, theology, and canon law; several Particular Councils of that period enact the same rule. Of preachers St. Charles Borromeo demands that they be proficient in the science of the Fathers, ecclesiastical history and the sacred canons; and to facilitate the acquisition of this last science he had a special teacher appointed to explain it.

Ancient regulations demanded that Bishops divide their parish priests into several groups and bring them in turn to the episcopal city, one of the purposes of these meetings being to give them instructions on the canons. (Thomassin, P. II, L. III, c. 74; vol. V. p. 358.)

52. 3°. If we take canon law in a broad sense as embracing the whole legislative work of the Church from the beginning to the present day, its study presents other advantages of a more general character.

"As a discipline of the intellect, it is for the cleric what the study of the civil law is for the secular, an influence ever broadening, tempering, and maturing his thoughts; a great school of patience, of moderation, of prudence, of measure. It shows how immovable firmness in essentials may be combined with admirable condescension in all else. In sustaining the divine law the Church is inflexible; in enforcing her own enactments she is full of considerateness and compassion for human weakness. Wherever she goes we find her tenderly accommodating her discipline to the degree of discipline she meets, commanding or forbidding, or tolerating, just as circumstances, present or prospective, seem to require. The ordinances of such Popes as St. Gregory the Great or St. Nicholas I are admirable in that regard; and all through the Decretals of the mediæval Popes we find the same gentle, reasonable, hopeful spirit, equally removed from weak indulgence and from undue rigor. To learn at such a school should be the ambition of all those who are called to share in the work of the Church, including even canonists themselves, some of whom, more erudite than judicious, are disposed to lift Church discipline almost above the natural and divine law, and make it into something rigid, unyielding, and ever so unlike that gentle, pliable, and, in the highest sense of the word, human rule, which it has been in the hands of the Church herself." (J. B. Hogan, l. c., p. 319.)

53. To the historian the study of canon law reveals the inner life of the Church, her aims, her ideals; the obstacles she had to overcome, the abuses she suffered from at different periods of her existence, the remedies she applied; the religious temperament of the races she had to deal with and the results of her action upon them. We do not really know the Church if we do not know her legislation, in which more fully than in anything else are reflected her mind and her aspirations.

The jurist will find in the *Corpus Juris Canonici* many provisions introduced first by ecclesiastical authority and accepted afterwards by the State; he will recognize in some of the rules formulated by ancient Synods or Popes principles which guide him even to this day; he will see the transforming influence exercised by Christianity on the law of pagan Rome and what it meant for modern legislations; and he, too, may learn how living men should be dealt with and how firmness may not be incompatible with human condescension.

54. The sociologist can hardly understand or account for present conditions unless he studies them in their antecedents and goes back to the origins of our modern civilization. This must infallibly lead him to inquire into the state of society in the Middle Ages. One of the most reliable, most abundant sources of information on that subject will be the Collections of ancient canons and of Papal Decretals. From the nature of the measures taken to correct more or less common abuses, from the cases proposed for solution, from apparently insignificant details given, he will, at times, get an insight into the life of the people and gather most interesting information not to be found elsewhere. This has been long understood by secular historians and jurists, as is shown by the publication of numerous scholarly works on various aspects of Church discipline.

VII. CODIFICATION OF CANON LAW. THE "CODEX JURIS CANONICI"

(Preface to the Code by His Eminence Cardinal Gasparri; J. Naval, Codificationis Juris Canonici Recensio Historico-Apologetica, Romae, 1918; P. Maroto, Institutiones Juris Canonici; vol. I, n. 154 ff., Madrid, Roma, 1918.)

55. 1. *Its Necessity.* Since the close of the *Corpus Juris* numerous new laws and decrees had been issued by Popes, Councils, and Roman Congregations. No complete Collection of them had ever been published and they remained scattered through the ponderous volumes of the *Bullaria,* the *Acta S. Sedis,* and other such compilations, which were accessible to only a few and for professional canonists themselves formed an unwieldly mass of legal material. Moreover, not a few ordinances, whether included in the *Corpus Juris* or of more recent date, appeared to be contradictory; some had been formally repealed, others had become obsolete by long disuse; others, again, had ceased to be useful or applicable in the present condition of society. Great confusion was thus engendered and correct knowledge of the law rendered very difficult even for those who had to enforce it.

Already in the Council of Trent the wish had been expressed in the name of the king of Portugal that a commission of learned theologians be appointed to make a thorough study of the canonical constitutions binding under pain of mortal sin, define their exact meaning, see whether their obligation should not be restricted in certain cases, and clearly determine how far they were to be maintained and observed.

56. The confusion had increased in the course of time, and in the Vatican Council several strong requests for a reform were drawn up by various groups of Bishops.

"The body of ecclesiastical laws," said the Bishops of the Province of Naples, "has become, in modern times, an almost unbearable burden—*ingens camelorum onus*—; contradictory texts abound in it, giving rise to endless disputes; often it is impossible to ascertain what is really of obligation." They recommend, then, that a new *Corpus Juris* be compiled, in which would be found clearly laid down the general principles of the ecclesiastical legislation, the laws actually in vigor, without those which have only a historical interest, and such new laws as would be necessary to settle controversies. (Acta et Decreta Sacrorum Conciliorum Recentiorum. Collectio Lacensis, Friburgi Brisgoviae, Herder; 1890, T. VII, p. 825d, 826a, b.)

Not less explicit was the *Postulatum* of French Bishops: "It is very evident," they said, "and has long been recognized by all and proclaimed everywhere that some revision and reformation of canon law is necessary and very urgent. For, owing to the changes that have taken place in society, many laws have become useless and others very difficult if not impossible to observe; of others it is doubtful whether they are still in vigor or not. Finally, in the course of centuries, their number has so multiplied and they have been so heaped up in voluminous Collections that, in a sense, we may say, we are buried beneath the laws. Hence it is that the study of canon law is beset with almost inextricable difficulties, the door is open to disputes and litigations, consciences are troubled with a thousand anxieties, and people are driven to despise the law." Therefore, they concluded, it is very desirable that the Council take up that great and important work of the reformation of ecclesiastical canons. For this purpose it was suggested that the Council itself indicate the principal reforms to be effected and give the general principles which would serve as a guide for the others. Then a commission would be appointed, composed of the most learned canonists and theologians together with men of consummate experience from all parts of the Church. The whole canonical legislation would be subjected by them to a careful revision; some of the old laws would be abrogated, some would be modified, and new ones might be added. Thus would be obtained a body of laws better adapted to the present needs of the Church, disposed in a logical order and formulated in clearer and more precise terms. (L.c. p. 840b.) Similar petitions were presented by the Bishops of Germany, p. 874b; by the Bishops of Belgium and Canada, p. 879b, c; by the Bishops of central Italy, and others. (P. 889a, b, c.) Unfortunately the Council was suspended before satisfaction could be given to these requests or the matter discussed.

57. Some canonists, Deshayes, in his *Memento*

Juris Canonici, Hollweck, in his *De Poenis;* Pillet, Pizzani, Colomiati, attempted, of their own private initiative, to gather together all the laws actually in vigor on a certain subject, to arrange them in a scientific order, and give them the form of clear, concise articles which they have in modern codes; but their work, however meritorious and useful, besides being unavoidably incomplete, lacked the official character which alone could invest it with the necessary authority.

A few portions of the ecclesiastical legislation were also codified with the sanction of the Holy See; the legislation on censures *latae sententiae,* in the Constitution *Apostolicae Sedis,* published by order of Pius IX in 1869; the legislation on prohibited books, in the Constitution *Officiorum et Munerum* published in 1897 by order of Leo XIII. An Instruction of the Congregation of Bishops and Regulars of June 11, 1880, contained a simplified form of procedure for the criminal and civil causes of clerics; and in the decree *Conditae a Christo* of Dec. 8, 1900, were summed up the rules regarding Religious with simple vows. These were happy innovations, but they covered only a small portion of the ground. The complete revision was deferred to the pontificate of Pius X.

58. 2. *Preliminaries to the Work of Codification.* On March 17, 1904, only a few months after his accession, Pius X published the *Motu Proprio, Arduum Sane, De Ecclesiae Legibus in Unum Redigendis,* in which, after enumerating the principal reasons which showed the insufficiency of the existing canonical Collections, he announced his project to prepare a new one without being discouraged by the magnitude of the task or the difficulty of the enterprise.

He therefore established a commission of Cardinals to whom would be committed the supreme direction of the entire matter. The Cardinals would be assisted by a certain number of consultors chosen amongst the most expert canonists and theologians; and, moreover, the whole body of Catholic Bishops would be called upon to cooperate in the work.

59. Soon after, on March 25th, the Cardinal Secretary of State addressed to all the Bishops of the world a circular letter in which he communicated to them the *Motu Proprio* and the list of consultors already appointed. The Metropolitans were directed at the same time to examine with their Suffragans which provisions of the present law would, in their opinion, particularly need change or correction; and to send a brief statement of their views to the Holy See as soon as possible and at least within four months from the reception of the letter. The Bishops of each nation were authorized, moreover, to send to Rome, at their own expense, a canonist or theologian, chosen by them, to act as consultor in the new commission. They might also, if they preferred, delegate one of the Roman consultors to represent them and speak in their name; or even select some one of their own nation who, without going to Rome, would lend his assistance by correspondence.

60. This letter was followed, on April 6th of the same year 1904, by an appeal from the Secretary of the Commission to all the Catholic Universities throughout the world, asking for their cooperation and giving them a general outline of the work to be done. The plan of the Holy Father, it said, is to sum up the whole law into aptly distributed canons or articles similar to those in modern codes. For the convenience of the consultors, the matter is tentatively divided thus: after introductory titles on the Holy Trinity and Catholic Faith, on Constitutions, Custom, and Rescripts, there will be five books treating successively of Persons, Sacraments, Sacred Things and Places, Crimes and Punishments, Judgments. That order will be modified if deemed advisable.

It is the wish of the Holy Father that all the Universities concur in that difficult and important undertaking; hence the rectors are requested to find out and let the Secretary of the Commission know as soon as possible what part of the ecclesiastical legislation their professors of canon law would be ready to formulate into articles or canons. On receiving their answer further instructions would be sent them and more complete directions. (Eccl. Rev., Dec. 1904, p. 603.)

61. 3. *The Codification. Method of Work.* The Commission of Cardinals announced in the Letter *Arduum sane munus* was appointed without delay; it consisted of sixteen members. A special committee of five was, however, formed soon after to secure quicker action.

The first care of the commission was to obtain the cooperation of a large body of able consultors. These were selected from among the most learned prelates of the Roman Curia, the members of Religious Orders, the secular clergy, in Italy and in other countries as well. Here also, lest time should be wasted in unprofitable discussions, two special commissions were appointed for the drafting of the canons, with the understanding, however, that no important piece of legislation would be finally adopted without being submitted to all the consultors, who would be invited to present observations and suggest modifications, if deemed advisable.

Precise directions were given by the Holy See to the members of the commissions to guide them in their work and privileges granted them to facilitate it. They had free access to all libraries and collections in religious houses or ecclesiastical institutions, and were permitted to borrow all books or documents they might need. Such of them as were members of chapters received dispensation from choir attendance when their presence was required on the commissions.

62. To each consultor was entrusted, for codification, that portion of the Church's legislation with which he was particularly familiar. At least two consultors were at work on each chapter of the Code, sometimes three or four, when the matter was of special importance. There were no communications between them and generally they did not even know one another.

63. The following directions had been given to the consultors:

(*a*) The Code is to deal only with disciplinary matters; it is not forbidden, however, it may even be necessary, to touch upon certain principles of the natural law or of the Christian faith.

(*b*) The disciplinary laws of the Church, setting aside those which have become obsolete or abrogated, are to be gathered from the *Corpus Juris,* the Council of Trent, the Acts of the Roman Pontiffs, the decrees of Roman Congregations or Ecclesiastical Tribunals, and reduced to short canons embodying only the enactment itself or *pars dispositiva* of the law, not the reasons for it, the occasion, etc. Each canon may be divided into paragraphs if necessary.

(*c*) The very words of the ancient documents

should be reproduced in the canons, as far as possible, always aiming at brevity and clearness; quotations from the same documents may be added by way of explanation, indicating the exact page, volume, and edition from which they are taken.

(*d*) In questions of importance and of a practical character about which authors differ a firm and definite solution should be proposed.

(*e*) Should a change in the present law be deemed advisable or necessary, it might be embodied in a canon, making mention of the modification involved and briefly giving the reasons for it. The same thing should be done if a new provision was to be introduced.

(*f*) The language to be used is Latin and it ought to be as worthy as possible of the majesty of the sacred canons so happily expressed in the ancient Roman law. (Preface to the Code, XXXII.)

64. The special commissions set to work on November 13, 1904; they met once a week, one of them on Thursdays the other on Sundays. The preliminary drafts of every canon, prepared by the consultors appointed for that purpose, had been handed in the day before to the president of the commission, who now submitted them, for discussion, to all its members, inviting every one of these to express freely his opinion and appreciation.

If a text thus presented proved satisfactory to all it was adopted at once, but this was not ordinarily the case, and the discussion seldom led to an agreement in the first meeting; the matter had to come again before the commission. The president, taking into account the modifications suggested, the additions asked for, the various criticisms offered, prepared another text, had it printed and distributed to the consultors, so that they might study it and be ready to discuss it the following week.

65. Even in its second form the canon rarely proved fully satisfactory; it had to be amended again and come before the commission a third, fourth, in some cases a tenth and even a twelfth time when the matter was particularly intricate, before a formula could be found which would receive universal approval. There were instances in which no such unanimity could possibly be reached. The canon was then drawn up in two forms, one in the sense of the majority or of the existing legislation; the other in the sense of the minority or of the proposed innovation. The entire body of consultors were called upon to give in writing their views on the proposed texts, and both the texts and the comments upon them were referred to the special commission of Cardinals who, after going over the whole question at least twice, pronounced the final decision. All this naturally demanded much time and labor, on the part principally of the president of the special commissions, on whom devolved the greater share of the work; it shows, on the other hand, with what care the laws of the Church are framed.

As the various parts of the Code were completed, the Sovereign Pontiff Pius X ordered copies of them to be sent to all the Bishops of the Catholic world and to superiors of Religious Orders.

A first volume containing the first and second books of the Code was thus sent out in 1912; the third and fourth books were ready in 1913, and the fifth in 1914.

Together with the text of the Code, Ordinaries received a letter requesting them to examine it carefully and to communicate to the Holy See, in all sincerity and freedom, their opinion of it, the objections they might have to some of its provisions, the amendments they might wish to suggest.

In the summer of 1914 war broke out in Europe and soon after occurred the death of Pope Pius X. Some feared that the preparation of the Code was going to be delayed considerably thereby or even suspended indefinitely. The work went on, however, under the protection and with the encouragement of the new Pontiff, Benedict XV, in spite of innumerable difficulties.

66. Meanwhile reports from Bishops all over the world had reached Rome; they were studied with all due attention and their contents classified. Whatever seemed of real importance and well grounded was embodied in some of the existing canons or in new ones framed for the purpose, and the texts thus corrected, modified, or completed had to go once more before the special commission of Cardinals. This meant a revision of the whole Code, a task almost as arduous as the first one. Three years sufficed, however, to bring it to a conclusion. In August, 1916, a revised text of the Code, in a volume of about 1,000 pages, containing 2,438 canons, could be presented to the commission of Cardinals and other competent persons for final examination. All was gone over again in detail and a few changes decided upon, none, however, of great importance. The most exacting critics pronounced the Code as perfect as could be expected and ready for publication.

Over twelve years of assiduous work had been required to complete it. Some had thought at first that seven or eight years would suffice, but the undertaking offered difficulties of which few could have a correct appreciation. Indeed, when one considers, on the one hand, the magnitude of the task and, on the other, the scrupulous attention given to its every detail, there is rather reason to wonder that it could be accomplished in so short a time.

67. 4. *Promulgation of the Code.* With sentiments of joy and profound gratification, Pope Benedict XV announced officially, in the Consistory of December 4, 1916, that the Code of Canon Law, so long and anxiously looked for, was now completed and would be published in the near future; an event, he added, so important and so full of promise for the Church, that it would suffice to render our age illustrious in the centuries to come. (A.A.S. Dec. 9, 1916, p. 465; Monitore, Gennaio, 1917.)

Conditions resulting from the war caused further delay and the promulgation took place only several months after, on May 27, 1917. On that day, the feast of Pentecost, Pope Benedict XV issued the Constitution *Providentissima Mater Ecclesia,* in which, after recalling briefly the principal steps that led up to this important event, in the fulness of the Apostolic authority with which he is invested, he pronounces the Code promulgated and having the force of law for the whole Church. In order, however, that all may have full knowledge of its prescriptions before they become effective, he decrees that they will not have the force of law till Pentecost of the following year, that is, till the nineteenth day of May, 1918.

On the 28th of June, in the Hall of the Consistory, the first copy of the Code was formally presented to the Holy Father, with great solemnity, by the president of the commission for the codification of laws, His Eminence Cardinal Gasparri, in presence of the Sacred College, numerous Bishops, prelates, and many of the consultors who had cooperated in the work.

The official edition of the Code appeared in the *Acta Apostolicae Sedis,* as a supplement to the June number. It was followed a few months later by another edition containing, besides the text of the law, a long preface by Cardinal Gasparri and a copious Index; a third edition was published a little later still, with notes and references to the sources of the law.

68. 5. *General Divisions and Contents.* The official title of the Code is: *Codex Juris Canonici, Pii X Pontificis Maximi Jussu Digestus, Benedicti Papae XV Auctoritate Promulgatus.*

It is divided into five books. The first contains general rules; the second treats of persons; the third of sacred things; the fourth of canoncial trials; the fifth of delinquencies and punishments. Each book is subdivided into titles and each title into canons. There are in all one hundred and seven titles distributed in five series corresponding to the five books. For the canons there is only one series of numbers running through the whole Code, so that each canon has a distinct number and to quote a special canon it will suffice to indicate its number, without having to mention the title or book.

The second book has three parts; the third, five; the fourth, two; the fifth, three. The first part of the second book and the second part of the third are divided into two sections each.

The longer titles are subdivided into chapters and the chapters into articles; some of the canons have several paragraphs.

The Bull of promulgation, *Providentissima Mater Ecclesia,* and the Profession of Faith have been inserted in the beginning, before the first book, and eight Papal Constitutions at the end, after the fifth. All these documents are authentic in the legal sense and whatever enactments they may contain have the force of law.

The headings of books, parts, sections, titles, chapters and articles are likewise authentic and part of the official text. As they do not form complete sentences they can not contain any distinct enactments, but they may serve to interpret the canons and the principle still holds: *a rubro ad nigrum valet illatio.* (P. Maroto, n. 167.) The Preface, Notes, and Index added afterwards, but not promulgated with the text in the *Acta Apostolicae Sedis,* have a great, but only doctrinal, authority.

69. 6. *Authority of the Code.* Its authority is public, universal, exclusive, and permanent.

Promulgation by the Pope gives it the character of an authentic Collection, every part of which has the force of law independently of the source from which it may be derived.

It is binding on the whole Latin Church both in the internal and the external forum and no other ecclesiastical laws continue in force than those contained in the Code or recognized by it. (Can. 1-6.)

Although it can not be immutable and absolutely final, measures have been taken to maintain its usefulness and secure the stability of the work therein accomplished. In the *Motu Proprio* of Sept. 15, 1917, instituting a commission for the interpretation of the Code, Pope Benedict XV decrees that, in future, Roman Congregations shall not enact general decisions unless some grave interest of the universal Church demands it. Their ordinary mission shall be to promote faithful compliance with the prescriptions of the Code, and to issue opportune instructions intended to explain these prescriptions and help their enforcement. (Canoniste Contemporain, Sept. 1917, p. 397.)

Should at any time the good of the Church call for a new decree it shall be drawn up by the Congregation which is competent in the matter and submitted to the Pope for approval; then it shall be referred to the Commission of Interpretation. If it modifies some provision of the Code, the Commission shall indicate which and the new text shall be substituted for the old one; if it introduces an altogether new provision, the commission shall determine where it is to be inserted, and this extra canon shall bear the same number as the one immediately preceding it, with the additional sign *bis, ter;* for example, Can. 115bis; so that the numbers of the canons may remain undisturbed. Thus the Code will continue to be the complete source of Church legislation and the need will not arise for a new Collection of general laws.

70. 7. *Character of the New Code.* (Il Monitore Ecclesiastico, Feb. 1919, p. 50.)

The present Code is the first authentic, complete Collection of the general laws of the Church arranged in a systematic, logical order and reduced to brief, concise formulae, after the example of modern civil codes.

Very different in form from previous Collections, it not infrequently differs from them likewise in substance. The legislator has codified the ancient legislation, but he has modified it also when needed to adapt it to present conditions. His main purpose in this, as shown in his work, was to promote more efficaciously the salvation of souls. *Salus populi supreme lex* has clearly been his guiding principle.

Hence in the organization of the Church and of the hierarchy those offices always have the particular favor of the law which are more directly connected with the care of souls.

Power is centralized to increase efficiency; more extensive faculties are granted to Bishops (*v.g.* in Can. 349, 386, 468, 534, 806, 1006, 1045, 1245, 1304), more freedom in the appointment to various offices, greater independence from chapters, less restricted jurisdiction over Religious, even those who are exempt.

The authority of pastors over the laity and also the clergy of the parish, whether secular or regular, is notably enhanced. The rights and duties of assistant pastors are more clearly defined than ever before.

In order that to a more suitable external organization may correspond a more intense interior spirit, special attention is given to the training of the clergy; rules are laid down for their personal religious life after ordination; certain exercises of piety are prescribed for them or strongly recommended; study is encouraged and even commanded; ecclesiastical learning is promised reward. (Can. 124-144.)

Occasions of sin are removed by the mitigation of many of the laws that affect the faithful directly; for example, the laws regarding fasting and abstinence, feast days of obligation, impediments of marriage, reservation of sin, the effects of ecclesiastical censures.

In the same spirit an effort has been made to bring the laws of the Church, particularly in mixed matters, into as complete conformity as possible with modern civil legislations. Thus on legal adoption (Can. 1059, 1080), prescription (Can. 1508), contracts (Can. 1529), the law of the State becomes, with some qualifications, the law of the Church. In many other cases the civil provisions have been adopted substantially or have served as models, particularly in the fourth book on Judicial Procedure and in the first part of the fifth book on Delinquencies and Penalties.

VIII. INTERPRETATION OF THE CODE

71. By the *Motu Proprio* of Sept. 15, 1917, Pope Benedict XV established a special Commission for the Interpretation of the Code as the Congregation called of the Council had formerly been established for the interpretation of the Council of Trent. It was feared that uncertainty and confusion would soon prevail again if private opinions and conjectures had to be depended upon to ascertain the meaning of the new law.

The commission is to answer questions proposed by or through the Ordinaries and superiors of Religious Orders. Its decisions have the force of law.

This official or legal interpretation is not intended, however, to exclude but rather to guide the usual, judicial, or doctrinal one.

Ecclesiastical tribunals will apply the law to particular cases, thus giving rise to a jurisprudence which in the course of time may become an authoritative norm. In spite of the effort made by the legislator to be clear, precise, and complete, the explanations of canonists will still be needed to bring out the full sense and bearing of many of the texts.

Nor does the publication of the Code dispense from the study of the former legislation and of ancient canonists; for "the Code for the most part retains the discipline thus far in force although it makes opportune changes. . . . Canons which restate former laws without any modification have to be understood in the same sense as the old laws and according to the interpretation given to them by recognized authors." (Can. 6.) Various rules are laid down in the Code itself for the guidance of official and private interpreters, particularly in Canons 6, 7, 17-24. (P. J. Noval, O.P., Codicis Piano-Benedictini Notitia Generalis, n. 60, 89.)

IX. SOURCES AND BIBLIOGRAPHY

72. The list of the ancient canonical Collections and of the principal works on canon law previous to the publication of the Code can be found in another part of this Introduction.

The sources of the individual canons in the present Code or the former provisions which they modify are indicated in the notes of Cardinal Gasparri in the following order: *Corpus Juris Canonici,* Councils, Pontifical Constitutions, Decrees of Congregations.

Works on the new Code:

Ph. Maroto, Institutiones Juris Canonici ad Normam Novi Codicis; T. I (Can. 1-214). Madrid, Roma, 1918; T. II, fasc. I (Can. 215; 264), 1919.

A. Blat, O.P., Commentarium Textus Codicis Juris Canonici; Lib. II, de Personis. Romae, Ferrari, 1919.

Lib. III, de Rebus, Pars prima, de Sacramentis.

J. Noval, O.P., De Processibus, Commentarium in Librum Quartum Codicis Juris Canonici, 1920; De Delictis et Poenis; Liber Introductivus; Liber Primus. Torino, Romae, Marietti.

J. B. Ferreres, S.J., Institutiones Canonicae juxta Novissimum Codicem Pii X a Benedicto XV Promulgatum. Barcinone, 1917.

P. C. Augustine, O.S.B., A Commentary on the New Code of Canon Law. Herder, St. Louis, 1918-1922.

M. Bargilliat, Praelectiones Juris Canonici, editio XXXIa, ad Canones Novi Codicis Redacta. Parisiis, 1918.

T. Albertus, Ad Codicem Juris Canonici Commentaria Minora, Romae, 1920.

J. Creusen, S.J., and A. Vermeersch, S.J., Summa Novi Juris Canonici Commentariis Aucta. H. Dessain, Malines, 1918.

G. Cocchi, Commentarium in Universum Codicem Juris Canonici. Marietti, Torino, 1920.

H. A. Ayrinhac, S.S., Penal Legislation in the New Code of Canon Law. Benziger Brothers, New York, 1920.

J. Sole, Praelectiones in Codicem Juris Canonici, Liber V, De Delictis et Poenis. Romae, 1920.

H. Papi, S.J., Religious Profession. A Commentary on a Chapter of the New Code of Canon Law. New York, Kenedy & Sons, 1918.

The Government of Religious Communities. A Commentary on three chapters of the New Code of Canon Law. Kenedy & Sons, New York, 1919.

F. Cappello, S.J., Tractatus Canonico-Moralis de Sacramentis juxta Codicem Juris Canonici. P. Marietti, Torino. Vol. I, De Sacramentis in Genere, De Baptismo, Confirmatione et Eucharistia; Vol. II, De Poenitentia, Ordine et Extrema Unctione; Vol. III, De Matrimonio.

D. Cerato, Matrimonium a Codice Juris Canonici integre desumptum, cum adnotatiunculis. Petavii, 1919.

A. Bevilacqua, Trattato Dommatico, Giuridico e Morale sul Matrimonio Cristiano. Roma, 1918.
P. Fourneret, Le Mariage Chrétien. Paris, 1919.
H. A. Ayrinhac, S.S., Marriage Legislation in the New Code of Canon Law. Benziger Bros., New York, 1918.
J. Petrovits, The New Law of the Church on Matrimony. J. J. McVey, Philadelphia, 1919.
F. M. Cappello, De Censuris juxta Codicem Juris Canonici. Marietti, Torino, 1919.
D. Cerato, Censurae Vigentes ipso Facto a Codice Juris Canonici Excerptae. Patavii, 1918.
J. B. Pighi, Censurae Sententiae Latae quas habet Codex Juris Canonici, cum Brevi Commentario. Veronae, 1917; De Sacramento Matrimonii, 1919.
J. Chelodi, Jus Matrimoniale, juxta Codicem. J. C. Tridenti, 1919.

Articles in Reviews:

Ecclesiastical Review, Philadelphia; Oct. 1917 ff.
Irish Theological Quarterly Review, Dublin; Oct. 1917 ff.
The Irish Ecclesiastical Record, Dublin; Nov. 1917 ff.
Civiltá Cattolica, Roma; 1917-1918.
Il Monitore Ecclesiastico, Roma; Jan. 1918 ff. (Cf. Aug. 1918, p. 247.)
Canoniste Contemporain, Paris; Juillet 1917 ff.
Revue du Clergé Français, Paris; Oct. Nov. 1917.
Revista Ecclesiastica, Valladolid; Oct. 1917 ff.
Resena Ecclesiastica; Barcelona, 1917, n. 104-107; 1918, n. 112-114.

PROFESSION OF FAITH

73. 1. The Decretals of Gregory IX, after the example of the Justinian Code, open with a title on the Blessed Trinity and the Catholic Faith. The first chapter taken from the Fourth Lateran Council (1215) contains the Profession of Faith drawn up by that Council against the errors of the Cathari and Waldenses. In the *Liber Sextus* and the *Clementinae* the first title is likewise *De Summa Trinitate et Fide Catholica.*

Arguments were not wanting to show the fitness of going back to the source of all authority at the beginning of an exposition of the Church's laws. (Reiffenstuel, Lib. I, Tit. I.) Some canonists recognized, however, that the discussion of the mysteries of religion was not within their province and that the canonical prescriptions on the Profession of Faith found their natural place in other parts of the legislation. Several of the old Collections, even among the authentic ones, did not have the title on the Blessed Trinity. (F. X. Wernz, Jus Decretalium, vol. I, n. 80; vol. III, n. 7.)

The first plan of the Code, as tentatively outlined for the convenience of the consultors, included an introductory title on the Trinity and the Catholic Faith. (Letter to the Rectors of Catholic Universities, Apr. 6, 1904.) This title was afterwards abandoned and only the formula of the Profession of Faith was retained, outside the regular series of titles and canons. The rules regarding the obligation of making the profession of faith were reserved for the fourth part of the third book, which treats of the ecclesiastical *magisterium.*

74. 2. The formula given here is that of Pius IV, completed by Pius IX, and called *Professio Piana.* There is no mention in this place nor anywhere else in the Code of the Profession of Faith or Oath prescribed by Pope Pius X against the modernistic errors (*Sacrorum Antistitum, Sept.* 1, 1910). From this silence some canonists concluded that it had ceased to be obligatory. (Ferreres, vol. I, n. 122.) That the inference was not legitimate the Holy Office declared explicitly March 22, 1918. The measures against Modernism were of a temporary character by their very nature and could not, for that reason, be embodied in the Code; but omission did not imply abrogation. Since the evil which they are intended to combat has not yet disappeared they remain in force until the Holy See decides otherwise. (A.A.S., Apr. 1, 1918, p. 136.)

PROFESSIO FIDEI

75. "Ego N. firma fide credo et profiteor omnia et singula, quae continentur in Symbolo Fidei, quo Sancta Romana Ecclesia utitur; videlicet: Credo in unum Deum Patrem omnipotentem, factorem coeli et terrae, visibilium omnium et invisibilium. Et in unum Dominum Jesum Christum Filium Dei unigenitum. Et ex Patre natum ante omnia saecula. Deum de Deo, lumen de lumine, Deum verum de Deo vero. Genitum, non factum, consubstantialem Patri, per quem omnia facta sunt. Qui propter nos homines et propter nostram salutem descendit de coelis. Et incarnatus est de Spiritu sancto ex Maria Virgine et homo factus est. Crucifixus etiam pro nobis sub Pontio Pilato passus et sepultus est. Et resurrexit tertia die secundum Scripturas. Et ascendit in coelum, sedet ad dexteram Patris. Et iterum venturus est cum gloria judicare vivos et mortuos; cujus regni non erit finis. Et in Spiritum sanctum Dominum et vivificantem, qui ex Patre Filioque procedit. Qui cum Patre et Filio simul adoratur et conglorificatur; qui locutus est per prophetas. Et unam Sanctam Catholicam et Apostolicam Ecclesiam. Confiteor unum baptisma in remissionem peccatorum. Et expecto resurrectionem mortuorum et vitam venturi saeculi. Amen.

"Apostolicas et Ecclesiasticas traditiones, reliquasque ejusdem Ecclesiae observationes et constitutiones firmissime admitto et amplector. Item Sacram Scripturam juxta eum sensum, quem tenuit et tenet sancta Mater Ecclesia, cujus est judicare de vero sensu et interpretatione sacrarum Scripturarum, admitto; nec eam unquam nisi juxta unanimem consensum Patrum accipiam et interpretabor.

"Profiteor quoque septem esse vere et proprie Sacramenta novae legis a Jesu Christo Domino nostro instituta, atque ad salutem humani generis licet non omnia singulis necessaria, scilicet Baptismum, Confirmationem, Eucharistiam, Poenitentiam, Extremam Unctionem, Ordinem, et Matrimonium; illaque gratiam conferre, et ex his Baptismum, Confirmationem, et Ordinem sine sacrilegio reiterari non posse. Receptos quoque et approbatos Ecclesiae Catholicae ritus in supradictorum omnium sacramentorum solemni administratione recipio et admitto. Omnia et singula quae de peccato originali et de justificatione in sacrosancta Tridentina Synodo definita et declarata fuerunt, amplector et recipio. Profiteor pariter, in Missa offerri Deo verum, proprium et propitiatorium sacrificium pro vivis et defunctis; atque in sanctissimo Eucharistiae Sacramento esse vere, realiter et substantialiter Corpus et Sanguinem, una cum Anima et Divinitate Domini nostri Jesu Christi, fierique conversionem totius substantiae panis in Corpus, et totius substantiae vini in Sanguinem, quam conversionem Catholica Ecclesia Transsubstantiationem appellat. Fateor etiam sub altera tantum specie totum atque integrum Christum verumque Sacramentum sumi. Constanter teneo Purgatorium esse, animasque ibi detentas Fidelium suffragiis juvari. Similiter et Sanctos una cum Christo regnantes venerandos atque invocandos esse, eosque orationes Deo pro nobis offerre, atque eorum reliquias esse venerandas. Firmissime assero, imagines Christi ac Deiparae semper Virginis, necnon aliorum Sanctorum habendas et retinendas esse, atque eis debitum honorem ac venerationem impertiendam. Indulgentiarum etiam potestatem a Christo in Ecclesia relictam fuisse, illarumque usum Christiano populo maxime salutarem esse affirmo. Sanctam, Catholicam et Apostolicam Romanam Ecclesiam omnium Ecclesiarum matrem et magistram agnosco; Romanoque Pontifici, beati Petri Apostolorum Principis successori ac Jesu Christi Vicario veram obedientiam spondeo ac juro.

"Caetera item omnia a sacris Canonibus et Oecumenicis Conciliis, ac praecipue a sacrosacta Tridentina Synodo et ab Oecumenico Concilio Vaticano tradita, definita ac declarata, praesertim de Romani Pontificis Primatu et Infallibili Magisterio, indubitanter recipio atque profiteor; simulque contraria omnia, atque haereses quascumque ab Ecclesia damnatas et rejectas et anathematizatas pariter damno, rejicio et anathematizo. Hanc veram Catholicam fidem, extra quam nemo salus esse potest, quam in praesenti sponte profiteor et veraciter teneo, eamdem integram et inviolatam usque ad extremum vitae spiritum constantissime (Deo adjuvante) retinere et confiteri, atque a meis subditis, vel illis quorum cura ad me in munere meo spectabit, teneri, doceri et praedicari, quantum in me erit, curaturum, ego idem N. spondeo, voveo, ac juro. Sic me Deus adjuvet, et haec sancta Dei Evangelia."

IURISIURANDI FORMULA

Juxta Motu Proprio *Sacrorum Antistitum* Primi Septembris, 1910

76. "Ego . . . firmiter amplector ac recipio omnia et singula, quae ab inerranti Ecclesiae magisterio definita, adserta ac declarata sunt, praesertim ea doctrinae capita, quae huius temporis erroribus directo adversantur. Ac primum quidem Deum, rerum omnium principium et finem, naturali rationis lumine per ea quae facta sunt, hoc est per *visibilia* creationis opera, tamquam causam per effectus, certo cognosci, adeoque demonstrari etiam posse, profiteor. Secundo, externa revelationis argumenta, hoc est facta divina, in primisque miracula et prophetias admitto et agnosco tamquam signa certis ima divinitus ortae christianae Religionis, eademque teneo aetatum omnium atque hominum, etiam huius temporis, intelligentiae esse maxime accommodata. Tertio: Firma pariter fide credo, Ecclesiam, verbi revelati custodem et magistram, per ipsum verum atque historicum Christum, quum apud nos degeret, proxime ac directo institutam, eandemque super Petrum, apostolicae hierarchiae principem eiusque in aevum successores aedificatam. Quarto: Fidei doctrinam ab Apostolis per orthodoxos Patres eodem sensu eademque semper sententia ad nos usque transmissam, sincere recipio; ideoque prorsus reiicio haereticum commentum evolutionis dogmatum, ab uno in alium sensum transeuntium, diversum ab eo, quem prius habuit Ecclesia; pariterque damno errorem omnem, quo, divino deposito, Christi Sponsae tradito ab Eaque fideliter custodiendo, sufficitur philosophicum inventum, vel creatio humanae conscientiae, hominum conatu sensim efformatae et in posterum indefinito progressu perficiendae. Quinto: Certissime teneo ac sincere profiteor, Fidem non esse coecum sensum religionis e latebris *subconscientiae* erumpentem, sub pressione cordis et inflexionis voluntatis moraliter informatae, sed verum assensum intellectus veritati extrinsecus acceptae ex auditu, quo nempe, quae a Deo personali, creatore ac domino nostro dicta, testata et revelata sunt, vera esse credimus, propter Dei auctoritatem summe veracis.

"Me etiam, qua par est, reverentia, subiicio totoque animo adhaereo damnationibus, declarationibus, praescriptis omnibus, quae in Encyclicis litteris *"Pascendi"* et in Decreto *"Lamentabili"* continentur praesertim, circa eam quam historiam domatum vocant.—Idem reprobo errorem affirmantium, propositam ab Ecclesia fidem posse historiae repugnare, et catholica dogmata, quo sensu nunc intelliguntur, cum verioribus christianae religionis originibus componi non posse.—Damno quoque ac reiicio eorum sententiam, qui dicunt, christianum hominem eruditiorem induere personam duplicem, aliam credentis, aliam historici, quasi liceret historico ea retinere quae credentis fidei contradicant, aut praemissas adstruere, ex quibus consequatur dogmata esse aut falsa aut dubia, modo haec directo non denegentur.—Reprobo pariter eam Scripturae Sanctae diiudicandae atque interpretandae rationem, quae, Ecclesiae traditione, analogia Fidei, et Apostolicae Sedis normis posthabitis, *rationalistarum* commentis inhaeret, et criticen textus velut unicam supremamque regulam, haud minus licenter quam temere amplectitur.—Sententiam praeterea illorum reiicio qui tenent, doctori disciplinae historicae theologicae tradendae, aut iis de rebus scribenti seponendam prius esse opinionem ante conceptam sive de supernaturali origine catholicae traditionis, sive de promissa divinitus ope ad perennem conservationem uniuscuiusque revelati veri; deinde scripta Patrum singulorum interpretanda solis scientiae principiis, sacra qualibet auctoritate seclusa, eaque iudicii libertate, qua profana quaevis monumenta solent investigari.—In universum denique me alienissimum ab errore profiteor, quo *modernistae* tenent in sacra traditione nihil inesse divini; aut, quod longe deterius, pantheistico sensu illud admittunt; ita ut nihil iam restet nisi nudum factum et simplex, communibus historiae factis aequandum; hominum nempe sua industria, solertia, ingenio scholam a Christo eiusque apostolis inchoatam per subsequentes aetates continuantium. Proinde fidem Patrum firmissime retineo et ad extremum vitae spiritum retinebo, de charismate *veritatis certo,* quod est, fuit eritique semper in *episcopatus ab Apostolis succesione;* non ut id teneatur quod melius et aptius videri possit secundum suam cuiusque aetatis culturam, sed ut *nunquam aliter credatur, nunquam aliter* intelligatur absoluta et immutabilis veritas ab initio per Apostolos praedicata.

"Haec omnia spondeo me fideliter, integre sincereque servaturum et inviolabiliter custoditurum, nusquam ab iis sive in docendo sive quomodolibet verbis Scriptisque deflectendo. Sic spondeo, sic juro, sic me Deus adjuvet et haec sancta Dei Evangelia."

BOOK I

GENERAL NORMS

(Can. 1-86.)

77. The first book, which is the shortest one of the five (eighty-six canons), contains general provisions and serves as a sort of introduction to the others.

After seven preliminary canons, it is divided into six titles: I, On Ecclesiastical Laws; II, On Custom; III, On the Reckoning of Time; IV, On Rescripts; V, On Privileges; VI, On Dispensations.

PRELIMINARY CANONS. (1-7.)

(Ferreres, n. 119; Maroto, n. 168; J. Noval, Codicis Piano-Benedictini Notitia Generalis, p. 42; Civiltá Cattolica, Jun. 1917.)

The preliminary canons, although only seven in number, are of the utmost importance for the interpretation and correct application of those which follow. They reveal the mind of the legislator as to the persons whom the Code is to affect, the matters which it is intended to regulate and those which remain outside of its scope. Therein is defined the effect which the Code will have on the discipline of the Oriental Churches, on liturgical law, on concordats, on acquired rights, privileges and indults, on customs, and on the existing legislation.

I. THE CODE AND THE ORIENTAL CHURCHES. (Can. 1.)

78. The Code is intended for the Latin Church; the Eastern Churches have their own canon law and the attitude of the Roman Pontiffs towards their customs as well as their liturgies has always been one of toleration and respect. (IV Lateran Council,

c. 4.) At Florence (1438-1439), after a detailed discussion of the differences which separated the Greeks from the Latins, the two parties agreed that each Church keep its own liturgy and discipline.

The theory that pontifical disciplinary laws are not meant to bind Eastern Catholics was explicitly set forth at the beginning of the seventeenth century by a theologian of great renown, Azor (Institutiones Morales, P. I, Lib. V, c. 11, sec. 7), and maintained by many others after him. Missionaries having interrogated the Congregation of the Propaganda on the subject, the question was examined in a particular meeting presided over by Cardinal Pamphili, afterwards Pope Innocent X, and on July 4, 1631, the answer came that the subjects of the four Eastern Patriarchs should not be considered as bound by Papal Constitutions except in three cases: (*a*) when the Constitutions dealt with matters of faith; (*b*) when the obligation was explicitly affirmed by the Pontiff; (*c*) when his intention of imposing the obligation was sufficiently clear from the nature of the law, as, for example, in the prohibition to appeal from the Pope to a General Council. (Collectanea C. de P.F., ed. 2a, n. 395, sec. 44.)

This decision never received formal papal approval and therefore it remains in itself a mere theological opinion (Coll., n. 113, or n. 1578), but it enjoyed great authority. Popes frequently referred to it and followed it in particular cases. (Clement VIII, Aug. 31, 1595; Benedict XIV, *Etsi Pastoralis,* May 26, 1742. Coll. n. 358; *Allatae sunt,* Jul. 2, 1755, Coll. 395.) On the same principle, Leo XIII declared (Nov. 8, 1882, Coll. n. 1578) that the Const. *In Suprema* of June 20, 1882, concerning the obligation of Bishops to say Mass for their people did not apply to Eastern prelates except in as far as it gives expression to the divine right, which demands that pastors pray and offer the sacrifice sometimes for their flock, but leaves to ecclesiastical regulations to determine how often; likewise the Congregation of the Council, on Feb. 1, 1908, returned a negative answer to the question whether the decree *Ne temere,* on the forms of marriage, affected the Eastern Churches.

79. 2. The Code now explicitly states that it regards only the Latin Church and binds the Eastern Churches only in matters which of their nature concern them also.

The canons which from their very nature and in accordance with previous decisions will bind them are those: (*a*) in which this obligation is explicitly mentioned; (*b*) those in which it is implied, because, for example, they contain a declaration of the divine right and are not purely ecclesiastical; *e.g.* Can. 805, on the obligation for priests to say Mass several times a year; Can. 864, on the obligation of receiving the Holy Eucharist when in danger of death; (*c*) those which are not strictly disciplinary but doctrinal and rather concern faith or morals; (*d*) the S. Penitentiary declared, July 7, 1917, that the faithful of the Oriental rites can gain the indulgences granted by general pontifical decree (A.A.S.; 1917, p. 399); canonists apply the same principle to all favorable laws, with some restrictions, however. On March 13, 1916, the Congregation for the Oriental Rites declared that the Apostolic Const. *Incruentum Altaris* of Aug. 10, 1915, granting permission to all priests to say three Masses on All Souls' Day, concerned only the Latin Church and that it was not expedient to extend the privilege to the priests of the East. (A.A.S., 1916, p. 104.) The reason seems to have been, not to make changes in their liturgy.

In all other matters Catholics who do not belong to the Latin rite are governed by the laws of their own particular Churches.

II. THE CODE AND LITURGICAL LAWS. (Can. 2.)

80. Revision and codification of liturgical laws were not part of the legislator's plan. The rules about the rites and ceremonies which are prescribed in liturgical books approved by the Latin Church for the celebration of Holy Mass, the administration of the sacraments and sacramentals and other sacred functions, retain all their force unless they are expressly corrected in the Code.

The special and constant attention which the Church, chiefly through the Congregation of Rites, gives to everything pertaining to divine worship rendered a revision of these rules unnecessary; they are so numerous and so minute that a new classification of them would prove a very arduous task. By their incorporation in it the Code would have grown to an inconvenient size without real advantage. They are, besides, of such peculiar nature that they could not easily be fused with the rest of the legislation.

By liturgical laws are to be understood, not only the rubrics of the Missal, Breviary, Ritual, Pontifical, and other liturgical books of the Church, but also Constitutions of Roman Pontiffs and decrees of Congregations really bearing on liturgy and intended to explain rubrics, facilitate their application, or promote their observance. Thus the decrees contained in the Collection which the Congregation of Rites commenced to publish in 1898 with the approbation of Pope Leo XIII, under the title: *Decreta*

Authentica Congregationis S. Rituum, will continue in force; as also those included in an additional volume issued in 1912. An exception should be made for the general decrees which are not strictly liturgical but bear on matters which have since ceased to be within the province of the Congregation of Rites; those, for example, dealing with questions of precedence, the application of the Mass for the people, etc. Particular decrees remain unchanged. (Maroto, n. 122, 171.)

III. THE CODE AND CONCORDATS. (Can. 3.)

(Cardinal Cavagnis: Institutiones Juris Publici Ecclesiastici, Romae, 1889; P. I, p. 380; Wernz, I, n. 164 sq.; Dictionnaire de Théologie Catholique, Concordats; The Catholic Encyclopedia, Concordat.)

81. 1. Concordats are agreements between the religious and civil power regarding matters which may interest both societies.

Examples of such agreements are met with in the twelfth century (London Pact, between Paschal II and Henry I, in 1107; Sutri Convention, between the same Pope and Henry V of Germany, in 1111; Concordat of Worms or *Pactum Callixtinum,* between Callistus II and Henry V, in 1122) and even at a much earlier date, if we include in the list of concordats the pact of Quierzy between Stephen II and Pepin the Short, in 754; those between Adrian I and Charles the Great, in 774; between Leo VIII and Otto I, in 963, and other similar ones. (Tardif, Histoire des Sources du Droit Canonique, p. 251; Concordata Nationis Germanicae, T. II, p. 5, 7; c. 22, 23, 30-33, D. LXIII.) According to some writers, there were six or seven concordats before the eighteenth century; twelve or fifteen during the eighteenth and many more during the nineteenth century. Cardinal Cavagnis counts fifty-two up to 1886. Among the best known ones may be mentioned the concordats of Bologna between Leo X and Francis I, in 1516; of Vienna between Eugene IV and German Princes, in 1447; of 1801 between Pius VII and Bonaparte. (Nussi: Conventiones de Rebus Ecclesiasticis inter Sanctam Sedem et Civilem Potestatem Variis Formis Initae, Romae, 1869, contains the text, in Latin, of most of them; in another edition of the same work by Bueck, Mayence, 1870, the documents are given in the chronological instead of the logical order. A more complete and more reliable Collection is: *Raccolta di Concordati su Materie Ecclesiastiche tra la S. Sede é le Autoritá Civili,* 1098-1914, in 4°, p. 1140, Tipografia Poliglotta Vaticana, 1919.)

82. 2. What is the real nature of a concordat? (*a*) For the regalists who look upon the Church as an inferior society subordinate to the State, concordats derive their binding force exclusively from the civil authority, which can therefore revoke them at will. This is called the legalist theory; it was solemnly proposed for the first time by the Bavarian government in 1770, and has been defended since by many writers or jurists, such as Hinschius, Sarway, and Friedberg.

(*b*) Numerous Catholic canonists see in concordats strictly bilateral contracts binding on both parties. (Cavagnis, o.c., P. I, p. 398; Soglia, Institutiones Juris Publici Ecclesiastici; Palmieri, De Romano Pontifice; Moulart, l'Eglise et l'Etat; Turinaz, Les Concordats; Giobbio, I Concordati.)

(*c*) According to others, concordats are, in themselves, privileges granted by the Church to the State, directly imposing obligations on the State alone.

(Cardinal Tarquini, Institutiones Juris Ecclesiastici; Hammerstein, De Ecclesia et Statu Juridice Consideratis, Treves, 1886; De Bonald, Deux Questions sur le Concordat de 1801; B. Ojetti, in The Catholic Encyclopedia, v. Concordat.)

83. 3. The present Code does not settle the controversy, but, without deciding whether the existing concordats might be modified by its provisions, it declares that they are not. They remain in full force notwithstanding contrary prescriptions of the Code.

IV. THE CODE AND ACQUIRED RIGHTS, PRIVILEGES, AND INDULTS. (Can. 4.)

84. 1. The rights legitimately acquired by a third party are not affected by the prescriptions of the Code. This is in accordance with the principle laid down in the eighteenth rule of the Apostolic Chancery. The Supreme Pontiff does not mean, by any declaration, letter, favor, even if granted *motu proprio et ex certa scientia,* to take away from other parties the rights they legally possess. (Reiffenstuel, L. VII, Tit. V, p. 106.) Whatever be, for example, the favors granted to pastors, they are not freed from the obligations contracted towards parishioners, unless by an express provision to the contrary.

2. Privileges are special favors granted by the legislator, in a somewhat permanent manner, outside or against the common law. This canon states that privileges of which physical or moral persons were in possession at the time the Code was published remain in force unless expressly revoked. This concerns only special privileges, as those contained in the old common law were abrogated with the law itself, unless confirmed by the Code.

As for the future, Can. 71 enacts that a general law would repeal contrary privileges contained in the Code but not others, unless explicitly declared or unless the law emanates from the superior of the grantor of these privileges.

Ancient canonists admitted likewise that a subsequent universal law abolishes contrary privileges embodied in the common law but not special ones.

85. 3. Indults are concessions by the Holy See of certain powers or exemptions from law. They partake of the nature of special privileges and follow the same rule; contrary prescriptions of the Code do not abrogate them unless it be explicitly so stated.

With privileges or indults should not be confounded here special dispositions of the law or Pontifical Constitutions, which have rather the character of particular legislation and are abrogated if contrary to the Code. Thus it has been declared that the provisions of the Second Plenary Council of Baltimore, n. 96, empowering Bishops or Metropolitans to appoint the Administrator of a diocese during the vacancy of the See are abrogated as contrary to Can. 427. (Nov. 24, 1918, A.A.S., 1919, p. 75.) In like manner, the question having been asked whether the Constitution *Provida* of Jan. 18, 1906, which exempted mixed marriages in Germany and Hungary from the regular form of contract, was abrogated in accordance with Can. 6, 1°, as a particular law contrary to Can. 1099, or whether as a privilege or indult it still remained in force in accordance with Can. 4, the answer given was: it is abrogated. (March 30, 1918; L. Wouters, C.SS.R., De Forma Promissionis et Celebrationis Matrimonii, 1919, p. 53.)

V. THE CODE AND EXISTING CONTRARY CUSTOMS. (Can. 5.)

86. 1. Customs may be *juxta, praeter,* or *contra legem.* This canon deals only with those which are contrary to some prescriptions of the Code. Those which are *juxta legem* retain evidently all their value; those which are *praeter* must be assimilated to laws, general or particular, and treated accordingly.

Again, customs may be universal or particular; no difference is made here between these. They may have existed from time immemorial, or for a hundred years, or for a shorter period.

2. In the Code some customs are explicitly maintained or tolerated, others are explicitly reprobated as corruptions of the law, others are not mentioned explicitly or implicitly.

(*a*) Customs explicitly maintained or tolerated by the Code remain in force.

(*b*) Customs expressly reprobated, whether universal or particular, of immemorial or of shorter duration, are abrogated, and it is forbidden to introduce them again.

(*c*) Customs not mentioned in any way and contrary to some provision of the Code, whether they be universal or particular, are abrogated unless they have existed from time immemorial, in which case the Ordinary of the place may tolerate them if, considering local and personal circumstances, he judges that they could not prudently be abolished.

VI. THE CODE AND FORMER CANONICAL LEGISLATION. (Can. 6.)

87. As already stated, the Code supersedes all previous canonical Collections and forms the complete source of the general ecclesiastical legislation; not that it introduces an entirely new system of discipline, rather it retains as much as possible and for the most part the one hitherto in force, only completing or modifying it when necessary. Hence:

1. All universal laws which are contrary to the prescriptions of the Code have been abrogated. The same principle applies to particular laws, except that some of these may be and have been maintained by special disposition. Therefore the decrees of the Baltimore Councils which are opposed to provisions of the new law have lost their legal value, unless an exception has been made in their favor by the legislator.

2. Such portions of the ancient legislation as have been embodied in the new one without any or with only verbal changes retain their former binding force and will have to be interpreted in the same sense as they were interpreted in the past by approved authors.

88. 3. Some of the ancient laws have entered into the new canons with modifications; these canons have to be interpreted in the light of the ancient law in so far as they agree with it; where they differ, their meaning is determined from the wording adopted by the legislator. His mind is generally manifested by a comparison between the former and the present text of the law.

4. An ancient law is not presumed to have been changed unless this be fairly clear. Whenever it remains doubtful whether a canon of the Code differs from the former prescription conformity should be supposed.

5. In penal matters, however, the intention of reform is more easily admitted and penalties not mentioned in the Code, whether spiritual or temporal,

medicinal or vindictive, *ferendae* or *latae sententiae,* must be considered as abrogated. In such matters the ancient law serves only as a source of interpretation; all the binding force is derived from the new law.

89. 6. In regard to other legislation: (*a*) Ancient general ecclesiastical laws not included in the Code, explicitly or implicitly, cease by that very fact to be binding. The legislator shows sufficiently, by leaving them out, his intention of abrogating them, since the new Collection is meant to be complete.

(*b*) This rule does not hold for particular laws, such as decrees of local Councils or measures taken, even by the supreme authority, in view of temporary needs, for example, the anti-modernistic prescriptions. The Code is not concerned with particular legislations and they remain unchanged as long as they do not go against the new universal law. (Cf. Can. 22.)

(*c*) Natural and divine positive laws retain, as is evident, all their binding force independently of canonical confirmation or sanction.

(*d*) Concordats, acquired rights, privileges, and indults do not come under this rule either, as explicitly declared, and because they are not part of the general legislation of the Church nor laws strictly so called.

(*e*) All liturgical laws are explicitly declared to remain in force and, therefore, need not be renewed individually.

90. (*f*) What laws should be considered as included in the Code, if not explicitly at least implicitly, may not be perfectly clear in all cases.

Can. 904, on the obligation of denouncing the crime of solicitation, refers to the Apostolic Constitutions, particularly to the Constitution of Benedict XIV, *Sacramentum Poenitentiae* of June 1, 1741; Can. 160 enacts that papal elections are governed by the Constitution of Pius X, *Vacante Sede Apostolica* of Dec. 25, 1904. It seems legitimate to conclude that all the dispositions contained in these Constitutions become thereby included in the Code, not simply the general principle which they enunciate.

On the other hand, although according to Can. 20, when there is neither general nor particular enactment by which to decide a certain case, the rule to settle it should be taken from laws given in similar matters, from the general principles of canon law, from the practice of the Roman Court, or from the common teaching of canonists; it does not follow that such a rule or the sources from which it is drawn become implicitly part of the Code.

Legal provisions should be considered as implicitly included in the Code when they are contained in some of its canons, "as the conclusion in the principle, as the species in the genus, as the part in the whole, as the lesser in the greater." (Noval, l.c., p. 47.)

VII. MEANING OF THE EXPRESSIONS "APOSTOLIC SEE," "HOLY SEE," IN THE CODE. (Can. 7.)

91. The term "Apostolic See" or "Holy See" serves to designate in the Code not only the Roman Pontiff but also the Congregations, Tribunals, and Offices through which the Pope usually transacts the affairs of the universal Church. The context or the nature of the matter in question shows whether it ought, in particular cases, to be understood exclusively of the Pontiff. In him resides the fulness of ecclesiastical jurisdiction; he communicates some of it to Congregations, which thus act in his name and as representatives of the Roman See, although there is always an important difference between their enactments and those emanating immediately from the Pope himself.

TITLE I

OF ECCLESIASTICAL LAWS

(Can. 8-24.)

(Decretales Gregorii IX et Bonifacii VIII, Lib. I, Tit. 2, De Const.; Reiffenstuel, Jus Canonicum Universum, Lib. I, Tit. 2; Suarez, De Legibus; Wernz, Jus Decretalium, vol. I, Tit. IV; Bouquillon, Theologia Moralis Fundamentalis, Tractatus III, Lib. VI; Maroto, l. c., n. 177 ff.)

I. NATURE OF ECCLESIASTICAL LAWS

92. 1. A law in general, according to St. Thomas, is an ordinance of the practical reason, for the common good, promulgated by him who has the care of the social order. An ecclesiastical law is one enacted by ecclesiastical authority for the good of a Christian community.

(*a*) Law implies command, obligation; in this it differs from mere counsel, exhortation, instruction, warning, or even rule, which may only contain a direction, a norm of life. It is not necessary that the law be formulated in formally imperative terms, as long as the legislator's intention of imposing an obligation is sufficiently manifest from the context or other circumstances.

(*b*) Law aims at the common good, *i.e.* it is enacted for the community or at least for a certain portion of it, for example, for the clergy, not for individual members. To be a fit subject for legislation a community must be complete or perfect; the Church, ecclesiastical provinces, dioceses, completely organized religious communities, are perfect societies in this canonical sense, but not, for instance, a parish, a chapter, a particular religious house, a confraternity.

The purpose of the law must, besides, be to promote the good of the community, not exclusively that of individuals, although it may be directly for the good of the individual members and thus promote the good of the community. The laws on annual confession, Easter communion, fasting and abstinence, are directly for the sanctification of the individuals, but the good of the community is closely connected with that of its members.

93. (*c*) Like the community for which it is intended, the law has some permanency if not absolute perpetuity.

(*d*) The author of the law is the superior who has power of ruling over a perfect community. In the Church this power is vested, for the whole Christian world, in the Pope and General Councils, in the Roman Congregations as representing the Holy See, in Plenary and Provincial Councils, in Bishops, Vicars Apostolic, Prefects Apostolic, Prelates Nullius, heads of Religious Orders under certain conditions; not, for example, in superiors of religious houses, Vicars-General, pastors, masters, parents, husbands; these have only private or domestic or, as it is called, "dominative" authority. Even judges, although possessing jurisdiction, have no legislative power.

94. 2. Laws are territorial when their effect is limited to a certain territory; they are personal when they follow the persons and bind them wherever they may be. Ordinarily laws are territorial. The communities for which they are made usually have a fixed residence; by which also they come under the authority of the legislator and it is conducive to good order that the same law should govern all who habitually live in the same place. Hence the exercise of legislative power has commonly been made to depend on territory. "Laws are not presumed to be personal but territorial, unless the contrary be proved." (Can. 8.)

General laws which bind everywhere are all, at least virtually, personal, since their efficacy is not limited to any province. Some of them, however, impose obligations to be fulfilled in definite places and may in that sense be called strictly territorial; for example, laws on residence, on diocesan visitation, etc. In other cases the object of a general law is, of its nature, personal, such as hearing Mass, going to confession, irregularities, impediments. The law may then be considered as personal also.

But it is especially in regard to particular laws that the distinction may prove of importance. Regularly they are territorial, but they may also be personal; this, however, is not to be presumed and should be proved with sufficient certainty from the object of the law, its purpose, or the explicit declaration of the legislator. If an Ordinary imposed on his clergy the obligation of abstaining from intoxicating drinks, of reciting the rosary, if he forbade them to read a certain book, to go to theaters even outside of his diocese, as, according to some canonists he has power to do under the present Code, these would be personal particular laws. (Maroto, n. 183.)

II. PROMULGATION OF ECCLESIASTICAL LAWS

95. 1. *Nature.* The promulgation of law is the act of the legislator formally and officially manifesting his will to impose a certain obligation on the subjects. It differs from divulgation or notification. It may require some time for a law after its promulgation to become generally known; on the other hand, should the law be known before it has been promulgated it would not be binding for that reason nor really be a law as yet.

2. *Necessity.* Laws are enacted when they are promulgated. (Can. 8.) The will of the legislator to impose an obligation must be made known publicly and officially before it can be binding on the subjects. There can remain no doubt that promulgation is an essential, even though perhaps not intrinsic and constitutive, element of law, whatever may have been the opinions of ancient canonists. (Bouix, De Curia Romana, Pars 3a, Sectio 1a, c. 2; Suarez, De Legibus, Lib. I, c. 11, n. 1.)

96. 3. *Mode of Promulgation.* No special form is necessary from the nature of things, provided the will of the legislator be sufficiently manifested and may gradually reach the persons concerned. It is for the legislator to decide what means should be used to attain this end.

(*a*) Under the old Roman law each new ordinance had to be published in every province of the Empire before it went into effect. The Sovereign Pontiffs often adopted a similar practice and sent copies of their Constitutions or Decrees to the various Bishops or Metropolitans. Some canonists, regalists, and Jansenists argued from this that it was essential for all papal laws to be published in every diocese or at least in every kingdom; and as the publication could be prevented by the civil rulers, the exercise of ecclesiastical jurisdiction became thus dependent on the good-will of the princes.

There is clearly no foundation for this theory and it never received any official recognition, directly or indirectly. Innocent III promulgated a Collection of his Decretals in a letter addressed to the University of Bologna (1210). Martin IV had the bull against Michael Paleologus posted on the doors of the principal church at Orvieto, where he then resided, declaring that this was sufficient promulgation.

From this time on the same mode of promulgation was frequently used. Apostolic Constitutions and Letters would be posted at the doors of the Roman basilicas St. John Lateran and St. Peter, or at the Apostolic Chancery and on the Campo de' fiori. The Encyclicals were generally sent to the Bishops. For some laws a special mode of publication was prescribed, *v.g.* for the Decree *"Tametsi."*

In the Const. *Promulgandi* of Sept. 29, 1908, Pius X enacted that beginning with the year 1909 all Papal Constitutions, laws, decrees and all other acts of the Pope or of the Roman Congregations should be inserted in the *Acta Apostolicae Sedis* and that, unless otherwise ordained, this would suffice for their promulgation.

97. (*b*) These provisions are maintained in the Code. The laws of the Apostolic See are promulgated by publishing them in the *Acta Apostolicae Sedis* unless in some special cases another mode of promulgation be prescribed. The laws begin to bind in conscience only three months after the date affixed to the number of the *Acta* in which they appear, unless the nature of the law requires that it go into effect at once, or unless the law itself expressly provides for a longer or shorter period of "vacation." (Can. 9.)

This mode of promulgation is sufficient and necessary for all papal laws. A pontifical document, even though of undoubted authenticity, would remain without binding force it it had not been inserted in the *Acta* unless explicitly provided otherwise.

The time which elapses between the publication of a law and the day when it goes into effect is called the "vacation" of the law. It is now a period of three months for the laws of the Apostolic See, except in some special cases. This time is counted from the date of the number of the *Acta*. A law published in the number which bears the date of February 8, 1919, goes into effect May 8.

Doctrinal decrees concerning faith or morals, those which contain a declaration of the divine law or of any law about which there is no real uncertainty, of their nature go into effect without delay.

Nothing is said here about the promulgation of any other laws than those of the Holy See. This is left for the legislators to determine.

Ordinarily episcopal laws have no "vacation" and go into effect as soon as promulgated; for the decrees of Particular Councils some delay is usually allowed.

III. OBJECT OF ECCLESIASTICAL LAWS

98. (*a*) The object of ecclesiastical as of other laws must be something just, reasonable, necessary, or useful for the community, and not too difficult. Heroic acts can be demanded by the Church only when the common good requires them or when a person has freely accepted an office or dignity which calls for them.

(*b*) Purely internal acts, according to many canonists, do not come directly under the jurisdiction of the Church in the external forum. All must admit, however, that the Church may command internal acts which are necessarily connected with the external ones, *v.g.* the dispositions required for the worthy reception of holy communion, and, in general, that the legislative power of the Church must extend as far as the interests of the Christian society demand. In practice it will seldom, if ever, happen that obedience can be refused to an ecclesiastical ordinance on the plea that its object is too purely internal. (Maroto, n. 185; Bouquillon, n. 114.)

(*c*) Laws concern the future, not the past, unless express mention be made of the past. (Can. 10.) To be the rule of action, law must precede it. It can not affect a past action in itself to render it unlawful, but it can pronounce on its moral character and regulate some, at least, of its consequences.

The ecclesiastical legislator can declare certain acts contrary to the divine law or to an existing ecclesiastical law, annul them when the matter is within his jurisdiction, or attach to them irregularities, impediments, disabilities, etc., which do not necessarily suppose a fault. He can likewise enact a punishment against past offences.

All this, however, is always by way of exception, and no law is supposed to have any such retroactive effect unless it be explicitly stated.

IV. EFFECTS OF ECCLESIASTICAL LAWS

99. 1. The immediate and essential effect of law is to impose an obligation. The obligation may be positive or negative, grave or light.

It may be *ad culpam* or only *ad poenam, i.e.* the

law may command or forbid something under pain of sin or of punishment only, thus binding the subjects either to fulfil its prescriptions or to undergo the penalty.

Canonists admit that ecclesiastical laws may be and that some, although very few, are merely penal. (Wernz, I, n. 112; Maroto, n. 220.)

2. Law may also render null and void or voidable an act which according to natural law or the general principles of positive law would be valid; it may likewise disqualify a person for certain actions, functions or dignities. We have examples of this in marriage impediments and censures.

These are, however, extraordinary effects of the law, and the Code decrees that "only those laws are to be considered as invalidating or disqualifying which state explicitly or equivalently either that the act is null and void or that the person is disqualified." (Can. 11.)

V. SUBJECTS OF THE LAW. (Can. 12-14.)

100. 1. *General Conditions.* To be bound by merely ecclesiastical laws a person must be baptized, enjoy the use of reason, and have completed his seventh year.

Men become members of the Christian society by baptism. The Church claims no authority over those who are outside her fold. They may be affected by her laws indirectly; for example, if they contract marriage with a Catholic. Nor is putative baptism sufficient; the sacrament must have been received validly to bring one under the Church's jurisdiction.

Divine laws are binding on all rational creatures,

but human laws require the use of reason, at least the habitual use.

As this condition is ordinarily fulfilled about the age of seven, the Church has decreed that her laws would not be obligatory before completion of the seventh year even though the full use of reason might exist before that, unless there be an explicit provision to the contrary. Thus the law on annual confession and communion is binding as soon as the age of reason is reached independently of the age, as the wording of the canons (859, 906) clearly implies and the Commission of Interpretation explicitly declared. (Answer to the Bishop of Valleyfield and the Archbishop of New York Jan. 3, 1918; E. R., March, 1918, p. 313; cf. Can. 854, 940.) The ecclesiastical law in these cases is frequently a declaration of the divine right.

Even after the age of seven one is not subject to ecclesiastical laws if he has not habitually the use of reason; the *impuberes* are excused from penalties *latae sententiae.* (Can. 2230.)

The Code has no special provision here for baptized non-Catholics or persons under excommunication. It can not be doubted that the Church has jurisdiction over them and that they are bound by her laws if such is her will. Such is certainly the case in regard to laws which are intended directly for the common good, like those on marriage impediments. From others they are explicitly exempted; for example, the law on the form of marriage. (Can. 1099, 2.) There are acts forbidden to them as long as they remain under censure, as assisting at the divine services; these can not be demanded of them, although there be an obligation to remove the obstacle and render them possible.

Some good canonists and theologians consider it as probable that the Church does not wish to impose on heretics and schismatics born and educated outside her influence the obligations which have for their direct and immediate object the sanctification of the individuals, like fasting, abstinence, hearing Mass on Sundays, etc. (Wernz, I, 103; Bouquillon, n. 154.) This does not apply to those who are responsible for their heresy or schism.

101. 2. *General Laws.* They are binding on all for whom they were intended, wherever they may be. Those made for the clergy in general bind ecclesiastics outside as well as in the place of their residence, unless they be in a place which is exempt, or the laws be territorial in the sense that they can be fulfilled only in a determined territory.

General laws of the Latin Church are not intended for Eastern Catholics even when they reside in Latin countries; they are considered as exempt or as strangers, *peregrini,* although they may have a domicile in the place. They remain bound by the legislation of their own rite and by such laws of the territory in which they live as pertain to the formalities of contracts and the public order besides the rules which may have been enacted for them by competent authority. (Maroto, n. 198.) The Const. of Pius X, *Ea semper fuit,* of Aug. 14, 1907, (A.S.S., vol. XLI, p. 3) and a few years later, Aug. 17, 1914, a decree of the Propaganda (A.A.S., vol. VI, p. 458) regulate the condition of the Ruthenians in the United States. A similar measure had been taken, Aug. 18, 1913, regarding the Ruthenians in Canada. (A.A.S., V, 393.)

102. 3. *Particular Laws.* Laws enacted for a limited territory are binding only on those whom they concern and who have both their domicile or quasi-domicile and their actual residence in the territory; unless the laws be also personal, in which case they follow the persons everywhere. Thus laws made for the clergy of a certain diocese bind the ecclesiastics of that diocese on two conditions: that they have their domicile or quasi-domicile in the diocese and that they actually reside there. As soon as they go outside its limits they cease to be bound, unless the laws be also personal.

That particular laws may be personal is evident from Can. 14, 1°; that such laws can be enacted by local Ordinaries is maintained by some modern canonists against the common opinion of ancient authors, principally on the strength of Can. 201, 3: Unless the nature of the case or law forbid, voluntary or non-judicial jurisdiction can be exercised . . . over subjects outside the territory. A Bishop might forbid his clergy to go *v.g.* to theaters even outside the diocese. (Maroto, n. 200.)

103. 4. *Strangers, Peregrini.* Persons having a domicile or quasi-domicile in another place but not in the one in which they are at present:

(*a*) Do not come under the particular laws of their place of domicile from which they are absent unless the violation of these laws would have its effect in the place of domicile, *v.g.* the violation of the law of residence, or unless the laws be personal. The principle holds even when one would go out of the territory for the express purpose of evading its legislation.

(*b*) Neither are strangers bound to observe the particular laws of the territory in which they happen to sojourn, except those which are intended to protect public order or concern legal formalities. Strangers are obliged to respect particular laws if non-observance by them would be calculated to cause scandal in the community or lead to the very disorders which they are meant to remedy. Good order may demand likewise that certain regulations be enacted for strangers; a Bishop must have power, for example, to lay down the conditions on which visiting priests will be allowed to say Mass in the diocese or exercise the sacred functions.

Crimes may be prosecuted and punished according to the laws of the territory in which they are committed; the formalities to be observed in contracts are those prescribed in the place.

104. (*c*) Strangers are bound to observe general laws in force where they actually reside, even though they be not obligatory in the place of their domicile. A person by leaving, even only temporarily, the place of his domicile, ceases to enjoy its privileges which act as territorial laws; but by explicit concession of the legislator he is entitled to the privileges of the place in which he actually sojourns, although not bound by its particular laws. Thus a person traveling through a diocese in which, by special indult, the feast of the Immaculate Conception is not kept as a day of obligation will not be bound to keep it, although in his own diocese it is observed in accordance with common law. On the other hand, if he had his domicile in a place in which the feast is not kept and would happen to reside actually in one in which it is, he would be bound to keep it, that is, to conform to the common law.

5. *Vagi.* Under the present law the proper Ordinary of persons who have neither domicile nor quasi-domicile anywhere is the Ordinary of the place in which they actually reside. (Can. 94, 2.) They

are consequently bound to observe all the laws, general and particular, actually in force in the place of their present residence. The contrary opinion of some ancient canonists can not be held any longer.

VI. DOUBT, IGNORANCE, ERROR ABOUT ECCLESIASTICAL LAWS. (Can. 15-16.)

105. 1. *Doubt.* The doubt may be about the law itself, its existence, its meaning and import, its abrogation; it is then a *dubium juris.* Or it may bear on a fact coming under the law, *dubium facti.* It may, for example, be doubtful whether violence and what kind of violence against a cleric is punished with censure or whether a certain person has been guilty of that offence.

In cases of *dubium juris* the laws are not binding. This applies also to annulling or disqualifying laws. When the doubt concerns a fact, whether or not it comes under the law, dispensation may be granted by the Ordinary, provided it be a matter in which the Sovereign Pontiff is wont to dispense. He might, for instance, dispense from the censure possibly incurred by violent proceedings against a cleric. Dispensation should be obtained, for the external forum, whenever it is not practically certain that the law does not apply to the case.

106. 2. *Ignorance and Error.* (*a*) Ignorance never excuses from a strictly annulling or disqualifying law unless the contrary be expressly stated. (Can. 16.) The rule is absolute and applies to invincible as well as to vincible ignorance. It would seem to apply also to the case when the annulling effect is penal, for example, the diriment impediment of crime.

Canonists generally held that when the annulment

is primarily penal, ignorance of the law which would excuse from sin would also excuse from the penalty; a few even maintained that ignorance of the penalty alone, that is of the annulling effect, would suffice to excuse from it. (Suarez, L. V., c. XXII, n. 5; Wernz, I, n. 110; D'Annibale, Summula Theologiae Moralis, I, n. 216.) This view receives no support from the present canon: "No ignorance of annulling or disqualifying laws excuses from them." The reason is that in such matters what should be considered above everything else is the common good. (Salsmans, Variationes in Jure Canonico, p. 6.)

(*b*) The Code does not treat here explicitly of the effect of ignorance on ordinary laws. (Its effect on penal laws is considered in the fifth book.) The teaching of canonists is that invincible ignorance of ecclesiastical law excuses from it and from the penalty attached to it; ignorance of the penalty alone does not excuse from the law, nor from the penalty except in the case of ecclesiastical censures; vincible ignorance does not excuse from sin nor from the penalty attached to the law, excepting some censures.

(*c*) Ignorance or error, when it concerns the law or its penalty, or a personal fact, or the notorious action of another, is not presumed but would have to be proved if invoked as an excuse. Ignorance of a fact concerning another which is not notorious should be presumed until the contrary has been proved.

VII. INTERPRETATION OF ECCLESIASTICAL LAWS. (Can. 17-19.)

107. 1. *Nature and Various Kinds.* Interpretation of law is the setting forth of its genuine meaning.

(*a*) It is called authentic when it emanates from

one having authority over the law, and may take the form of general declaration or of judicial sentence on a particular case or of rescript addressed to a particular person.

The explanation of the law given by private doctors is called doctrinal interpretation. Custom, the manner in which a law is understood and observed, constitutes its usual or customary interpretation. The application of the law to individual cases by the courts gives rise to a special kind of usual interpretation, which has received the name of jurisprudence.

(*b*) From a different point of view interpretation is said to be declaratory when it merely defines the meaning of a law in itself doubtful or uncertain, or simply asserts its meaning which is sufficiently clear but perhaps contested. It is extensive if it applies the law to cases which its wording would not include; restrictive, if it excludes from the application of the law cases which would be included if the text was taken literally.

108. 2. *Authority to Interpret Ecclesiastical Laws.* (*a*) Authentic interpretations can be given by the legislator, his successor, his superior in the matter, and those to whom this power has been delegated.

The Pope has authority to interpret authentically all ecclesiastical laws in declaratory, extensive, or restrictive manner. He delegates this power to the Roman Congregations and Tribunals, within certain limits prescribed for each of them. The Code is to be interpreted exclusively by the commission instituted especially for that purpose.

Local Ordinaries are the interpreters of diocesan legislation; Metropolitans or Patriarchs have no special authority, but it may be given them and often is by Particular Councils. Ecclesiastical tribunals have power to apply the laws to particular cases.

Interpretations given by Roman Congregations are ordinarily declaratory; they may be also extensive or restrictive when power is granted to that effect; then they receive usually a special approbation from the Pope, which is indicated by the formula: *facto verbo cum Sanctissimo.*

The Commission of Interpretation of the Code merely declares the meaning of the law, and the Tribunals of the Rota and Signatura, as also other ecclesiastical tribunals, pronounce on particular cases in accordance with the law without extension or restriction.

(*b*) Any Catholic has the privilege of giving his own interpretation of ecclesiastical laws unless it be prohibited by the legislator and provided he conform to the rules on the subject; but this work is usually left to skilled canonists and theologians.

(*c*) The source of customary interpretation is the practice and conduct of those who are subject to the law.

109. 3. *Value of Interpretation.* (*a*) Authentic interpretations given in the form of a law have the same force as the law itself. If they are mere declarations of a law which is neither obscure nor uncertain they do not require promulgation and their obligatory effect goes back to the moment when the law itself commenced to be binding. If they define the meaning of a text obscure or uncertain, and if they are extensive or restrictive, they need promulgation and have no retroactive effect.

Authentic interpretations given in the form of a judicial sentence or of a rescript bearing on a particular matter have not the force of law; they are binding only on the persons for whom they were given and affect only the matter on which they bear.

(*b*) Doctrinal interpretation has weight according to the skill, experience, legal knowledge of those who make it and the value of the reasons on which it is based. An interpretation which would have the unanimous support of canonists and theologians would practically be obligatory.

(*c*) Customary interpretation has very great authority, since custom is recognized as "the best interpreter of the law." When it has the required conditions, as explained further on, custom becomes law.

110. 4. *Rules of Interpretation.* (*a*) Ecclesiastical laws must be understood in the natural and obvious sense of the terms considered in the text and the context. If the words are clear there is no room for interpretations; hence the axioms: *Verba clara non admittunt interpretationem; ubi lex non distinguit nec nos distinguere debemus; verba generalia generaliter sunt sumenda.*

(*b*) If the text of the law even considered in the light of its context remains obscure and its meaning doubtful or unsatisfactory, the will of the legislator should be ascertained by the study of parallel texts in the Code if there are any bearing on the same or a similar subject; by the consideration of the scope of the law, of the occasion or circumstances of its enactment. The views of the legislator on the matter, his dispositions, his purpose in framing the law, if known, will help also in determining its real meaning.

111. 5. *Laws to be Strictly Interpreted.* Some laws are to be interpreted strictly, *i.e.* not applied to matters which are not clearly included in the text.

These are: (*a*) laws enacting penalties, according to the principle: *odiosa sunt restringenda,* and, *in poenis benignior interpretatio facienda est.*

(*b*) Laws which restrict the exercise of rights, *v.g.* laws which would restrict the right possessed by Bishops to appoint to parishes in their dioceses.

(*c*) Enactments which establish an exception to the law. They may be in the form of privileges, personal favors, special laws.

VIII. SUPPLETORY LAW. (Can. 20.)

112. Should it happen that no law could be found, general or particular, covering a certain matter, the deficiency would have to be supplied and a norm of action obtained by recourse to the following sources: the general principles of law applied with the equity proper to canon law; the practice of the Roman Court, or what it called the *stylus Curiae;* the common and constant teaching of doctors. These are not sources of law properly speaking, but they may furnish a practical solution of a particular case or a rule of action in certain matters.

In the application of penalties, however, it is not permitted thus to supply what may be wanting in the legislation.

IX. LAWS MADE IN VIEW OF A GENERAL DANGER. (Can. 21.)

113. A law which has been enacted in view of a general danger is binding also in the particular cases in which the danger might not exist. Mixed marriages, for example, are forbidden because they are generally dangerous and they remain unlawful by ecclesiastical law even in those cases in which it might be considered as practically certain that no evil effect will result from them; the same may be said of the prohibition to read certain books. It holds also for those for whom this would not be dangerous. The danger must be general, *i.e.* threatening the whole community or a portion of it, *e.g.* the clergy.

X. ABROGATION OF LAWS. (Can. 22, 23.)

114. Laws cease to bind principally in three ways: (*a*) by cessation of their end, so that they no longer attain, even partially, the purpose for which they were enacted and have become useless, if not hurtful, for the community; (*b*) by revocation or withdrawal by the legislator; (*c*) by the introduction of a contrary custom or simple non-observance, through which laws fall into desuetude. The Code treats here only of revocation, which includes: abrogation, or the total withdrawal of the law by direct action of the competent superior; derogation, or partial abrogation; abrogation, or abrogation by a contrary law.

1. A subsequent law enacted by competent authority abrogates a former law in three cases: when it contains an explicit statement to that effect, or when it is directly contrary to the previous ordinance, or when it takes up and re-orders the entire subject-matter of the older law. A later general law abrogates a former general one to which it is directly contrary; likewise a later special or particular law would abrogate a former special or particular one if it was directly contrary to it, *i.e.* covering the same matter in such a manner that both laws can not exist at the same time.

But a subsequent general law does not abolish or affect in any way existing special or particular laws, statutes for particular places or persons, like diocesan statutes, rules and constitutions of Orders, etc., unless the general law would have an explicit provision to the contrary. Thus Can. 6, 1°, expressly states that particular laws opposed to the prescriptions of the Code are abrogated unless some special provision be made in favor of them. Except for that declaration they would have continued in force according to the general principle which is laid down here.

2. In case of doubt whether or not an existing law is revoked by a new one, revocation is not to be presumed, but as far as possible both laws should be retained and so interpreted that they do not contradict but rather supplement each other.

XI. OF PRECEPTS. (Can. 24.)

115. 1. *Nature.* A precept is a command given by the legitimate superior to individual persons or to a community for a particular case. When it is given to individual persons it is called strictly personal or individual; when it is given to a community it is general or social.

Like law, the precept imposes an obligation; it supposes authority in him by whom it is issued and must be promulgated or made known to the persons concerned. But unlike the law, it does not necessarily require power of jurisdiction; economic or dominative power suffices. It may be given to imperfect societies, like families, parishes, etc., or even to individual persons. Its purpose may be the particular good of the subject or even of the superior himself; ordinarily it is personal, not territorial, of a transitory, not permanent character.

2. *Who Can Issue Precepts?* (*a*) All who possess in the Church ordinary or delegated power of jurisdiction, whether legislative or judicial, whether of the

internal or of the external forum; (*b*) those who, like pastors, have some power of governing although it is not a power of jurisdiction in the external forum; (*c*) those who have what is called dominative or quasi social power over an imperfect community or society, such as the superiors of religious houses that are not exempt, rectors of colleges and seminaries, etc.; (*d*) in the family the husband, the father, the master can give commands.

116. 3. *Personal and Transitory Nature of Precepts.* (*a*) The Code explicitly states that individual precepts are personal, although, no doubt, their effect might be limited to a definite territory if such was the manifested will of the superior. Nothing is said of general precepts, but the common opinion of canonists was that they also are ordinarily personal, and their teaching is rather confirmed than disproved by the legislator. It may, however, occur more frequently in their case that they are territorial, from the nature of the subject-matter or by the will of the superior.

(*b*) Precepts can not be juridically enforced unless they were imposed by a legal document or in presence of two witnesses. Thus, if a superior had given an order to one of his subjects in private and without the required formalities, he could not afterwards allege disobedience as a legal ground for dismissal.

(*c*) Precepts given to individual persons cease to bind when the superior who issued them loses his authority, unless they were given in writing or in the presence of two witnesses. If this formality has been observed, they do not, therefore, cease to bind with the death of the superior, whatever may be their subject-matter or other circumstances, since no distinction is made by the law and no other condition mentioned. And what is said by the Code of particular or individual precepts must apply also to the general ones, for which an even greater stability is often desirable.

TITLE II

OF CUSTOM

(Can. 25-30.)

(Reiffenstuel, Lib. I, Tit. IV; Bouquillon, l. c., De Lege Ecclesiastica, n. 118; Wernz, I, n. 184.)

117. 1. *Nature, Species, and Legal Value.* (*a*) Considered materially, custom or usage is a constant and uniform manner of acting; considered formally and as a right it is the obligation or freedom from obligation produced by these repeated acts. In canon law custom is defined as an unwritten legal right introduced by long continued acts of the Christian community with the approbation of the competent lawgiver.

(*b*) A custom is universal when it prevails over the whole Church; general, when it extends to a large portion of it, like a province; special, when it is limited to minor communities, such as dioceses.

It is against the law when it, totally or partially, abrogates an existing ordinance; beside the law, when it introduces an obligation which does not exist by law; according to law, when it interprets and confirms the law.

(*c*) Great importance was attached to custom in the early Church and it is to continued practice that many of the later disciplinary laws owe their origin; for example, the law on clerical celibacy. But for several centuries customs against the law, at least particular customs, were not easily admitted. Even

Gratian would seem to reject them, although in another place he grants that laws can be abrogated by contrary practices. (C. 4, D, 11; c. 3, D. 4.) This doctrine was more clearly explained and defined by the Glossators and then officially confirmed by Gregory IX. (C. 11, *De Consuetudine*.)

118. 2. *Efficient Cause of Customary Right or Consent of the Superior.* (*a*) In the Church, all legislative authority resides in ecclesiastical superiors; therefore it is from their consent alone that custom derives its binding force. (Can. 25.)

(*b*) It is not stated in the Code in what manner this consent should be given. Explicit consent certainly suffices, but it is not necessary. Tacit consent must also be admitted as sufficient. It exists when the superior, duly cognizant of a certain custom, does not condemn or oppose it, although he could do so without inconvenience. Silence due to motives of prudence would not have the same meaning, chiefly in a case of custom against the law.

Canonists commonly require for custom only a legal consent, which consists in an antecedent approval given by the legislator to any custom fulfilling the necessary conditions. Such approval of future customs was contained in the ancient law (c. 11, X, I, 4) and has, at least implicitly, been renewed in the Code. (Can. 25.)

(*c*) To introduce a custom, general or particular, against the common law or a general custom beside the law, the consent of the supreme legislator is needed; the consent of the Bishop suffices to introduce a diocesan custom beside the common law or against the diocesan law, but not against the law of a higher authority. (Wernz, n. 188.)

119. 3. *Subject of Custom.* (*a*) Custom can be

introduced only by a community or corporate body which can be the subject of law, such as an ecclesiastical province, a diocese, but not a parish, a chapter, imperfect societies, or private persons.

(*b*) The introduction of the custom must come from the greater part of the members of the community who are competent to give assent. The acts by which it is introduced must not be due to ignorance, error, fear, or violence. There must also be the intention of contracting an obligation if the custom is beside the law; of abrogating one if it is against the law. Acts performed merely out of devotion, charity, or courtesy do not create an obligation.

4. *Object of Custom.* (*a*) There can be no custom against the natural or the divine positive law, because no human authority has power to abrogate them.

(*b*) Custom against or beside the ecclesiastical law can be legitimate only if it is reasonable, for it partakes of the nature of law, which is an ordinance of reason; it must have all the conditions required for a law to be just or for the revocation of a law to be lawful. It is not reasonable if it is hurtful to the common good, subversive of ecclesiastical discipline, an occasion of sin, or if it is reprobated by the law. Canonists give a number of customs which are thus condemned as unreasonable. (Reiffenstuel, Tit. IV, n. 3.) When a law has a clause simply abolishing all customs to the contrary, no customs opposed to it remain legitimate except those which exist from time immemorial or for over a hundred years. Customs condemned as pernicious, an incentive to sin, etc., are abolished and could not be introduced again, unless the circumstances having changed, they would cease to be unreasonable.

120. 5. *Time Required for Customs.* (*a*) A custom which has the express or tacit approval of the lawgiver obtains by that very fact force of law (Suarez, De Legibus, Lib. VII, c. 8, n. 11, 16; Wernz, n. 190), at least if it is a custom contrary to law (Bouquillon, l. c. n. 118; Reiffenstuel, Tit. IV, 91, 92); but some canonists would refuse to consider this as custom in the legal sense of the term.

(*b*) For custom strictly so called, depending for its value on the merely legal consent of the legislator, some time is required; consent exists only in favor of customs legitimately prescribed. What that time should be, no text in the former legislation expressly defined. Ancient canonists demanded forty years at least for a custom against the law. Among modern canonists it was thought that ten years would probably be sufficient both for customs beside the law and against it.

(*c*) The Code removes all controversy or doubt on this point. For custom according to law, of which it is declared to be the best interpreter, no special time is required nor any other condition. (Can. 29.)

A custom beside the law must be reasonable in its object and have been observed by a community, knowingly and with the intention of binding itself, for forty full and continuous years. (Can. 28.)

A custom against the ecclesiastical law, besides being reasonable, must have prevailed for forty full and continuous years. If the law contained a clause prohibiting future customs, only those having existed for a hundred years or from time immemorial could have any force against it. (Can. 27.)

121. 6. *Abrogation of Customs.* Customs may lose their juridical value from the same internal and external causes as laws: cessation of the end, change in the object, abrogation by contrary law, custom, or desuetude.

(*a*) Contrary customs or simply desuetude abrogate the customs to which they are opposed and in the measure in which they are opposed to them.

(*b*) As to the effect of law on customs, the following rules are given:

An ordinary, general custom is revoked by a contrary general law, without mention of it; and also by a particular law as far as it is contrary to the custom.

A centennial or immemorial custom is not abrogated by a contrary law, unless explicit mention is made of it, or it is expressly reproved.

Particular customs are revoked by particular laws contrary to them, but not by general laws, unless these contain an explicit provision to that effect. Even the particular customs which were contrary to the prescriptions of the Code have been declared abrogated unless they were centennial or immemorial, in which case they might be tolerated by the Ordinary for reasons of prudence. (Can. 5.) Ordinarily, to revoke a particular custom a general law must have the clause: customs to the contrary notwithstanding, or a similar one; the words, "even centennial or immemorial" must be added if privileged customs are to be affected. (Can. 30.)

TITLE III

OF THE COMPUTATION OF TIME

(Can. 31-35.)

I. PRELIMINARY REMARKS

122. 1. The application of laws frequently involves a question of time: generally three months must elapse after their promulgation before they go into effect; some obligations have to be fulfilled within a certain number of days, or weeks, or months. Hence the need of the rules for the computation of time, which the legislator formulates here with a clearness and precision they never had before.

2. These rules hold in all canonical matters: universal ordinances, precepts, rescripts, privileges, judicial sentences; but they have nothing to do with problems of chronology or such questions as the determination of the date for the celebration of Easter.

3. They are not absolute rules, but should be followed when no others have been expressly laid down; liturgical laws regarding, for example, the beginning of the ecclesiastical year, of the solemnity of a feast, remain unchanged. Special provisions have been made concerning indulgences (Can. 921, 922, 923, 931), and it is stated that in what pertains to the fulfilment or enforcement of contracts, the prescriptions of the civil law should be complied with, unless there has been some other agreement to the contrary. Nothing prevents inferior legislators from adopting different rules for the application of their own laws, and it is clearly implied that private persons themselves have the same right in matters which depend on their will, like determining when an article sold should be delivered, paid for, etc.

II. GENERAL DIVISIONS OF TIME. (Can. 32.)

123. 1. The divisions of time considered here are the days, weeks, months, and years; the others would be without importance for the present purpose.

(*a*) The day is taken to consist of twenty-four consecutive hours, in accordance with the usual way of reckoning, if not with strictly scientific accuracy. The hours are counted from midnight to midnight, after the Roman method; not from sunrise to sunrise or sunset to sunset, as has been or still is the practice in some countries. A week consists of seven days.

(*b*) In law a month means a period of thirty days, and a year a period of three hundred and sixty-five days, unless it be stated that the month or year must be taken as it is in the calendar; for in the calendar certain months have thirty days, others thirty-one, and one of them has twenty-eight or twenty-nine. Some years have three hundred and sixty-six days.

2. Time and its divisions are reckoned physically, not morally; the principle *parum pro nihilo reputatur* does not hold in this matter, nor is there *parvitas materiae.* Thus the law of abstinence, of the eucharistic fast, commences to bind at midnight, not one minute before nor one minute after; the impediment of age for marriage, for religious profession, or for ordination, continues to exist till the last moment of the day which completes the required number of years. When the clock strikes midnight it becomes at once impossible to discharge an obligation attached to the day just elapsed.

124. 3. The days, weeks, months, and years specified by law must be complete; a part of a day, for example, is never counted as a full day if it is counted at all. Under the former legislation it was commonly admitted that, at least in certain matters, if the first day or week, etc., of a series was incomplete it would be counted as complete or not counted at all, according as the interest of the party concerned would suggest. In like manner, the last day could be considered completed as soon as commenced. The present law does not permit this, certainly not in the computation of days (Can. 34, §3), nor, it may be inferred, in the computation of months or years; for frequently it distinctly specifies that they ought to be complete. (Can. 12, 27, 28, 88, 504, 539, 555.) When this is not necessary the wording of the law clearly shows it. Thus the law of fasting is said to be binding till the beginning of the sixtieth year. (Can. 1254.)

4. Time may be reckoned *de die ad diem* or *de momento ad momentum,* from day to day or from moment to moment. In the first case the period begins and ends with the beginning and end of a day, *v.g.* from the first of January to the first of February would be a month *de die ad diem.*

In the second case the period begins and ends at a certain moment within a day, week, month, or year, *v.g.* from half past ten o'clock A. M., May 15th to half past ten o'clock A. M. July 15th would be a period of two months from moment to moment. Some call this the natural as opposed to the civil mode of reckoning.

III. RULES FOR RECKONING THE HOURS OF THE DAY. (Can. 33.)

125. 1. *General Rule.* In reckoning the hours of the day, the common usage of the place should be followed, unless some other provision has been made or an exception be allowed. The usage may be considered as sufficiently common when it is adopted by the greater part of the community, whether it was introduced by popular choice, by law, by explicit agreement, or some other cause.

2. *Exceptions.* A greater latitude in the reckoning of time is permitted by the legislator in the application of four laws: the law (*a*) on the private celebration of Holy Mass, which should not begin earlier than one hour before dawn nor later than one

hour after noon (Can. 821); (*b*) the law on the private recitation of the canonical hours, which is binding every day from midnight to midnight and particularly at certain definite moments within that period, so that the obligation can not be fulfilled once the day is over nor before it begins, except that Matins and Lauds may be anticipated from two o'clock of the previous day; (*c*) the law of the eucharistic fast; (*d*) the law of fasting and abstinence, the obligation of which extends likewise from midnight to midnight.

In relation to these laws it is permissible to follow the local time, mean or true, or the legal time, regional or extraordinary.

Astronomers in their calculations use what they call the sidereal time as the most accurate and true, but for ordinary purposes the solar time is found more practical. Its unit is the period in which the earth returns to the same position under the sun. This varies, but twenty-four hours is the mean time and, therefore, has been adopted, for the sake of convenience, as the division of every day.

Again, because the solar time, mean or true, differs in every locality with the difference of longitude, in order to have some uniformity the time at some important or central place is often selected and made the legal time for the whole country or sections of it. In the United States four zones are distinguished with the 75th, the 90th, the 105th, and the 120th meridian as their center, giving respectively the Eastern, the Central, the Mountain, and the Pacific standard time. The difference is one hour between each and the previous one. This is a regional and, for most places that follow it, a mean time.

The Daylight Saving Bill, which ordered all the

clocks in the country advanced one hour, supplies an example of extraordinary legal time.

IV. RULES FOR RECKONING THE WEEKS, MONTHS, AND YEARS

126. 1. If the months and years are designated by their own names or in some equivalent manner, *v.g.* the month of February, the year 1919, next year, etc., they must be taken as they are in the calendar.

2. If the time when the months or years are to begin is not assigned either implicitly or explicitly, the starting point is determined by some other cause and the reckoning is *de momento ad momentum;* for instance, if an offence is punished with suspension for a month and the declaratory sentence is pronounced so as to go into force on the fifteenth of January at two o'clock P. M., it will expire on the fifteenth of February at two o'clock. If one has a three months' vacation and chooses to take it beginning at noon on a certain day, the three months will be calculated from that moment.

Here another distinction must be made: the time may be continuous, as in the example of suspension for a month, or it may admit of interruptions. A three months' vacation may be taken in periods of two weeks or thereabouts. When the time is continuous, the months and years must be taken as they are in the calendar. In the example given, the suspension will last thirty-one days. When the time is interrupted, a week means seven days, a month thirty, a year three hundred and sixty-five.

127. 3. If the starting point is determined explicitly or implicitly and the time or period consists of one or several months or years, of one or several weeks or of several days:

(*a*) The months and years should always be taken as they are in the calendar and the time counted from day to day, not from moment to moment. The first day may or may not be included in the period.

(*b*) It is included if it is complete, that is, if the starting point coincides with the beginning of a day, and in that case the period ends when the day of the same number begins. For example, if one is given a month's vacation to begin on the tenth of May, the vacation ends when the tenth day of June begins, because the tenth day of May is included in it, since the beginning of the vacation coincides with the beginning of that day.

(*c*) If the starting point does not coincide with the beginning of a day, the first day, being incomplete, is not counted and the time ends with the end of the last day of the same number. The year's novitiate, the fourteen years for puberty, the ten days of the vacancy of an episcopal see, the ten days granted for appeal from a judicial sentence, do not commence exactly at midnight of a certain day, and thus the starting point does not coincide with the beginning of a day; hence the first day is not included in the reckoning of the time. Supposing, then, that the year's novitiate begins on the tenth of May, 1920, it is completed with the end of the tenth day of May, 1921, or the beginning of the eleventh.

128. (*d*) If the month has no day of the same number, *v.g.* a two months' vacation beginning December 31st should end February 31st, but as this month has no day of that number, the period ends with the last day of the month, at the beginning or at the end, according as the first was included or not in the time, that is, according as the starting point coincided or not with the beginning of a day.

In the example, the vacation will end on the twenty-eighth or twenty-ninth of February, according to the years, and either at the beginning or at the end of that day, according as the beginning of the vacation coincided or not with the beginning of the thirty-first day of December.

(*e*) In the case of actions of the same kind to be repeated at stated intervals, the term expires on the same recurring day, but the act may be renewed at any moment of that day. We have examples of this in a religious profession, which has to be renewed after three years; in elections, which have to be repeated every two years. Supposing that the religious profession was made on the first of June, 1920, the term expires only at the end of the first day of June, 1923, but the profession may be renewed at any moment during that day. It should even be renewed on that day if there is to be no interruption.

V. USEFUL AND CONTINUOUS TIME. (Can. 35.)

129. By useful time is meant in law the time granted for the exercise or prosecution of one's rights, in such a way that it does not run if one is prevented from using it through ignorance or some other cause.

Continuous time suffers no delay or interruption from one's ignorance or impossibility to act.

Thus colleges which possess the right of appointment to a vacant office are given three months of useful time to exercise it, which implies that if they were prevented, *v.g.* for ten days, from meeting for the election they would have that many additional days to exercise their right. On the contrary, capitular chapters have eight days after the vacancy of the episcopal see has been made known to them to elect a Vicar Capitular, and it is specified that if no election has been made within that time, whatever be the cause, the right devolves upon the Metropolitan. (Can. 161, 432.)

TITLE IV

ON RESCRIPTS

(Can. 36-62.)

(Decret. L. I, Tit. III, De Rescriptis; Reiffenstuel, 1, 3; Wernz, I, n. 149; Putzer, Commentarium in Facult. Apostol., p. Ia; Maroto, l. c., n. 278.)

I. GENERAL NOTIONS

130. 1. A rescript, in general, is a written reply. It was the custom of Roman emperors to answer in writing the petitions presented by magistrates or private citizens, and often the answer would be inserted into the document which contained the request; hence the name of *subscriptum* or *rescriptum*.

The Roman Pontiffs also, at least since the fourth century, received frequent consultations and petitions from both the Bishops and the faithful, and their written replies were likewise called rescripts or decretal letters. These had become very numerous in the twelfth century, after the introduction of the system of benefices and beneficial reservations, as also of a more complicated form of ecclesiastical trials, for which special delegations and instructions were often needed.

Bernard of Pavia devoted a title to rescripts in his first compilation (1189-1191) and the example was followed in subsequent Collections. The theory of rescripts was thus gradually developed in the decretals and completed in the rules of the Apostolic Chancery. (J. B. Riganti, Commentaria in Regulas Constitutiones et Ordinationes Cancelleriae Apostolicae, Romae, 1741, 4 vol. in fol.)

The Code has retained the title on rescripts, only omitting, as no longer of any practical value, some of the ancient prescriptions, chiefly in regard to beneficial and judicial matters. At present, dispensations and particularly marriage dispensations, form the main object of rescripts.

131. 2. A rescript, then, may be defined as a written papal or episcopal ordinance issued in reply to a petition for a favor, to a report on some particular affair, or a consultation on some private matter.

It is written, not merely oral like the *oracula vivae vocis.*

It differs from a constitution, which is addressed to the whole world or a portion of it and ordains something permanently; from a decree, which is issued *motu proprio* and does not presuppose a previous request; from a decretal, which, although sent in reply to a particular question, settles a point of law and has the force of precedent to rule subsequent analogous cases; from encyclicals, which are letters sent to all the Bishops of the Catholic world or at least to those of one country.

Constitutions are issued in the form of bulls or briefs; rescripts being directed to individuals and concerning matters of relatively minor importance require less solemnity. They are of a more private, particular character. When they are said to be granted *motu proprio,* this means that the concession is due to the generosity of the superior independently of the motives proposed in the request, not that there had not been any request made.

132. 3. When rescripts concern the administration of justice, appointing a judge, settling a controversy, prescribing a certain form of trial, etc., they are called rescripts of justice; when they grant a favor without any relation to judicial contentions, like indulgences, matrimonial dispensations, they are called rescripts of grace.

If the favor is actually granted in the rescript and applied to the petitioner by the grantor himself without intermediary, it is called a *gratia facta,* and the rescript is said to be in *forma gratiosa;* if the execution of the rescript is committed to another, it is said to be in commissory form, *in forma commissoria,* and the favor is a *gratia facienda.*

Rescripts may also be general or special, *i.e* for a certain class of persons or cases, or for well-determined persons; they may be according to, against, or beside, the law; *ad instantiam,* on request, or *motu proprio,* in the sense already explained.

4. According to the traditions of the Roman Court, *stylus Curiae,* a petition for a favor should contain three parts: an exposition of the facts, the reasons for the request, and the object of the request; and in the answer or rescript there are regularly found likewise three parts: a statement of the case, *pars narrativa;* the reasons of the concession or reply, *pars motiva seu doctrinalis;* and the concession itself or consultation, *pars dispositiva.* At present, however, Congregations do not adhere so strictly to this form and the first two parts are often reduced to the strict essentials.

II. BY WHOM CAN RESCRIPTS BE OBTAINED? (Can. 36, 37.)

133. 1. "Rescripts may be freely asked for both from the Apostolic See and from other Ordinaries by all who are not expressly forbidden."

Application for rescripts is usually made to the Holy See; but, as clearly implied in the law, other Ordinaries also may grant them, but only within the limits of their legislative power and to their own subjects.

Under decretal law, the prohibition to seek rescripts, under penalty of nullity of the act, existed against false or revoked procurators, heretics and schismatics, and persons under major excommunication, except in relation to the cause of the censure or appeal from it; hence the practice of absolving from censures, *ad cautelam,* before applying rescripts. (Putzer, l.c., n. 46, 47; Wernz, I, n. 151; Gennari, Cons. Can. 96.)

Pius X, in the Const. *Sapienti Consilio,* on the reorganization of the Roman Curia, decreed that, beginning with Nov. 3, 1908, pontifical favors and dispensations of all kinds would be valid and legitimate even when granted to persons under censure, unless these were excommunicated by name or suspended *a divinis* by the Holy See. (*Normæ speciales,* p.2a, c.3, n. 6; A.A.S., I. p.64.)

In the present law even that exception is not made and rescripts either of justice or of grace may be sought and granted to all Christians; only when they are issued by the Holy See in favor of one who is excommunicated, suspended, or personally interdicted by sentence, it is required, for validity, that mention be made of the censure.

This formality is not obligatory if there has not been any declaratory or condemnatory sentence, even though the censure is certain and publicly known, as, *v.g.* in the case of Protestants.

It will be noted, moreover, that this concerns only rescripts emanating from the Holy See; the strictly episcopal ones do not come under this rule. They are not exclusively episcopal when the Bishop acts in the name of the Holy See and by virtue of powers delegated to him even habitually. (Cf.Putzer, p.65, Gennari, l.c., p.219, n.2.)

134. 2. A rescript may be obtained for another even without his consent. He is not obliged to take advantage of the favor thus secured for him, but whether he accepts it or not the rescript is in itself valid and produces its effect, unless there be some clause to the contrary. It may, *v.g.* be explicitly stipulated that the rescript will take effect only on acceptance.

Only rescripts of grace could be obtained for another without special mandate under the ancient law, and acceptance by the interested party was always required for the validity of the act. In modern times custom had introduced the discipline now sanctioned by the Code.

III. WHEN RESCRIPTS TAKE EFFECT. (Can. 38.)

135. 1. Rescripts in *forma gratiosa,* that is, those by which a favor is granted without intermediary, become effective from the moment they are issued or signed; the concession can not, however, be taken advantage of until official notification of it has been received. Private information, however reliable, does not suffice. Thus, if faculties were granted for three months and the rescript had been issued on the third day of June, the time would be reckoned from that date.

2. Rescripts in the commissory form take effect from the moment they are presented to the executor, or rather from the date of execution in case the latter would not coincide with that of presentation.

Ordinarily rescripts of justice are to be executed by the judge, and they become effective when presented to him.

IV. DEFECTS ANNULLING RESCRIPTS. (Can. 39-47.)

136. Some defects are only accidental and render rescripts merely unlawful, others are essential and render them invalid.

Conditions demanded in a rescript must be considered as essential, so that their non-verification would have a nullifying effect, only when they are expressed by the particles *if, provided,* or others of similar meaning, by the ablative absolute or equivalent conditional clauses.

The law treats here of three general obstacles to the validity of rescripts: want of truth in the petition, previous refusal by another superior, and want of the proper object.

1. *Want of Truth in the Petition.* (*a*) In all rescripts this condition must be understood even when not expressed: "If the request is based on truth." Rescripts given *motu proprio* (Can. 45) and those containing a dispensation from minor impediments (Can. 1054) are an exception to this rule, as will be explained later.

(*b*) In rescripts which require no executor, the reasons on which the petition is based must be true at the moment the rescript is granted or signed; in others, it suffices that they be true at the time of execution.

137. (*c*) Want of truth in the petition may be due to subreption, concealment of what should be stated; to obreption, allegation of falsehood, or to mistakes about the names of the parties concerned, the object of the request, or the names of places.

Subreption is substantial and vitiates the rescript only when something has been omitted which the law of the Roman or of the episcopal court, the *stylus Curiae,* requires for validity. What this is can not be defined by a general rule, for it varies with the courts, the Congregations, and the cases.

Obreption or falsehood in rescripts usually bears on the reasons for the concession of the favor. Canonists distinguish two kinds of reasons: those which they call motive, which move and determine the superior to grant the request; and those which exercise some influence on his will but not an efficacious and determining one. They are called impulsive. Several reasons, each one of which taken in itself is only impulsive, may, when presented together, suffice to move the will; they form then one motive reason. As long as the petition contains one motive reason which is true the rescript it not vitiated by obreption.

Errors about the names of the parties concerned and their place of residence or about the object of the petition would render the rescript null only if the persons could not be identified with sufficient certainty or the nature of the request could not be known. In case of doubt, it is for the Ordinary of the place in which the rescript is to be used, or for the personal superior if the petitioners are Religious enjoying the privilege of exemption, to judge whether the petition is sufficiently definite in spite of errors. The present law is less severe on this point than the former one.

138. (*d*) Nor does the law distinguish any longer between the cases in which subreption, obreption, or error are due to inculpable mistake and those in which they should be ascribed to fraud and malice. (Can. 991, §1, 2249, §2 are no real exceptions.) If these defects are not substantial in the sense explained above, they do not render the rescript null because of the bad faith of the petitioner. On the other hand, his good faith does not prevent a substantial defect from vitiating the rescript.

(*e*) When a rescript contains several independent parts and they are not all affected by the defect, only those are vitiated which it affects. Thus, if a person applied for a twofold dispensation and the reasons given for one were all false, but those for the other were true, the second dispensation would be granted validly.

(*f*) The law implies that rescripts vitiated by some substantial defect are null *ipso facto;* the declaratory sentence demanded, in some cases, by ancient canonists is not needed. (Wernz, 1, 156.)

(*g*) The clause *"motu proprio"* in a rescript, implying that it is granted from pure liberality independently of the petition, secures its validity in spite of subreption or even of obreption, except in cases in which the very reason determining the concession is false.

Dispensations from minor impediments of marriage would, however, be valid in spite of any obreption or subreption. (Can. 1054.)

139. 2. *Previous Refusal by Another Superior.* In order to avoid confusion and perhaps prevent fraud, Innocent XII, in the Const. *Ut occurratur* of June 4, 1692, forbade, under pain of nullity, to apply to one of the Roman Congregations for a rescript of grace or justice which had already been refused by another. The need for this rule was not the same after the reorganization of the Roman Curia under Pius X, by which the attributions of each Congregation were carefully defined and limited. Still it was maintained then (*Normae speciales,* c. 1, n. 2) as it is maintained now in the Code and applied to the refusal of favors by local Ordinaries as well as by the Holy See.

140. (*a*) Refusal by the Holy See. A favor denied by one of the S. Congregations or Offices of the Roman Curia can not validly be granted by another Congregation or Office or by a local Ordinary, although having otherwise the power, without the consent of the Congregation or Office to which application was made first, an exception being made for the S. Penitentiary in matters of conscience. (Can. 43.)

(i) It is supposed that the Congregation or Office to which application had first been made was competent in the matter, for if it was not competent it would not be forbidden to have recourse to the one which is.

(ii) Nor can it be forbidden to go from a Congregation to the Pope personally, whose power is not bound or limited in any way by the action of his inferiors. But, although this is not explicitly stated here, it must be evident that a favor refused by the Pope personally could not be granted validly, without his authorization, by a Congregation or other Ordinary; not that in itself the power of the inferior is necessarily taken away by the action of the superior, but by a positive disposition of law clearly implied in this canon.

Usually when the Pope grants a favor he does so through the Congregation which is competent in the matter; a previous refusal fraudulently concealed would thus be detected. This, however, is not necessary.

(iii) Refusal of a favor by one of the Congregations does not prevent the S. Penitentiary from granting it for the *forum internum* alone; but inasmuch as favors granted by other Congregations affect the internal as well as the external forum, if they have been denied by the S. Penitentiary they could not, without its consent, be obtained from another Tribunal or Congregation.

(iv) Favors denied by the Holy See can not, without its consent, be obtained from the local Ordinary, even though he could have granted them had the petition been presented to him first. But if they have been refused by the Ordinary they may, without having to mention this fact, be asked of the Holy See. Often, however, a recommendation from the Ordinary will be required and if the matter is within his jurisdiction the petitioner will be referred back to him.

141. (*b*) Previous Refusal by other Ordinaries, like Legates of the Apostolic See, Bishops, superiors of exempt Religious Orders.

Two cases are considered here: recourse from one Ordinary to another having distinct, independent authority, and recourse from the Vicar-General to the Bishop or from the Bishop to the Vicar-General.

(i) A favor refused by one's own Ordinary should not be asked of another without making mention of the refusal, and the second Ordinary should not grant the request until he has been informed by the first of the reasons for his action. (Can. 44, § 1.)

It will be noted that this canon has no annulling clause; violation of the rule it contains, whether by the petitioner or the grantor, would render the rescript unlawful, not invalid. Two different Ordinaries constitute two independent tribunals, not one, like the Vicar-General and his Bishop, or even in a sense a local Ordinary and the Roman Curia.

The rule applies only when the favor has been refused by one's own Ordinary and is asked of another, whether the latter is also the petitioner's Ordinary or not; it does not, strictly speaking, apply if the favor has been first refused by a superior who is not the petitioner's Ordinary.

Nor would it apply in case the favor refused by the Ordinary is asked of his successor or even of himself and granted by him without remembering his previous refusal.

(ii) A favor denied by the Vicar-General and afterwards obtained from the Bishop without mentioning the refusal is invalid; if it was denied by the Bishop it could not be granted by the Vicar-General without the Bishop's consent. The reason for these rules is obvious; a Bishop has power to grant favors refused by his Vicar-General, but he is not supposed to have the intention of doing so. Such an intention has to be manifested, and for that the previous refusal must be known. The Vicar-General holds his power from the Bishop and can not exercise it against the latter's will.

142. 3. *Want of a Fit Subject or Proper Object.* (*a*) A rescript even granted by the Pope and *motu proprio* remains invalid if the grantee is disqualified by common law from receiving it, unless the very purpose of the rescript would be to remove the disqualification, or it would contain a clause destined to secure its validity in spite of canonical obstacles, as when it is stated that the concession will hold, disqualifications or censures notwithstanding. Petitioners must be qualified by law for the favor they ask; if they are not, the superior is supposed unwilling to grant it, unless he manifests a different disposition, at least in general terms.

(*b*) The object of rescripts, like that of laws, must

be just and reasonable; but there are, besides, certain favors which ecclesiastical superiors do not grant, as a rule, and which for this reason are not presumed to have been granted unless a derogatory clause in the rescript manifests the intention of making an exception. Without such a clause favors against legitimate local customs or particular statutes or the acquired rights of another person are invalid.

V. CONFLICTING RESCRIPTS. (Can. 48.)

143. It may happen that two or more rescripts pertaining to the same matter are so opposed to one another that they can not all be used at the same time; as for example, if a Bishop received authorization to tax all the parishes of the diocese for a certain object and Religious in charge of several parishes had obtained a rescript exempting them from all taxation for a definite number of years. The question arises in such cases which rescript is to prevail. To determine this, the first thing to be considered is whether and how far the different concessions are incompatible with one another.

1. When one of the rescripts is general and the other particular, the particular provisions of the latter have their full effect, then those of the former as far as remains possible. It is an application of the principle: *generi per speciem derogatur.* If the general rescript was given first, the particular one is considered as an exception to it; if it was issued last, it is not supposed to affect particular concessions previously made, in the same manner as a subsequent general law does not abrogate the existing particular legislation or customs unless the contrary be stated. Thus both the general and particular laws or re-

scripts are upheld and the action of the superior does not remain without effect.

144. 2. When the opposition between two rescripts is complete because they are both general or, if particular, of equal extent and bearing on the same matter, the one granted first generally prevails, unless mention of it be made in the second, or unless the first petitioner has not made use of his rescript through fraud or negligence. *Prior tempore potior jure.*

(*a*) Priority is determined by the date of concession, not of application or execution. This is clearly implied in the text of the present law (Can. 48, 1; Can. 206); nor is there any distinction to be made between the rescripts of grace and those of justice, the rescripts granted in the gracious form and those granted in the commissory form, whether free or necessary.

(*b*) Priority of time secures the preference, because the superior is presumed to have granted the second rescript by mistake and not to be willing to annul the first one if he knew or thought of it. But this is only a presumption, and there exists no foundation for it when the first rescript is mentioned in the second.

(*c*) As explicitly declared here, earlier rescripts cease to enjoy the favor of law if they are not made use of through fraud or notable negligence. When will the negligence be notable? Under the former discipline a delay of a year was generally demanded, at least for the rescripts of justice; but nothing is determined in the present law, and the appreciation of the negligence as well as of the fraud is left to the discretion of prudent men, particularly of the ecclesiastical judges.

Ancient canonists gave likewise the preference, although for a different reason, to a later rescript which had been executed and had obtained its full effect before the earlier one had been used, without fault or negligence on any one's part. (Reiffenstuel, L. I, Tit. III, n. 99.)

145. 3. In the case of rescripts bearing the same date and granted the same day, it may still be possible to know which was granted first. If this is not possible, none of them can prevail, supposing that they are contradictory, and all become void. The superior who granted them should be consulted, when it is possible, that he may decide who shall be favored.

If the rescripts were granted by different superiors having independent authority, the matter might be referred to a higher one, *v.g.* to the Holy See. If one of the grantors was the other's superior, the favor granted by him would prevail. A papal rescript would in such cases be preferred to an episcopal one. (C. 12, 31, III, 4, in Sexto.)

VI. INTERPRETATION OF RESCRIPTS. (Can. 49, 50.)

The meaning of a rescript may be clear or doubtful.

146. 1. The text of a rescript which is sufficiently clear and makes reasonable sense ought to be interpreted according to the proper meaning of the words and the common use of the terms, without extending it to cases not expressly included therein, that is, its interpretation must be merely declarative, not extensive nor restrictive.

2. When the meaning of a rescript is doubtful, a broad interpretation is ordinarily permitted, for

rescripts are favors, and *favores ampliandi sunt.* There are exceptions to this rule. The law explicitly mentions four kinds of rescripts which must be interpreted strictly.

(*a*) Rescripts of justice or pertaining to judicial controversies, because they frequently curtail the jurisdiction of the Ordinary and are to the detriment of the other party in a trial.

(*b*) Those which impair the acquired rights of other persons, for this is of odious effect.

(*c*) Those which are contrary to the common law and derogate from it in favor of private persons; this also is considered odious as tending to sacrifice the common to private good. Thus dispensations, privileges against the law, are of strict interpretation. The authorization to grant dispensations, on the other hand, is a favor or privilege outside the law, and should be interpreted in a broad manner.

(*d*) Rescripts obtained for the attainment of an ecclesiastical benefice or conferring such benefice, because they may favor inordinate ambition and encourage indiscreet requests.

VII. PRESENTATION OF RESCRIPTS. (Can. 51, 52.)

147. Before they are used, rescripts may have to be presented to the executor or to the Ordinary.

1. Rescripts granted in the gracious form do not require any executor to whom they should be presented. If they emanate from the Ordinary, there is no one else to whom they need be submitted.

For papal rescripts the Council of Trent decreed that they were all to be presented for recognition to the Ordinary of the parties. (Sess. XXII, de Ref., c. 5), but this rule had fallen into desuetude. In the reorganization of the Roman Curia by Pius X the necessity of that presentation was maintained for only two classes of rescripts: those containing favors which may be used in public, like permissions to expose a relic to popular veneration, to impart general indulgences, to wear a special dress, etc.; and those which demand the verification of certain conditions. Thus the privilege of a private oratory can not be used until the Ordinary of the place has inspected the oratory and convinced himself that it is in a fitting condition for the purpose; promises must be made before dispensations from the impediment of mixed religion can take effect.

The present law makes the same general dispositions and adds that presentation is also necessary whenever enjoined in the rescript, which supposes that it may be, as it frequently is, enjoined in other cases not included in the general rule.

2. Rescripts in the commissory form require an executor and must be presented to him. Under the former discipline rescripts of justice had to be presented within a year of their reception. The present Code states only in a general way, without making any distinction between the different kinds of rescripts, that they may be presented to the executor at any time, provided there be no fraud or deceit.

VIII. EXECUTION OF RESCRIPTS. (Can. 53-59.)

148. 1. *Who may be Executor.* By decretal law the execution of pontifical rescripts of justice was committed only to ecclesiastical dignitaries such as Bishops, Vicars-General, Prelates Regular, members of cathedral chapters, not to canons of collegiate chapters unless they held a *dignitas* or *personatus,* nor to rural deans or pastors; the execution of rescripts of grace pertaining to the external forum was reserved to ecclesiastics having external jurisdiction; the execution of those pertaining to the internal forum was entrusted to doctors in theology or canon law, to certain confessors, or to other ecclesiastics well qualified for the office. (C. 11, 1, 3, in Sexto.)

The Code does not require any special qualifications in the executors of rescripts in general, and Ordinaries are free to choose such ecclesiastics as they consider fit for this office. The practice of the Holy See in modern times has been to commit the execution of the rescripts of the S. Penitentiary for the internal forum to some confessor approved by the Ordinary and that of rescripts of the external forum to the Ordinary of the place. This was even the rule for marriage dispensations, at least since the decree of the Holy Office of Feb. 20, 1888 (Cf. Conc. Trid. Sess. XXII, c. 5), and the rule is maintained in the Code. (Can. 1055.)

149. 2. *Office of the Executor.* Executors or their commission are said to be necessary or voluntary, that is, they may be simply commissioned to carry out the rescript; the favor is already granted, it is a *gratia facta;* they have a *nudum ministerium* and serve as instruments; or they may be empowered to grant the favor if they see fit; the favor is a *gratia facienda,* and they act rather as delegates.

The commission is necessary or compulsive when it is expressed in preceptive terms, dispenses, absolves, etc., even though the concession be conditional, *v.g.* absolve provided restitution be made, dispense from the impediment of mixed religion after obtaining the required promises. The clause *pro tuo arbitrio et conscientia,* or a similar one, which may be added is a formula of politeness without canonical import.

(*a*) Executors who are merely commissioned to carry out the rescript can not refuse to do it except in three cases: when after a summary and extra-judicial investigation it is evident that the rescript is void in consequence of obreption or subreption; when the rescript is conditional and the conditions have not been fulfilled; when the petitioner is so unworthy of the favor, in the estimation of the executor, that to grant it to him would give offence to others. In this last case the execution is to be withheld and the grantor immediately notified. (Can. 54.)

(*b*) Voluntary or free executors may grant or refuse the favor according to their judgment and conscience. This implies that refusal without reasonable cause would not be fair on their part, although not strictly unjust.

150. 3. *Duties of Executors.* (*a*) Before proceeding to the execution they must, under pain of nullity, demand the rescript and ascertain its authenticity and integrity, unless they had been informed of its existence and contents by authority of the grantor himself. This may be done by telegraph or telephone, but only in exceptional cases. (S. O. Aug. 24, 1892; Litt. Ency. Sec. Stat., Dec. 10, 1891.) A copy of the document would ordinarily not suffice, the orginial must be produced; nor would any other information coming from some unofficial source, however reliable otherwise.

This certainly applies now to the execution of all rescripts, even of the rescripts of grace, and the contrary opinion of some ancient canonists is no longer tenable. (D'Annibale, I, n. 241.)

(*b*) The executor must not exceed the limits of his mandate nor grant more than is expressed in the rescript, nor less if his commission is a necessary or compulsive one; he must observe these limits as to persons, time, conditions, and other circumstances; he can not, for example, extend a privilege or dispensation from one person or place to another.

Failure to comply with one of the essential conditions laid down in the rescript or neglect of the substantial form of proceeding would render the execution null; it would be unlawful if the omission or neglect were only accidental.

151. 4. *Form of Execution.* (*a*) The execution of rescripts pertaining to the external forum should regularly be in writing (Can. 56); canonists do not, however, consider this as strictly essential and admit the validity of an execution by word of mouth, by telegraph or telephone.

(*b*) Nothing is prescribed regarding the rescripts which concern the internal forum; ordinarily they are executed orally.

5. *Execution through a Substitute or by a Successor.* (Can. 57, 58.) In the execution of a rescript may be distinguished the preparatory acts, recognition of the document, summary investigation of the case, etc., and the granting of the favor or execution proper. Under the ancient legislation the use of a substitute was allowed for the preparatory acts, but not for the execution itself (D'Annibale, I, n. 241; H. O. Feb. 20, 1888; Sept. 5, 1900); the present law is less severe.

(*a*) It is left to the discretion and good judgment of the executor to appoint some one in his place, if he chooses, except in two cases: when substitution is prohibited, or the substitute designated should one be used; and when the executor has been selected by reason of his personal qualifications.

(*b*) It was held before and is now expressly decreed that unless the executor has been chosen on account of his personal qualifications the commission passes to his successor in dignity or office.

6. *Errors in Execution.* The law explicitly permits one to repair them by repeating the execution.

7. *Fees for the Execution of Rescripts.* Canon 1507, to which we are referred here, provides that they shall be fixed for each province by the Provincial Council or by the Bishops and approved by the Holy See.

IX. DURATION OF RESCRIPTS. (Can. 60-63.)

152. Regularly rescripts are perpetual, but various causes may limit their duration. They may be granted for only a definite period or until a certain condition is fulfilled, and they cease by lapse of time and fulfilment of the condition; they cease also by the death of the grantee or by renunciation, if they are purely personal favors; they may be revoked by special act or general law, or expire when the grantor dies or loses his power. Only the last three causes are mentioned here by the legislator.

1. Rescripts may be withdrawn by the one who granted them, his successor or competent superior; this may be done formally and directly by special act or more indirectly by another rescript mentioning and contradicting the first. But the withdrawal has no effect until it has been duly intimated to the party concerned.

2. Laws may likewise annul existing rescripts, but this is only by way of rare exception and occurs in two cases, when the law expressly provides that contrary rescripts are revoked and when it emanates from the superior of the grantor. Thus a pontifical

law cancels all contrary rescripts issued by other Ordinaries.

153. 3. Ancient canonists held that rescripts of justice expire by the death or resignation of the grantor, *re integra;* the present law enacts that by the vacancy of the Apostolic See or of an episcopal see rescripts do not expire, except two classes of them:

(*a*) Those which contain some clause manifesting the intention of the superior to grant the favor only during his own life-time *v.g. ad beneplacitum nostrum; donec voluero,* the superior's good pleasure or will ending with him. The clause *ad beneplacitum S. Sedis* has not the same import, because the Holy See continues during vacancies; nor the one *donec revocavero,* which supposes a positive act for the withdrawal of the favor.

(*b*) Those which have been issued in favor of particular persons mentioned expressly, have been committed to an executor with discretionary power and have not received even a beginning of execution before the vacancy occurs, *re adhuc integra.* (Cf. Can. 1725.)

Nota. Rescripts often contain privileges or dispensations; the rules laid down in the next two titles on privileges and dispensations then apply to them.

TITLE V

ON PRIVILEGES

(Can. 63-79.)

(Commentaries on Title 33 of the fifth Book of Decretals; Reiffenstuel, V, 33; Suarez, De Legibus, L.VIII; Wernz, I, n. 158; D'Annibale, I, n. 227; L. Thomassin, Ancienne et Nouvelle Discipline de l'Eglise, P. I, L. 3, c. xxix; F. Piatus Montensis, Praelectiones Juris Regularium, vol. ii, P. v. De Regularium Privilegiis; Maroto, n. 290; Nouvelle Revue Théologique, Jan. Fév. Mars 1922.)

In Decretal Collections the question of privileges comes only in the fifth book and is treated chiefly under its penal aspect in the title on the abuse of privileges. In the Code it occupies the place which logically belongs to it as a source of right and obligation, after the titles on laws and customs. The new law embodies the theory of privileges first outlined by Gratian (C. 25, q. 1) and completed afterwards by canonists.

I. NOTION OF PRIVILEGE

154. 1. Among the ancient Romans the word *privilegium,* from *priva* or *privata lex,* served to designate, in general, special enactments concerning private persons, whether favorable or unfavorable. Cicero and others frequently use it in the sense of decree against a private person (De Legibus, iii, 19; Forcellini Totius Latinitatis Lexicon, Patavii, 1871, v. Privilegium); gradually its meaning became restricted to favorable laws or dispositions.

155. 2. In canon law the term is used in a broad and in a strict sense.

(*a*) By privilege in the broad sense is meant a special prerogative granted by common law to a person or class of persons; thus we speak of clerical or episcopal privileges, of privileges of regulars, of minors, or even of churches.

(*b*) A privilege in the strict sense is a provision of the legislator granting a special favor, of a somewhat permanent character, or the favor thus granted.

Privileges differ from laws properly so called inasmuch as they do not ordinarily impose any obligation on the grantee and only an indirect one on others; their immediate object is the private, not the common, good, and they imply departure from the common law.

They differ from rescripts, which are written answers to a question or request and do not necessarily contain a favor. Privilege always implies favor; it may be granted orally or in writing, and does not necessarily presuppose a petition for the concession.

Privileges differ also from dispensations. These are usually granted only for individual cases and always mean an exception to the law; privileges have a permanent character and may be outside the law, as well as against it.

II. PRINCIPAL DIVISIONS OF PRIVILEGES

156. 1. Privileges may be against the law, *v.g.* exemptions from common taxes, from episcopal jurisdiction; or beside it, *v.g.* faculties to absolve from reserved irregularities, to bless certain objects.

2. They are called personal when granted immediately to physical or moral persons, and real when granted to "things," for example, to a place, an office, etc.

3. They may be purely gratuitous, not based on special merits or services rendered, nor imposing any correlative obligation; or remunerative, onerous, or conventional.

4. They are favorable when the favor to the grantee causes no prejudice to others; otherwise they are odious.

5. Positive privileges allow the performance of acts otherwise forbidden; negative ones exempt from acts otherwise obligatory.

6. Privileges may also be absolute or conditional, perpetual or temporary, useful or merely honorary, oral or written.

III. ACQUISITION OF PRIVILEGES. (Can. 63-65.)

The Code recognizes three ways of acquiring privileges: direct concession, communication and legitimate custom or prescription.

157. 1. *Direct Concession.* (*a*) Privileges can be granted by him alone who has power over the law, who can exempt from it and impose upon others the obligation of respecting the prerogatives of the privileged party, that is, the legislator.

In the Church the Pope can grant privileges outside and against all ecclesiastical laws; inferior prelates can also grant privileges, but only within the limits of their jurisdiction as to both matter and subjects.

This power was exercised rarely in the first centuries, when strict observance of all ecclesiastical laws was urged upon all. With the growth of Church organization and the development of papal authority, in the eleventh and twelfth centuries, privileges became more frequent.

(*b*) Privileges against the law can be granted by the superior to those only over whom he has the jurisdiction necessary to exempt them from the law.

Privileges outside the law, being more in the nature of a donation, do not require jurisdiction over the grantee but only over those who must not be permitted to interfere with his privilege. (Wernz, n. 159.)

(*c*) Concession may be made in writing or orally, provided there remain no doubt as to its reality and it can be proved if contested.

No formal promulgation is needed, at least for privileges strictly so called; it suffices that the parties concerned be duly notified.

Acceptance by the grantee is not in itself necessary; but as the Church does not intend to force favors on any one, unless a contrary intention be manifested, a privilege goes into effect only when it has been accepted. This may be done implicitly or explicitly, directly and immediately, or by proxy. (Wernz, n. 160; J. Putzer, Commentarium in Facultates Apostolicas, n. 35.)

158. 2. *Communication or Extension to One of Privileges Granted to Another.* (Can. 63-65; Piatus, n. 141-149.)

(*a*) There exist two forms of this communication: one called principal, absolute, perfect, complete; the other accessory, relative, imperfect.

Privileges acquired by communication in the accessory or relative form are increased, diminished, or lost to the second grantee by the mere fact of increase, diminution, or loss in the principal or original one. Communication in the principal form gives absolute, independent possession and is practically equivalent to direct concession.

Usually confraternities share, in the accessory manner, in the privileges of the archconfraternities with which they are affiliated; numerous examples of full or absolute communication exist among Religious Orders. A decree of Leo X (Const. *Dudum,* 1519) made common to all Mendicant Orders the privileges granted to one of them. To the Friars Minor of the strict observance Clement VIII gave communication, besides, of the privileges special to non-Mendicant Orders. Participation in the Mendicants' privileges was gradually extended to all Regulars. Modern Religious Congregations have obtained, by indult, similar concessions, although generally not so extensive. Thus Leo XII (Sept. 12, 1826) communicated to the Oblates of B.V.M. all the indults, privileges, indulgences, and exemptions granted to the Congregation of the Most Holy Redeemer; the Redemptorists themselves had received communication of the privileges of the Passionists and two other Orders. For the future all communication of privileges between Religious is excluded. (Can. 613.)

Sometimes the communication is limited to privileges possessed at the time by the principal or original grantee, sometimes it extends also to future ones.

159. (*b*) Privileges, to be included in a general communication, must have been obtained by direct concession; under the present law the Oblates would not, by the decree of Leo XII, become sharers in the privileges of the Passionists which the Redemptorists possessed by communication. Some ancient canonists held a different view.

Another condition is that privileges should be perpetual, not temporary, and that they should not have been granted for a reason special to a certain place, thing, or person, those, for example, granted to a particular sanctuary of which an Order might have charge, or to an individual Religious or a group of Religious because of a special work they are engaged in.

The capacity of the second grantee has also to be taken into consideration; Nuns share in the privileges of Regulars whose rule they follow and to whose authority they are subject, but this evidently does not include privileges pertaining to clerical functions.

3. *Legitimate Custom or Prescription.* By legitimate custom or prescription privileges are acquired in the same manner as laws are abrogated or new obligations introduced.

Centenary or immemorial possession is declared to create a presumption that a privilege has been originally obtained by valid concession. This is a simple presumption and would cede to truth if proved to be groundless.

IV. INTERPRETATION OF PRIVILEGES. (Can. 67, 68.)

160. 1. Privileges, being special concessions made for special reasons, admit of declarative interpretation exclusively; they must not be restricted nor extended to similar cases, in accordance with the old rule: *Quod alicui gratiose conceditur trahi non debet ab aliis in exemplum.*

2. When the wording or purport is not clear, the same principle holds for privileges as for rescripts: they must be interpreted strictly if they pertain to litigations, or infringe upon the acquired rights of others, or go against the common law in favor of private persons, or have been obtained for the purpose of acquiring some benefice. In other matters a broad interpretation is permitted.

3. They should not, however, be so understood that they would really become of no value to the holder.

V. USE OF PRIVILEGES. (Can. 69.)

161. 1. Privileges should not be used before notification of the concession has been received, and this even under pain of nullity of the act if the privilege had been granted *motu proprio* or at the request of a third party. (Piatus, n. 165.)

2. Regularly no one is bound to take advantage of a privilege granted him solely for his personal benefit; this obligation may exist *per accidens* arising from some other cause, as when non-use would be-

come injurious to the common or private good, *v.g.* a confessor possessing the privilege of absolving from reserved sins should not refuse to use it in favor of a penitent who has made his confession to him. More probably the same holds good when the privilege makes the fulfilment of an obligation possible, for example, according to many theologians one having the privilege of the domestic chapel would be bound to use it should he be unable otherwise to hear Mass on a Sunday. (Suarez, L. VIII, c. xxiii, n. 8.)

3. When the direct object of privileges is the common good, whether they be granted to places or things, to communities or certain classes of persons, like the clerical privileges, individuals are not free to refrain from using them. (Maroto, 300; Wernz, n. 161.)

162. 4. Privileges may be granted to a community, but directly in favor of the individual members; in such cases, although the individual members can not renounce the favor, they are not, in particular instances, obliged to take advantage of it except for some special reason, such as the precept of a superior prescribing uniformity of practice in the matter.

5. Some privileges are granted in the form of command, as is clear from the text of the concession; for example, the Holy See may, in approving the Constitutions of an Order, which have the force of law, permit a mode of elections simpler than the one prescribed in the Code. This permission imposes an obligation, and elections made in a different manner would be null.

VI. LOSS OR CESSATION OF PRIVILEGES.
(Can. 70-78.)

Privileges are supposed to be perpetual, unless the

contrary be proved; they may be lost or cease in several ways.

163. 1. *By Revocation.* (Maroto, n. 301; Wernz, n. 162, IV.) (*a*) Privileges, like laws, can be revoked by the grantor himself, his successor or superior. A just and proportionate cause is always required, even in the case of merely gratuitous privileges. It would be a condition for the validity of the act if the privilege was an onerous or conventional one, besides the compensation which might be due.

(*b*) The superior may recall privileges directly and expressly by a special act, taking care to notify the person concerned; or indirectly and tacitly by enactment of a contrary law.

(*c*) A general law abrogates the privileges of a general character, that is, those contained in the Code.

(*d*) Particular privileges are not abolished by a general law unless it contains the clause *ad beneplacitum nostrum* or an equivalent one; or unless it has been enacted by the superior of the prelate who granted the privilege.

164. 2. *By Renunciation.* To be effective the renunciation must be accepted by the competent authority and emanate from one who has the right to renounce the privilege.

(*a*) Any person may renounce a privilege granted him for his private, personal benefit.

(*b*) Private persons can not renounce privileges granted principally in favor of a community, dignity, or place; a cleric can not renounce, even for himself, the privilege of the special court, nor a Bishop the privileges attached to his see or to the episcopal dignity.

(*c*) A community is free to renounce privileges granted to the body, not those, however, which were granted by the way of law or in words implying command. A special mode of election conceded to a Religious Order becomes obligatory once it has been accepted and made part of the rule. Nor are such renunciations permitted which would turn to the detriment of the Church or of other persons.

3. *By the Grantor's Loss of Power.* Privileges do not cease to be in force because the grantor loses his authority whether by death, transfer, resignation, or otherwise, unless the privileges have been granted with the clause *ad beneplacitum nostrum* or some equivalent one.

165. 4. *By the Death of the Privileged Person.* (Can. 74.) Strictly personal privileges are attached to the person and die with him; but at times it may not be clear whether a privilege is merely personal, or real, or mixed; whether, for example, it was granted to a particular Bishop or to the Ordinary of the diocese, to an individual superior or to the incumbent of the office. The wording of the concession, its purpose and subject-matter must be examined closely and, should any serious doubt still remain, the grantor might, perhaps, be consulted or a confirmation of the privilege obtained from the successor if needed.

5. *By Destruction of Thing or Place.* (Can. 75.) Real privileges, such as are granted, for example, to an office, a dignity, or a community, or to a church or monastery, last as long as the thing or place with which they are connected. If these perish or are destroyed absolutely, without hope of restoration or revival, the privileges are lost. They would be only suspended if the destruction was known or expected

to be temporary and did not, in fact, prove permanent. Even if the destruction was thought to be permanent, local privileges would revive upon restoration of the place within fifty years. Until this period of time has elapsed they may, therefore, be considered as only suspended. This would not apply, however, to privileges attached, for example, to a dignity or office.

166. 6. *By Non-Use or Contrary Use.* (Can. 76.) By non-use or contrary use privileges not onerous to others, and called also favorable, do not cease. Onerous privileges do, if non-use or contrary use implies renunciation or gives occasion to legitimate prescription.

(*a*) There is non-use of a positive privilege when the acts it permits are omitted; and contrary use of a negative privilege when those acts are performed which it permits to omit.

(*b*) Favorable positive privileges are not extinguished by non-use, nor favorable negative ones by contrary use, because one is free to take advantage of a favor when he chooses, and the mere fact that he delays doing so does not prove that he renounces his right to it, nor is there any reason, since the privilege is not onerous, to urge the presumption this might give rise to or invoke prescription.

(*c*) When, however, a privilege is onerous to others, in favor of those to whom it may be objectionable, the law recognizes that non-use or contrary use, although in themselves not sufficient to annul it, may, in certain cases, imply renunciation; for example, when one repeatedly neglects the opportunity of using his privilege or acts as if he had no privilege at all. The interested party is permitted to invoke prescription against an onerous privilege in the same manner as against any other burden.

167. 7. *By Change of Conditions.* (Can. 77.) A privilege does not expire by the mere fact that its final cause or the main reason for its concession ceases to exist; the privilege of having a domestic chapel granted to a priest unconditionally because of his present infirmities is not lost by him on being restored to health. The change of conditions must be such that, in the judgment of the superior, the privilege becomes hurtful or its use illicit.

8. *By lapse of the time,* or completion of the number of cases for which it was granted, a privilege ceases *ipso facto.* The law provides, however, but for the internal forum only, that an act performed, through oversight, after the expiration of the required delegation will not be null. (Can. 207, 2.)

9. *By Abuse of the Privilege.* (Can. 78.) Persons who abuse a privilege deserve, the law declares, to be deprived of it. They do not lose it *ipso facto,* but the competent superior may, supposing the offence serious enough, take it away from them. He should regularly do so, and in order to make this possible Ordinaries are directed to notify the Holy See when they know of any grave abuse of pontifical privileges.

VII. HABITUAL FACULTIES. (Can. 66.)

(P. Corradus, Praxis Dispensationum Apostolicarum, Migne, XIX, 7; J. Putzer, Commentarium in Facultates Apostolicas, 1898; Wernz, I, n. 163; Maroto, n. 297.)

168. 1. *Notion.* A faculty, in the legal sense, means a power. In a more restricted sense, faculties, as understood here, are special powers granted by an ecclesiastical superior having jurisdiction in the external forum. They may be powers to absolve from reserved sins and censures, to dispense from irregularities, vows, or ecclesiastical precepts; they may be an authorization to bless certain objects, to do what otherwise is unlawful, *v.g.* reading forbidden books, celebrating Mass twice on the same day, etc.

Faculties granted for determinate persons and specified cases are called particular. When their use has not been thus determined, they are called general, whether they have been granted forever, or for a fixed period of time, or for a limited number of cases.

169. 2. *Origin and Development.* Concessions of special faculties by the Holy See, although not unknown before, have become particularly frequent since the sixteenth century. On the other hand, with the progress of canon law and of centralization in Church organization during the preceding period, the limits of the jurisdiction of inferior prelates had been defined with greater strictness; on the other hand, the discovery of the New World having given fresh impetus to missionary activity, the Gospel was brought to distant countries, where often difficult situations would be met with and communication with Rome impossible. Special powers were granted, therefore, to Vicars Apostolic and to missionaries, through the Holy Office first, as usually involving questions of faith, then, with its sanction, through the Congregation of the Propaganda and also through the S. Penitentiary, for matters pertaining to the internal forum.

Common formulas were soon drawn up containing the faculties more frequently needed in different regions. (Urban VIII, Const. *Operosum,* Feb. 10, 1637.) Thus there were the Form I, C, D, E, for Bishops in the United States; Form T, for Canadian

Bishops; Form VI, for Irish Bishops; Form IV, for Vicars Apostolic; the Pagella S. Poenitentiariae.

Even in regularly organized dioceses, Bishops often found their ordinary powers insufficient to meet the needs of modern society, and they, too, applied for special faculties.

170. In the New Code, however, the common law has been adapted to present conditions and the power of Ordinaries extended whenever deemed necessary. (*V. g.* Can. 239, 349, 468, 534, 822, 914, 1006, 1043, 1045, 1245, 1304.) The special faculties formerly granted to them thus cease to be useful and would be calculated to cause confusion. Therefore, in order to secure greater uniformity in Church discipline, Pope Benedict XV, by decree of the S. Consistorial Congregation of April 25, 1918, withdrew all faculties for the external forum granted to Ordinaries of dioceses subject to the common law and declared that they could not be used any longer after May 18, 1918.

This applies to the faculties contained in the Brief of twenty-five years, as it was called, or in the printed formulas granted for ten, five, or three years.

This does not affect the faculties granted to Ordinaries who are under the jurisdiction of the Propaganda, nor those pertaining to the internal forum and usually obtained from the S. Penitentiary. Special indults which some Ordinaries may have remain likewise in force.

3. *Interpretation and Application.* General faculties habitually granted to Ordinaries are assimilated by the present law to privileges beside the law, and the same rules govern them. They are interpreted and applied according to the same principles and cease by the same causes.

171. 4. *Communication and Transmission.* Formerly some canonists, considering faculties as strictly personal privileges, concluded that they could not, without special permission, be communicated or subdelegated and that they did not pass on to the successor in office. (Putzer, n. 28; Wernz, Jus Decretalium, vol. iv, n. 622, note 104.) The opposite view, however, has been confirmed, in recent years by several decrees of the Holy Office. (Nov. 24, 1897; Ap. 20, June 22, Dec. 14, 1898; May 3, Dec. 20, 1899; Sept. 8, 1900.) The decree of Dec. 14, 1898, formally allowed the subdelegation, either in a general manner or for particular cases, of faculties granted by the Holy See, unless the indult contained provisions to the contrary.

According to the present Code, faculties obtained from the Apostolic See, by any Ordinary, Bishop, Abbot, Prelate Nullius, Vicar and Prefect Apostolic, superior of exempt Religious Order, Vicar-General, Administrator, regularly continue in force after the Ordinary has gone out of office, even if he had commenced to execute them, and they pass over to the successor unless there be in the indult some provision excluding such a transmission, or the faculties had been granted as a personal privilege or on account of special qualities or merits. This, however, would have to be proved; faculties are presumed to be for the office, not for the person, even if in the indult a Bishop would be designated by name.

5. *Powers Implied in Faculties.* They imply all the powers necessary for their exercise; hence the faculty of dispensing includes the power of absolving from the censures which might be, but only in as far as they would be, an obstacle to the reception of the dispensation.

TITLE VI.

ON DISPENSATIONS

(Can. 80-86.)

(Suarez, Lib. VI, c. x-xxiv; Pyrrhus Corradus, o. c.; Putzer, o. c.; Reiffenstuel, II, n. 449 sq.; D'Annibale, I, n. 230 sq.; Wernz, I, n. 119 sq.; Thomassin, Ancienne et Nouvelle Discipline de l'Eglise, P. II, L. III, c. 24-29; Dictionnaire de Théologie, Dispenses; Catholic Encyclopedia, Dispensation; Marotto, n. 302 sq.)

172. 1. *Nature.* (*a*) The term dispensation is usually employed in ancient classical writers in the sense of administration, distribution, stewardship. In ecclesiastical texts it often has also the same meaning. (Council of Antioch, c. 24, 25; Chalcedon, c. 24; Lateran, 1123, c. 4; C.X, q.1, c.5; C.XVI, q.7, c.11-21; C.XXV, q.11, c.2.)

In the administration of law prudence demands that particular circumstances be taken into account, burdens apportioned according to individual strength, and general legislation adapted to special needs. For the sake of the common good or to avoid greater evils illegal actions may be legitimized afterwards so that they have all their juridical effects; or exemption may have to be granted from a law which it would not be just or wise to enforce in a particular case.

(*b*) To these last acts of administration has been reserved by jurists the name of dispensation, which in a technical, legal acceptation may be defined as a relaxation of the law in a particular case by the lawful superior. The law continues in force, but it is suspended by the competent authority in a particular case, *i.e.* in favor of an individual person, physical or moral, or of a whole community, but for only one act or fixed, determined time. Dispensation thus differs from abrogation or derogation, by which the law is suppressed partially or totally; from permission, which does not suspend the law but rather brings the act into conformity with it; from interpretation or *epikeia,* which does not require jurisdiction nor the intervention of the superior but aims only at ascertaining the meaning of the law or the intention of the legislator; from absolution, which supposes a violation of the law and removes the guilt or censure incurred thereby; from privilege, which implies a more permanent concession and does not so much suspend as substitute a private for the common law for certain persons.

(*c*) Dispensations may be total or partial, temporary or perpetual, explicit, implicit, or tacit, direct or indirect, absolute or conditional, for the internal or external forum, in *forma gratiosa* or *commissoria;* these terms are sufficiently clear of themselves or have been explained already.

173. 2. *Historical Development.* (*a*) It is not possible for a human legislator so to frame his laws that their application will not in some cases offer serious difficulties calling for exceptions. This must be particularly true in a society which comprises men belonging to different races and countries with various customs and needs. Hence, from the beginning, the Church, ever solicitous for the welfare of each individual soul, showed herself ready to mitigate the strictness of her discipline when circumstances demanded.

St. Augustine highly praises the wisdom and charity of Pope St. Melchiades (314) who, in order to heal dissensions in the African Church, allowed Donatist Bishops consecrated by their leader Majorinus to retain their sees on return to unity when by law they should have been permanently excluded from them. (Thomassin, c.24.) At the request of Spanish

Bishops, Pope St. Siricius authorized penitents and bigamists to exercise the functions of the Orders which they had received unlawfully (398).

Dispensations, however, remained rare for a long time, and most of them, although not all, were granted to legitimize already illegally accomplished facts rather than to render them lawful beforehand; they were usually dispensations *post factum* and seldom *ad faciendum.*

Of matrimonial dispensations in particular, whether *post factum* or *ad faciendum,* we find some examples in the sixth and seventh centuries. (Epaonne, 517 c.30; Orleans, 538, c.11; Verberie, 756, c. 1.) St. Gregory the Great dispensed temporarily the newly-converted Anglo-Saxons from the impediment of consanguinity beyond the fourth degree. (C. xxxv, q.II, c.20.) These were general concessions. For papal dispensations of marriage in individual cases we have to come down to the eleventh century and to the beginning of the thirteenth for the first certain instance of an antecedent individual one.

In other matters there seem to have been antecedent individual dispensations at an earlier date. Pope Pelagius (590) permitted the promotion to the diaconate of a widower legally debarred from it by former incontinence. (D. xxxiv, c.vii.) Charlemagne is said to have obtained from Pope Adrian I, with the approval of the Council of Frankfort (794, c.55), for the Bishops of Metz and Cologne, dispensation from the law of residence, that they might live in the imperial palace. Antecedent dispensations are nevertheless still relatively rare in the Middle Ages. The Decretal Collections mention only few and they have no title on dispensations. The law was rigorously enforced whenever possible. In the sixteenth century the Holy See grants ampler faculties to missionaries in distant lands and in the seventeenth similar privileges are extended to other countries.

174. (*b*) It is not that any serious doubt was entertained as to the existence of the power of dispensing in the Church. Its necessity is too evident. In the words of St. Cyril of Alexandria, "as on a stormy ocean, when the ship is in danger, part of the cargo is thrown into the sea that the rest may be saved, so in the affairs of the world, when all can not be saved something is sacrificed that all be not lost." (Epist. lvi, Migne, P.G., vol. XXXVII, col. 319, C. I, q. 7, c. 16.)

The theory of dispensations, outlined by Pope Martin I (649-653, P.L., vol. LXXXVII, col.159), was more fully developed by the canonists of the Gregorian and post-Gregorian period (1060-1140), immediate predecessors of Gratian, who first attempted a scientific treatment of ecclesiastical law and whose work prepared the way for the *Decretum*. Pope Urban II (1088-1099) brought out with peculiar clearness and authority the distinction which ought to be made between what is immutable in canonical legislation and what is subject to change by dispensation, and this doctrine passing, through the writings of Bernald of Coutances and Yvo of Chartres (Migne, P.L. vol. 161, col. 50 sq.), into the teaching of the schools helped considerably to remove all possible misconception on the subject. (Paul Fournier, Un Tournant de l'Histoire du Droit, 1060-1140; Paris, 1917.)

175. (*c*) As long as dispensations continued to be looked upon as nothing more than necessary acts of a prudent administration, Bishops, as guardians of all ecclesiastical laws, whether general or particular, considered themselves authorized to grant them, individually or in Provincial Councils. When, however, time and other circumstances permitted, they frequently referred such cases to the Pope, even from the Eastern Church, particularly the more important and unusual ones. This practice grew more and more common as time went on.

During the persecutions recourse to Rome often proved impossible or dangerous and most of the dispensations had to be obtained from the local Bishops. In the course of the third and fourth centuries the custom was gradually introduced of referring these matters to the Councils as enjoying higher authority and likely to use greater firmness for the maintenance of ecclesiastical discipline.

Particular Councils still exercised dispensing power in the eighth, ninth, and even tenth centuries, but recourses to the Holy See were now much more common (Thomassin, 26), and soon the principle was universally accepted that dispensations from general laws must come from the supreme lawgiver. This change was due to several causes; a clearer understanding of the nature of dispensation and of the power it presupposes, excessive leniency of some Bishops, who lacked the energy or independence necessary to resist local influences, respect for the See of Peter, progress in the centralization of authority.

176. (*d*) Bishops, however, had to dispense from general laws in some cases. Necessity usually accounted for the practice, but to reconcile it with the theory now admitted by all, canonists proposed various explanations. According to one, which met with little success, Bishops would retain all the dispensing power formerly exercised by them and not formally withdrawn. (Glossa in c. 4, De Judiciis, 5°,

De Adulterio.) The more common teaching was, at the end of the fifteenth century, and had substantially remained thereafter, that Bishops can dispense from general laws when urgent necessity or great utility demands it and when this power is granted to them by custom or by law, explicitly or implicitly; in all cases, for example, in which the legislator permits dispensation without reserving it to the Holy See. Modern canonists added all doubtful cases. (Ferraris, Prompta Bibliotheca, Dispensatio, n.23 sq.; Dictionnaire de Théologie Catholique, Dispenses, col. 1435.)

177. (*e*) About the extent of the Pope's dispensing power there existed, for a time, some uncertainty. That he should not dispense without grave reason, all readily admitted; but some asked whether he had any power over apostolic decrees, the canons of the first great Councils which formed the basis of ecclesiastical legislation, and general statutes. In support of the negative answer they brought forward, besides other arguments, a declaration attributed to Pope Urban and now recognized as apocryphal. (C.XXV, q.1,c.6.) For the opposite view could be quoted certainly authentic texts and facts of history, showing that the Roman Pontiffs claimed and exercised such power.

The controversy was settled, if any remained, by Pope Innocent III, who after a formal discussion of the subject decides that he can dispense from the decree of Alexander III and the Lateran Council (1179, c. 3) forbidding the promotion to the episcopate of a man of illegitimate birth. His authority, he says, is equal to that of his predecessor and therefore he can not be bound by his decisions. (C. 20,X,I, Tit. VI.)

178. 3. *Author of Dispensations.* To dispense from a law requires a power equal, yet not necessarily superior, to that which enacted it.

(*a*) The Pope. (i) Of his own right, *i.e.* by virtue of his office, the Pope has power to dispense from all ecclesiastical laws, general or particular, whether enacted by an individual Pontiff, by an Oecumenical Council, or even by apostolic authority.

(ii) He dispenses from vows, oaths, religious profession, unconsummated marriage, by derived power communicated to him as the Vicar of Christ. In such cases, the obligation, although one of divine right, is conditioned on previous human consent, and the Pope, in the name of God, remits for the faithful over whose will he has a real authority that obligation which results from their free act and the consequences flowing from it by natural or divine positive law. (Suarez, De Legibus, L.II,c.14; Noldin, De Principiis, n.182.)

(iii) From the absolute precepts of the natural or divine positive law, *i.e.* those which do not presuppose human consent, the Pope can not dispense even by derived power; he only interprets them. (Suarez, l.c., n.25; Wernz, n.122.)

179. (*b*) Bishops and other local Ordinaries inferior to the Pope. (i) In all diocesan legislation they dispense of their own right, whether it was enacted by themselves or their predecessors, in or out of Synod. (Can. 82.)

(ii) From the laws of Provincial or Plenary Councils they are authorized by the Code, as by the former discipline, to dispense in particular cases only. (Can. 82, 291, §2.)

(iii) From the general laws of the Church or pontifical laws enacted for a particular territory,

Bishops and other Ordinaries can not dispense of their own right; this power may be granted them explicitly or implicitly, by common law or special delegation.

The present Code explicitly grants it to them: in all doubtful cases (doubt of fact, Can. 15); in cases in which recourse to the Holy See is difficult and at the same time there is grave danger in delay, provided the needed dispensation be one of those which the Holy See is wont to grant; and in certain particular matters. (*V.g.* Can. 990, 1043, 1045, 1245, 2237.) There is no explicit mention of the cases of frequent occurrence or of minor importance which had formerly been assimilated to urgent cases in regard to the Bishop's dispensing power.

(*c*) Pastors. They can dispense neither from general nor from particular laws, unless that power has been expressly granted them. (Can. 83.)

The Code grants to them explicitly the power of dispensing their subjects, in particular cases, from the law of fasting or abstinence and the Sunday law; they were generally considered before as having these powers by custom or tacit concession of the Holy See. They may now dispense also from certain marriage impediments. (Can. 1043-45, 1098.) Similar powers are granted to superiors of Religious Orders (Can. 1245), to confessors. (Can. 1044, 1045, 990.)

180. 4. *Subjects of Dispensations.* A superior can exercise his dispensing power only in favor of those over whom he has jurisdiction. He has sufficient jurisdiction for the purpose of dispensation over all *incolae* whose domicile is in his territory, whether they are actually present in it or not; over *advenae,* or persons who have their quasi-domicile and are actually present within the limits of his jurisdiction;

over *vagi,* who have no domicile or quasi-domicile anywhere and are now in his territory; also, at least probably, over *peregrini* who, although they have a domicile or quasi-domicile in some other place, become his subjects, in some degree, by the fact of their presence in his territory. (H.O., Nov.22,1865, S.C. de Prop. Fid., Sept. 19, 1861; March 13, 1886; Wernz, n.123; D'Annibale, n.232; Putzer, n.49; Maroto, n.305.)

A superior having general powers may use them in his own favor unless the dispensation would have to be granted in the tribunal of penance. Dispensing is an act of voluntary jurisdiction which does not require distinction of persons.

181. 5. *Causes for Granting Dispensations.* (Can. 84.) (*a*) It is always unlawful to dispense from ecclesiastical laws without a just and reasonable cause. The dispensation is even invalid if it is granted by virtue of derived, vicarious, or delegated power which is supposed to be communicated only on condition of sufficient reason for its use. A superior who dispenses of his own right acts unlawfully when he does so without just cause, but his act is valid, as the binding force of the law depends entirely on his will.

(*b*) The gravity of the cause must be in proportion to the importance of the law from which dispensation is sought. When there is doubt as to its sufficiency, the dispensation is lawfully asked for and, if granted, will be both valid and lawful.

(*c*) The cause must be verified at the moment of the real concession of the dispensation, as said when speaking of rescripts. (Can. 41.) Not only should it truly exist, but it should be known to exist; this, however, is required only for its lawfulness, unless it had been made a necessary condition, which is usually not done at present.

182. 6. *Interpretation of Dispensations.* Dispensations, like rescripts contrary to the law (Can. 50), must be interpreted strictly. The same holds true of the power of dispensing when it is granted for a certain case.

The general power of dispensing, whether ordinary or delegated, may be interpreted broadly since it is a favor and its object is the common good, unless the interest of a third party be at stake or there be some provision to the contrary in the law or the delegation.

183. 7. *Cessation of Dispensations.* Dispensations granted for a single act obtain their full effect as soon as really granted; they can not cease. There can be cessation of only such dispensations as admit of successive applications or have not as yet produced any effect.

Dispensations cease in the same manner as privileges and, moreover, by the certain and complete cessation of the motive cause. By the disappearance of a merely influencing reason, or by a doubtful or only partial cessation of the motive or determining cause, dispensations would not be nullified, for they still remain, at least probably, reasonable.

Usually dispensations from impediments or irregularities are granted absolutely, *i.e.* they do not permit successive application but obtain their full effect from the moment of concession or execution. Provided that at that moment the motive cause be true, even if afterwards it would cease to be so, before, *v.g.* the marriage has been contracted, the dispensation remains effective. (Lehmkuhl, Theologia Moralis, I, n. 268.)

BOOK II

OF PERSONS

(Can. 87-214.)

After laying down the general principles of ecclesiastical law, in the first book, the Code passes, in the second, to the legislation on persons. In a society, the constituent elements and the organization have to be considered first, then the means by which it can attain its end.

This book includes substantially the matter of the first and third in Decretal Collections, Judex, Clerus. It is divided into three parts corresponding to the three classes into which the members of the Church may be distributed: the clergy, the religious, and the laity. A few preliminary canons containing general notions serve as an introduction.

PRELIMINARY NOTIONS. (Can. 87-107.)

(Commentarium Textus Codicis Juris Canonici, Liber II, De Personis, Auctore Alberto Blat, O. P.; Maroto, l.c., n. 389.)

The legislator here defines canonical personality and the main juridical aspects under which both physical and moral persons may have to be considered for the application of law.

I. PHYSICAL PERSONS. (Can. 87-98.)

184. 1. *Definition.* (*a*) A person in the physical sense is, according to the classic definition of Boethius (De Persona et Duabus Naturis, c. ii), an individual substance of a rational nature; or, a rational substance, complete, existing in itself, independent, and centre of attribution of its own powers and activity.

To be a person in the juridical sense one must, besides, be recognized by law as enjoying certain rights. Every human being is, by nature, the subject of rights as well as of duties: but this has not always been admitted by legislators, particularly in the case of slaves, to whom in pagan times all rights were often denied; moreover, the State may confer upon citizens further accidental prerogatives of its own. (Wernz, I, n. 103; D'Annibale, I, 82.)

Personality in the canonical sense, or personality in Christ's Church, implies the right to the Christian privileges with the corresponding duties.

(*b*) Canonical personality evidently does not flow from our human nature; it is obtained through baptism, by which one acquires all the rights and assumes all the obligations of Christians.

Baptism without qualification means baptism of water, received validly, whoever may have been the minister.

185. (*c*) This personality is as inamissible as the baptismal character itself. Any one who has been validly baptized remains forever a member of Christ's Church, *i.e.* the Catholic Church, and subject to her authority. Apostates, heretics, schismatics, excommunicates are bound, not only by the divine positive, but also by the ecclesiastical, laws unless the Church, explicitly or implicitly, exempts them from the latter. (Maroto, n. 196; Wernz, I, n. 103, 80.)

A Christian may, however, be deprived of his rights, owing to some obstacle which separates him from the ecclesiastical communion or to some ecclesiastical censure. Apostasy and heresy separate from the unity of faith, schism from the unity of obedience; some censures, like excommunications, separate also from the communion of the faithful, whilst others, like suspensions and interdicts, only take away some particular rights.

Separation from ecclesiastical communion implies separation from the body of the Church and loss of those privileges which are attached to external membership, not necessarily separation from Christ and from the soul of the Church nor loss of all supernatural means of salvation.

186. 2. *Age.* The physical and moral development which usually go with age serve to determine a person's legal status.

(*a*) Majority and minority.—In the Church, persons are presumed to reach the development which entitles them to the full use of their rights when completing their twenty-first year. This is only presumption, which yields to convincing evidence. Under that age they are minors and subject to the authority of their parents or guardians, except in those matters in which law grants independence, *v.g.* in the choice of a state of life. (Can. 1034, 1648, § 3.)

(*b*) Puberty. The age of puberty is legally reached, whatever be the reality, at the end of the fourteenth year by boys and at the end of the twelfth year by girls. *Impuberes* do not incur penalties *latae sententiae* (Can. 2230), nor are they supposed ordinarily to contract irregularities or other canonical impediments to the reception of Orders. (Can. 994.)

(*c*) Minors under seven are called infants (*infans, puer, parvulus*); they are presumed not to have the use of reason, and purely ecclesiastical laws do not bind them even if *de facto* they have the use of reason (Can. 12), unless otherwise explicitly stated. (*V.g.* Can. 854, § 2.) After completing their seventh year they are supposed to enjoy the use of reason and to be responsible for their acts, unless the contrary be proved.

The law assimilates to infants older persons who are not habitually rational; they are not subject to ecclesiastical laws or penalties even in their occasional lucid moments. (Can. 2201.)

187. 3. *Place of Origin and of Residence.* Very frequently laws affect persons through the place with which these are connected; hence the juridical importance of local relationships.

Connection with place may be by birth or by residence; the latter, admitting of various degrees of stability or duration, gives rise to corresponding relations known in law as domicile, quasi-domicile, transitory residence, vagrancy.

(Commentaries on Title III, Book IV of Decretals, De Clandestina Desponsatione; Treatises De Matrimonio or De Sacra Ordinatione; D'Annibale, I, n. 82; Wernz, IV, n. 177; Fourneret, Le Domicile Matrimonial, Paris, 1906; J. Alberti, De Domicilio Ecclesiastico Acquirendo et Amittendo deque ejus Effectibus, Acquapendente 1909; Catholic Encyclopedia, Domicile; Dictionnaire de Théologie Catholique, Domicile; Irish Theological Quarterly, April, 1915, Jan., 1916, July, 1916, July, 1917; Irish Ecclesiastical Record, March, 1918.)

188. 1°. Origin. (*a*) Among the ancient Romans the term origin, *origo, jus originis,* designated the bond of prerogatives and obligations which united a person to his family, taking this word in its broad sense. The family having become identified with the place in which it settled, the relationship was transferred to the latter, that is, to the city or municipium. *Origo* thus corresponded substantially to what is now called nationality. Children inherited it from their parents, for they belonged to the same municipality and enjoyed the same city rights independently of their real place of birth.

The Barbarian invasions caused these notions and the Roman law generally to be lost sight of for a time. They reappeared with the revival of legal studies in the twelfth century, but in a somewhat modified form. The jurists of the Bolognese School interpreted origin as a species of domicile acquired by birth in the place in which one is normally born, which is the place of the parents' residence at that moment. A person born accidentally in some other locality would have for his place of origin his father's real, even though not legal, birthplace. Later jurists defined the place of origin more absolutely as that in which one was born or should have been born, that is, the place of the father's domicile at the time of the son's birth. (Voet, Commentarius ad Pandectas; Neapoli, San Giacomo, 1827-1833.)

189. (*b*) The jurists' deformed concept of origin passed into canon law, slowly, however, and soon to be abandoned almost entirely, without ever finding much application except in the question of the legitimate minister of ordination or of baptism.

The Decretals of Gregory IX make no mention of it, nor does the great canonist of the fourteenth century, Bernard of Parma. The Sixth Book of Decretals (L. I, Tit. IX, De Temporibus Ordinationum) contains a decree of Clement IV (1268) and one of Boniface VIII (1299) declaring it lawful for a Bishop to ordain candidates who are natives of his diocese, *oriundi*. To determine when one can truly be considered as *oriundus* of a place, canonists had recourse to the jurists' theory of origin, some laying particular stress on the father's domicile, others on the place of birth. (Reiffenstuel, In Tit.,

n. 88.) Clement XII, in the celebrated Const. *Speculatores* (Nov 4, 1694), which remained the law on the matter till the publication of the Code, gave the official rule in which the two views were combined. A candidate for Orders must be considered as the subject, by reason of his origin, of the Bishop in whose diocese he was born, provided this was not due to a merely accidental occurrence. If at the time his father did not have, in the place, a somewhat stable residence—the Pope does not use here the word domicile—it is not the son's but the father's actual place of birth that has to be considered. Should, however, the father acquire afterwards a domicile in the son's accidental place of birth this would become the latter's legal place of origin. (S. Many, S.S., De Sacra Ordinatione, n. 29.) In practice, the interpretation and application of this rule did not go without some difficulties.

From the general principles of law canonists concluded that, in the case of illegitimate or posthumous children, what is regularly said of the father applies to the mother. The legal place or origin for exposed children was presumed, in the absence of proofs to the contrary, to be the place in which they happened to be found. In favor of converts, Paul III granted (*Cupientes,* March 21, 1542) and Clement XI confirmed (*Propagandae,* March 10, 1704) that the place of their baptism or spiritual birth would enjoy the privileges of place of origin.

190. (*c*) Under the present law the place of origin is determined, even for converts or neophytes, by the domicile of the father, or his quasi-domicile if he had no domicile, at the time of the son's birth. For illegitimate or posthumous children the mother's domicile or quasi-domicile serves the same purpose.

Would a person have two places of origin if his parents had a twofold domicile? St. Alphonsus answered in the affirmative, under the former discipline, but many canonists maintained that the place of origin must necessarily be one like the place of birth, with which they identified it; the present law does not imply such identification, except when the parents have neither domicile nor quasi-domicile. The place of birth is then always the place of origin.

The provision of the Bull *Cupientes* and the privilege of converts are abrogated. The place of origin for exposed children is absolutely decreed to be the place in which they were found. If, however, their parents became known afterwards, they might probably cease to be considered as foundlings. (Blat, p. 9.)

Origin no longer suffices to give jurisdiction to a Bishop over candidates for ordination (Can. 956); it retains its importance in regard to the administration of baptism (Can. 738).

191. 2°. Domicile. (*a*) In Roman law domicile was an extension of *origo,* a communication to outsiders of the legal status belonging to native citizens by right of birth. A stranger who settled in a municipium would be expected to take his share of the common burden, to pay taxes, etc.; he had to be granted some of the common advantages also. Thus he became a member of the community, the *patria,* not as citizen by origin, but as inhabitant, *incola,* by residence and domicile.

Jurists needed some time to develop a theory of domicile; after long discussions they at last recognized as its real essential element the intention of permanent residence and as its normal proof actual residence together with transfer of one's effects or any other sign of stable settlement. In some cases the law presumed or supplied these conditions. A married woman shared the domicile of her husband even though she did not live with him, and minors that of their father, at least probably; senators had a domicile in Rome even when dispensed from residence. By a special disposition of the Justinian Code students acquired a domicile in a city after a residence of ten years. A man could have several domiciles, as he could have several places of origin.

Domicile was lost by change of intention as manifested in removal of residence.

The *Lex Romana Wisigothorum* which, after the Barbarian invasion, prevailed generally, ignored domicile, and the name itself ceased to be used in legal documents. Race and actual residence served, in its place, to determine a man's juridical standing.

After the return to Roman law, in the twelfth century, the idea of domicile underwent some important alterations at the hands of glossarists. They transformed, as said before, origin into a species of domicile. In the acquisition of domicile proper they distinguished two essential elements, the material and the formal one, residence and intention, and gave the same importance to the one as to the other. They required for all, as formerly for students, a ten years' test, unless the intention was clearly manifested otherwise.

192. (*b*) Ancient canon law contained no independent theory nor any official definition of domicile. Ecclesiastical legislation simply adapted itself first to the Roman then to the Barbarian law, ecclesiastical superiors endeavoring to solve practical cases and regulate the exercise of local jurisdiction on the principles of justice and equity, in conformity with prevailing customs.

After the renaissance of the twelfth century, domicile remains for some time without any special importance in Church discipline. Gratian barely mentions the name in his Decree. Criminals were brought, not before the court of the territory in which they lived, but of the territory in which the offence had been committed or the object in dispute happened to be located; candidates for Orders became a Bishop's subjects by birth or previous ordination, not by domicile; funeral dues went to the church in which the deceased had during life received the sacraments. In other matters similar rules were followed.

193. The connection, however, between civil and canonical law was too close in those days and domicile played too great a part in the former not to receive soon some recognition in the latter. Moreover, for the application of the Lateran decree on paschal communion and later on of the decree *Tametsi* on the form of marriage, it was necessary to have a simple and easy way of determining the *proprius sacerdos* from whom communion should be received at Easter and the pastor before whom marriages had to be contracted under pain of nullity. Hence, after the Council of Lateran (1215), and especially after the Council of Trent, the new interest shown by canonists in questions of domicile. Some adopted the interpretation of the Bolognese jurists, others favored more the older theory. The Gloss of the Decree and that of the *Liber Sextus* admit the doctrine of the ten years' residence, but it is positively rejected by Bernard of Parma, and as late as the seventeenth century Fagnani still holds that intention is the only essential element in domicile and that no residence of any kind is strictly necessary for it. The general tendency, however, was to lay stress on the material element, *i.e.* residence, as easier to ascertain; Sanchez gave to it the same importance as to intention (De Matrimonio, III, 23-25), and his view soon prevailed. On the other hand, the ten years' test was gradually abandoned like the domicile of origin, except in connection with ordination. Here again the Bull *Speculatores* demanded that to become a Bishop's subject by reason of domicile a candidate should reside in his diocese for ten years or transfer there the greater part of his property and reside there for a considerable time, which was ordinarily interpreted three or four years. The intention of remaining permanently had, besides, to be confirmed by oath.

194. For ordinary, acquired, as distinct from legal, domicile, two conditions came to be recognized after the Council of Trent as necessary and sufficient: residence in a certain place and intention of remaining permanently unless something would call the person away. The ten years' residence had no other value than to create a strong presumption in favor of the intention.

Some uncertainty still remained as to the exact meaning of the term "place." In Roman law domicile was attached to the city; the same principle obtained for a long time in canon law, but as in Church discipline domicile has its most frequent applications to such acts as baptisms, marriages, funerals, which are of a parochial character, the parochial aspect of domicile itself assumed such prominence that any other was lost sight of, and many concluded that domicile could be acquired only in a parish and not in a diocese except through the parish. This view became prevalent after the Council of Trent and the more complete organization of parish life which followed it. Innocent XII in the Bull *Speculatores* (1694) still speaks of domicile *in loco,* but this was interpreted as equivalent to *in parochia,* or if the words had to be taken in a broader sense they were applied only to domicile for ordination. (S. Many, De Sacra Ordinatione, n. 33.) Though some canonists do not give up the domicile in a city or locality, *in civitate, in castro, in loco* (3, Lib. III, Tit. XII, in Sexto; Sanchez, De Matrimonio, L. III, Disp. 23, n. 14), the common opinion is against them. (D'Annibale, I, n. 83; Gasparri, De Matrimonio, n. 981.)

For the diocesan domicile there seems to be no analogy in Roman law nor any support in ancient canon law.

195. (*c*) Present legislation. Domicile is acquired by residence in a parish or quasi-parish, or at least in a diocese, vicariate apostolic, prefecture apostolic; provided this residence be either united to the intention of remaining there permanently unless called away or prolonged for ten complete years. (Can. 92.) The Code retains the hitherto accepted definition of domicile, but admits residence as sufficient in some cases and introduces the diocesan domicile.

(i) As under the former discipline, residence is an essential element of domicile. It supposes personal presence in the place, and transference of property would not be sufficient. The latter is not of itself necessary, although in practice it will always be very useful to distinguish a passing visit from a stable settlement. (F. Deshayes, Questions Pratiques sur le Mariage, Domicile, p. 5.)

(ii) Residence is now sufficient for the acquisition of domicile if it continues for ten years without moral interruption. (Blat, o. c., p. 12.)

(iii) When to residence is joined the intention of remaining permanently domicile is acquired at once. Canon law accepts as proof of such intention the testimony of the parties concerned, provided there be no reason to suspect their honesty. Other evidence may be found in their acts, the business they are engaged in, the purpose of their coming, etc.

There are thus now two ways of acquiring domicile: residence for ten years and residence with intention of remaining permanently. Intention ceases to be an absolutely essential element since it can be dispensed with, and greater importance is given to residence than ever before.

(iv) Domicile in the city or locality is clearly abrogated now if it was not before, but domicile in the diocese, vicariate apostolic, or prefecture apostolic receives official recognition. A person remaining ten years in a diocese acquires a domicile therein, even though he may have been wandering from place to place during all that time without settling in any parish; he has also a diocesan domicile as soon as he comes into the diocese with the intention of remaining permanently and before he has chosen any particular parish for his place of residence.

196. 3°. Quasi-Domicile. (*a*) Quasi-domicile is an extended or attenuated domicile; the idea was developed exclusively by canonists, slowly and haltingly, under the pressure of necessity and to meet practical difficulties.

The faithful could not reasonably be expected always to go to the church of their domicile for their annual confession, paschal communion, weddings, funerals, etc.; they had to be allowed to discharge these obligations and become parishioners in places of less stable residence. This concession was frequently made in particular cases before the principle received general acceptance, which does not seem to have come till the period subsequent to the Council of Trent, when the application of the decree *Tametsi* gave rise to so many complications. Only in 1702 did the Congregation of the Council declare that the pastor of the domicile or quasi-domicile of the parties was the *proprius parochus* for marriage. What constituted this less stable yet sufficient residence or quasi-domicile remained still to be defined. (Nouvelle Revue Théologique, Sept., 1907, p. 513, s.)

197. Boniface VIII had decreed in 1298 (c. *Is qui,* Lib. III, Tit. XII, in Sexto) that in regard to funeral rights a deceased person should not be considered as a parishioner in a place to which he had come *recreationis causa vel ad ruralia exercenda,* for the purpose of recreation or of rural business. Canonists generalized the principle and applied it to students, servants, refugees, and various other classes of persons.

Sanchez, who wrote about the year 1592, was one of the first to depart from the common teaching. He maintained that the words of the Pope should be understood of persons whose residence in the locality was of brief duration, not of those whose business kept them there for a considerable time, and by considerable time he meant the greater part of the year. (De Matrimonio, Lib. III, disp. 23.) Why the greater part of the year, asked Fagnani almost a century later (1661); for him actual residence with a slight fixity of tenure sufficed. Provided a man had not come to a place with the positive intention of merely passing through he was entitled to the privileges of a parishioner; he quoted the decision of the Congregation of the Council in the case of two persons from Utrecht whose marriage was pronounced valid from the mere fact that they had been for a month in the place of the celebration. (In caput Significat, De Parochiis.) In other cases, it is true, the Tribunal of the Rota had declared three or four months insufficient. Reiffenstuel (1703) insisted on six months but it was not six months of actual residence. Distinguishing in quasi-domicile as in domicile itself a formal and a material element, the intention and the residence, he demanded for acquiring it actual residence with intention of remaining for the greater part of the year. This theory was destined to prevail, but only after prolonged controversies; meanwhile the same uncertainty continued and the same variety of practices. Asked for a general rule that could be followed in this matter, Benedict XIV preferred to limit himself to the solution of particular cases. (Inst. Ecc. n. 33, 38.) When urged by the Bishop of Goa to explain what quasi-domicile consisted in, he answered that before contracting marriage the party had to live in the place for at least one month, and he referred to Fagnani and the decision of the Congregation in the Utrecht case. (Const. *Paucis abhinc*, March 19, 1758.) From these words many canonists and theologians concluded that according to the Pontiff a month's residence was what constituted quasi-domicile, at least in matrimonial matters. Several rituals or particular Councils adopted this as a rule to guide the clergy, except that some extended the time of the necessary residence to two, four, or six months. This, however, did not harmonize with Roman decisions.

198. At last the Holy Office, on June 7, 1867, issued a decree officially declaring that to constitute a quasi-domicile two things are necessary: residence in the place and intention of remaining there for the greater part of the year; as soon as these two conditions are fulfilled quasi-domicile is acquired. If there is no certainty regarding the existence of the intention, recourse must be had to the various indications which may manifest it, and special use should be made of the rule confirmed by Pope Benedict XIV, that is, it should be found out whether the party resided in the place for at least one month, and if such be the case this may be taken as a presumption in law that the intention of remaining for the greater part of the year was not wanting.

The decree was quite clear and explicit; yet the old erroneous views it condemned were not abandoned at once and completely. Some interpreted the words *per majorem anni portem* as implying simply a notable part of the year, some months, probably four months according to Lehmkuhl (II, n. 775), or even one month according to Santi (III, n. 75), provided the stay be not *rusticationis causa.*

Roman Congregations did not accept this interpretation, but concessions were made in favor of some dioceses. At the request of the Archbishop of Baltimore the Holy Office granted that in the United States, under certain circumstances, quasi-domicile could be acquired, for matrimonial purposes, by residence for one month independently of intention. (May 6, 1886.) The Archbishop of Paris obtained in 1898 that a six months' residence should have the same effect in his episcopal city. These were special regulations, as the Assessor of the Holy Office explicitly stated in answer to a question of the Congregation of the Council (Jan. 26, 1903); they should not be transformed into rules, as some seemed inclined to do. At the same time several decisions of the Rota showed that a residence of six or more months, without being sufficient of itself to constitute a quasi-domicile, could be accepted as implying the necessary intention unless the contrary would be clearly demonstrated. (May 5, 1914.)

The decree *Ne Temere* (Aug. 2, 1907) had abrogated quasi-domicile in matrimonial matters (March 28, 1908), but the Code restores it.

199. (*b*) Present legislation. Quasi-domicile is now acquired in a parish or diocese by actual residence with the intention of remaining for the greater part of the year at least, or by actual residence during the greater part of a year. Its similarity to domicile and difference from it are obvious.

The Code thus maintains the classic conception of quasi-domicile, consisting of a material and a formal element, residence and intention; but it permits, on the specified condition of residence, to dispense with the intention, which may be so difficult to prove. Satisfaction is given to the persistent demand for a rule which can easily be applied when the intention remains uncertain or indefinite.

On the one hand, quasi-domicile can be acquired without having to wait for a whole month; on the other, a person who has resided in the same place for the greater part of a year will not be without quasi-domicile there, whatever may have been his state of mind during that time.

Residence and intention are understood here and

proved in the same manner as for domicile. A month's residence has the same value as before, in accordance with the teaching of Benedict XIV, as a presumption of intention to reside for the greater part of the year.

200. 4°. Legal Domicile or Quasi-Domicile. A legal domicile is one conferred or imposed by law independently of residence or intention. In Roman law, as said before, a wife shared necessarily in her husband's domicile, a minor in his father's or guardian's; prisoners had a domicile in the place of imprisonment, soldiers in the place of actual service, and senators in Rome or Constantinople. Most of these regulations passed into the Church law and canonists admit a legal domicile for wives, minors, prisoners, exiles, and generally for all persons exercising a perpetual office or having a residential benefice, such as Bishops, canons, parish priests. The Code mentions it only for three classes of persons: married women, persons deprived of the use of reason, and minors, to whom religious are, in certain matters, assimilated. In reality, the others acquire it in the usual way, only their special position may be a proof or constitute a presumption that the necessary conditions are fulfilled. Dependence on the will of another does not necessarily exclude personal intention.

(*a*) Married women. They necessarily retain the domicile of their husbands as long as they are not legitimately separated, *i.e.* freed from the obligation of cohabitation, in accordance with the provisions of Can. 1131.

They may, however, acquire a quasi-domicile of their own; not a domicile, as evidently implied.

When they are legitimately separated they may

also acquire a domicile of their own on the ordinary conditions, but if the causes for separation ceased to exist they would have to return to their husbands' domicile.

201. (*b*) Minors necessarily share the domicile of those in whose charge they are—father, mother, guardians, the institution in which foundlings, for example, are cared for if they have no individual legal guardian.

After the years of infancy they can acquire a quasi-domicile of their own; this implies naturally that they can not do so before, and clearly this would have been impossible under the former legislation, since infants are incapable of any intention, but at present quasi-domicile can be acquired by the mere material fact of residence, and some canonists would apply this also to children. (Creusen, Vermeersch, o. c., n. 51.)

When they reach their majority they can acquire even a domicile of their own, but they retain the former one, which now becomes personal, until they leave it without intention of returning. Such intention would have to be proved conclusively, for the presumption is against it, but there is nothing to show that paternal domicile is not lost in the same way as any other nor that it can not be lost until a new one is acquired.

(*c*) The insane share the domicile of their guardians and they are assimilated by law to infants. There is, therefore, no mention of quasi-domicile to be acquired by them, but here, also, the question may be asked whether, for example, an insane person who has spent ten years in a certain institution should be considered as a *vagus,* supposing that his guardian has no domicile anywhere.

Some canonists hold that quasi-domicile is imposed by law in about the same cases as domicile, but Can. 93, which establishes legal domicile, is absolutely silent on legal quasi-domicile. (Blat, n. 410, 3.)

202. 5°. Loss of Domicile or Quasi-Domicile. They are both lost in the same manner: by leaving the place with the intention of not returning. The two conditions are always necessary. Neither would the determination to abandon the place forever suffice if there had been no execution, nor mere absence as long as the intention of returning would continue. Such intention, however, when the absence is prolonged, has to be proved.

The rule given here does not apply to legal domicile, which, as said before, the insane can never lose, children can lose only after reaching their majority, and married women when they are legally separated from their husbands.

Seeing how much more readily domicile and quasi-domicile can be acquired than lost, there should remain no doubt at present that a person can have several of them at the same time.

203. 6°. Juridical Effects of Relationship to Place. (Can. 91, 94.) (*a*) In Roman law a person was a citizen in the place of origin or in the municipality to which he belonged by right of birth; if, although born elsewhere, he had become a member of the community by domicile, he was an *incola,* or inhabitant; if he had spent some time in the place without, however, acquiring a domicile, he remained a stranger, *advena;* those making but a passing sojourn were transients, *peregrini.* In canon law, the *incolae* are those who have a domicile; the *advenae* those who have a quasi-domicile in the place; the *peregrini* those who have neither in the place but one or the other somewhere else. Persons who have neither domicile nor quasi-domicile anywhere are called *vagi.* For jurists who considered origin as a species of domicile every person had at least one domicile, since no one can be without place of birth.

204. (*b*) Domicile, quasi-domicile, and residence determine every one's proper Ordinary and pastor.

(i) Persons having a domicile or quasi-domicile in a certain parish belong to the pastor of that parish and to the Ordinary of the diocese in which it is located. Should they have domiciles or quasi-domiciles in several distinct parishes or dioceses they have also several pastors or Ordinaries, and they may go to the one they choose, except in a few matters. (Can. 90, § 1.)

(ii) Those who have a domicile or quasi-domicile in a diocese, vicariate apostolic, or prefecture apostolic, not in any particular parish, are subjects of the Ordinary of that diocese, vicariate, or prefecture, and parishioners of the pastor in whose territory they actually reside.

(iii) *Peregrini,* or transients, have no proper Ordinary or pastor in the place (they have one elsewhere), still they may be subject to some of its laws (Can. 14, § 1) and to the penalties attached to them (Can. 1566, § 1; 2226, § 1); they may also, under specified conditions, receive there baptism (Can. 738, § 2), confirmation (Can. 783, § 1), holy communion even at Easter (Can. 859, § 5), absolution from sins (Can. 874, § 5), even from sins reserved in their own diocese (Can. 900, 3°), extreme unction (Can. 938, § 2, cf. 397, 514), Christian burial. (Can. 1218, § 1.)

(iv) For the *vagi,* the pastor and Ordinary of the place in which they actually happen to be is their proper pastor and Ordinary, with the same rights and duties as if they had domicile in the territory.

There is thus no one who does not come under the authority of some pastor and Ordinary.

205. 4. *Consanguinity and Affinity.* There may exist between physical persons certain bonds of union and relations producing important juridical effects; for example, relationship by blood, by marriage, by adoption, by baptism, etc. The Code treats in this place of the first two only.

1°. Blood relationship, or consanguinity. The canonical effects of consanguinity are seen chiefly in the legislation on marriage; here the legislator merely gives the rules for computing it.

(*a*) Consanguinity is the bond that unites persons of the same blood, that is, persons who descend one from the other or from one common ancestor within certain limits. The common ancestor from whom related persons descend is called the *stipes,* stock; the series of persons descending from the common stock form the line. When persons descend one from the other they are said to be related in the direct line; when they descend, not one from the other, but all from one common ancestor their relationship is in the collateral, transversal, oblique line. In a collateral relationship there are two lines or two series of persons, one on each side of the common stock. Thus, if James and John are second cousins, there is a line connecting James and another connecting John with their great-grandfather, who is the common stock.

The lines may be equal, as in the example given, or unequal, as between uncle and niece. The measure of the distance between persons who are related to one another is called degree.

206. (*b*) In the direct line there are as many degrees as there are persons, not including the common stock, or as many degrees as there are generations.

In the collateral line, according to the way of reckoning of the Roman law, of modern civil legislations generally, and also of the Eastern Church, there are as many degrees as there are generations or as many degrees as there are persons, in the two series or lines, the common stock not included. Second cousins would thus be related in the sixth degree.

According to the way of reckoning commonly in use among the Germanic tribes and adopted by the canon law of the Latin Church, there are as many degrees as there are generations between one of the parties and the common stock, or as there are generations on one side, or as there are persons on one side of the line, not including the common stock. Second cousins are related in the third degree. If the two series of persons or the two sides of the line are unequal, it is the longer one which determines the distance of relationship. For greater precision, however, it may be asked that the distance be indicated for either side. (Wernz, IV, n. 406 ff.; Esmein, Le Mariage en Droit Canonique, Paris, 1891; Catholic Encyclopedia, Consanguinity.)

207. 2°. Affinity. (*a*) Roman law called *affines* the relations of the husband and wife, *viri et uxores cognati.* (L. 4, § 3, D. XXXVIII, 10.) The foundation of affinity was legitimate marriage, whether consummated or not.

The law of Moses contains no definition of affinity, but it forbids marriage between a man and his daughter or grand-daughter-in-law, between a man and his deceased brother's widow, or the widow of his father's brother (Lev. xviii, 8-18; xx, 20), thus implying that marriage gives rise to new relations which have some juridical effects.

The early Church apparently accepted and sanctioned the doctrine and prescriptions of both the civil and the Mosaic law on the subject.

(*b*) Gradually, however, the juridical effects of affinity in regard to matrimony were extended (Elvira, 300, c. 61; Neocaesarea, 314-325, c. 2) and then its concept itself was changed. It came to be a relation arising, not from marriage as such, but from carnal relations.

The germ of this theory may be found in a text of St. Augustine quoted in the *Decretum* and often after. (C. 15, C. XXXV, q. 2, 3.) If husband and wife, he says, are not two but one flesh, little difference is to be made between daughter and daughter-in-law. From this principle it could legitimately be inferred that all the relations of the wife are almost equally related to the husband, and that affinity arises from unlawful as well as from lawful intercourse, but not from unconsummated marriage. The conclusion was drawn, probably in the course of the eighth century, by custom rather than formal legislation. The new doctrine is clearly expressed in some of the False Decretals reproduced by Gratian. (C. 10, C. XXXV, q. 2, 3.) The Pseudo-Isidorian Collection certainly helped to spread it without, however, being responsible for its introduction into canon law, as traces of it are met with at an earlier period. (Compiégne, 757, c. 13; Wernz, IV, n. 429; Esmein, p. 377.) At the time of the Council of Tuzey (860) Hincmar of Rheims considered it as commonly received.

Nor did the development stop here. In the eleventh or twelfth century, to the affinity which exists between a person and the blood relations of the one with whom he had intercourse, was added a second kind existing between one party and the relations by marriage of the other; and a third kind existing between the blood relations of one and the blood relations of the other; and even a fourth kind existing between the kin of a first husband and the children born of a second marriage. Benedict XIV illustrates this by the following example: Titius, brother of Caius, contracts and consummates marriage with Bertha; the latter is akin to Caius by the first kind of affinity. Titius dies and Bertha marries Sempronius; there arises the second kind of affinity between Sempronius and all the blood relations of Titius. Bertha dies and Sempronius marries Noevia; the blood-relatives of Titius become akin to her also. (De Synodo Diocesana, L. IX, c. 13.) The Fourth Lateran Council maintained only the first kind of affinity and abolished all the others. (C. 50.)

208. (*c*) The present law brings back the original conception of affinity, for which only valid marriage was considered, not carnal intercourse. Affinity is now produced by every marriage provided it be valid, whether consummated or not. It is not produced by any carnal relations outside of marriage.

It exists only between the man and the blood relations of the woman, and likewise between the woman and the blood relations of the man, not, for example, between the brother of the wife and the sister of the husband. The principle still holds: *affinitas non parit affinitatem.*

The husband and the wife are considered as one flesh and the impediment is reckoned in this wise, that the blood relations of the man are related to the woman by affinity in the same line and the same degree as they are related to him by blood, and *vice versa.*

209. 5. *Rite.* (Can. 98.) (*a*) By rite is ordinarily meant a religious ceremony or prayer; thus we speak of the rite of baptism, of ordination, of the Congregation of Rites. The ceremonies, prayers, mode of worship special to particular religious bodies or Churches are also called their rites, for instance, the rite of the Carthusians, of the Carmelites, of the Dominicans; the Ambrosian and Mozarabic rites. Under the name of rite is also sometimes included, together with the liturgy, the whole disciplinary legislation special to a Church. Of rites understood in this comprehensive sense there exist two great groups: the Occidental or Latin one and the Oriental, which includes the Greek, Armenian, Syriac, and Coptic rites, subdivided into several branches. (Catholic Encyclopedia, Rites.)

The Code here merely defines in a general way the relations of individual persons to rites understood chiefly in the last sense, what determines the rite to which they belong, and on what conditions they may pass from one to another.

The attitude of the Latin Church towards Oriental rites has always been one of reverence, manifesting itself by the great care to preserve them intact. Roman Pontiffs have enacted numerous regulations for this purpose, particularly Benedict XIV (*Etsi Pastoralis,* May 26, 1742; *Demandatum,* Dec. 24, 1743; *Allatae sunt,* Jul. 26, 1755); Leo XIII (*Praeclara,* June 20, 1894; *Orientalium,* Nov. 30, 1894); Pius X (*Tradita ab antiquis,* Sept. 14, 1912.)

210. (*b*) The present law embodies substantially the provisions of the documents just mentioned:

(i) Among the Catholic rites a person belongs to the one in which he was baptized. There are three exceptions to this rule. It does not hold if a person has been baptized in a certain rite by fraud, that is, in violation of a law which demands that he should be baptized in another; nor does it hold if baptism has been received in a certain rite because a minister of the proper one could not be secured. In these two cases the sacrament is supposed to have been received in the rite regularly called for by canonical prescriptions (Can. 756), *viz.* in the rite of the parents or in the rite of the father if the parents belong to different rites, or in the rite of the Catholic parent when one parent is a non-Catholic.

The third exception is the one which may be made by apostolic indult granting permission to be baptized with the ceremonies of a certain rite without obligation of adhering to it.

These enactments of the common law concern only Catholics and Catholic rites. Converts who were baptized in one of the Eastern non-Catholic rites are allowed by the Cong. P. F. (Nov. 20, 1838) to join the one among the Catholic Oriental rites which they prefer. If they are baptized again they still have their choice, but they will belong to the rite in which they choose to be baptized.

211. (ii) Passing from one rite to another is considered in law as odious, particularly passing from the Latin to an Oriental rite and *vice versa;* hence:

Ecclesiastics are strictly forbidden to proselytize and try by whatsoever means to induce Orientals to pass to the Latin rite or Latins to Oriental rites. Benedict XIV and Leo XIII punished this offence with suspension, but the Code mentions no penalty.

Permission from the Apostolic See is required to pass from one rite to another or to return to the former one after a legal transfer. A married woman may, however, join the rite of her husband either at the time of, or during, marriage; after dissolution of the contract, not before, she is free to return to her former rite, unless paticular law, local decree, or custom forbid.

The custom, even if continued for a long time, of receiving holy communion in another rite does not imply change of rite.

According to the Const. *Orientalium* (n. 11), if communities, families, or individual persons separated from the Church have returned to the fold on the express condition that they will embrace the Latin rite they temporarily belong to that rite, but they are at liberty some day to return to the native one. If no such condition was laid down but sacraments have been received from Latin priests only because no others were at hand, return to the proper rite is obligatory as soon as Oriental priests can be found.

II. MORAL PERSONS. (Can. 99-102.)

(Cavagnis, Institutiones Juris Publici Ecclesiastici, Pars 2a, n. 344; Blat, o. c., p. 27; Maroto, o. c., n. 458.)

212. 1. *Nature.* Canonical personality or capacity to acquire and exercise rights in the Church which goes by divine ordinance with individual human nature and the reception of baptism, may also be conferred by public ecclesiastical authority upon corporate bodies or institutions, which thus obtain prerogatives normally reserved to individual rational beings and, for that reason, are called moral or legal, as distinct from physical or individual, persons.

2. *Divisions.* Moral persons, in the Church, may be collegiate or non-collegiate, corporate or non-corporate.

Collegiate or corporate persons, *v.g.* chapters, confraternities, Religious Orders are made up of several individual persons but in such a manner that the personality of the college or corporate body is distinct from that of the members; it does not receive its existence and rights from them and may continue to have legal existence for some time after they have all died. In this it differs from a collective body, which in reality is not a person but, as the name implies, a collection of persons who have put together some of their powers and rights.

As examples of non-collegiate persons the Code quotes churches, seminaries, benefices, etc., to which law recognizes certain rights to be exercised through administrators, yet in themselves distinct and independent.

Moral persons may also be of divine or ecclesiastical origin, lay or clerical, public or private.

213. 3. *Constitution of Moral Persons.* To constitute a moral person several general conditions are required: proper authority, formal institution, legitimate object, and necessary material elements.

(*a*) Authority. In the civil society the will of the individual members may suffice to give legal personality to an organization, but canonical personality pertains to the supernatural order and, therefore, can come only from God, immediately or through the Church.

(i) The Catholic Church and the Apostolic See being of divine institution hold their legal personality from God Himself; they are independent of any human power both in their origin and in the exercise of their prerogatives. Apostolic See here does not include Roman Congregations, Tribunals, or Offices, as the context clearly shows. (Can. 7.)

(ii) Other moral persons in the Church owe their existence to the ecclesiastical authority. To some the legal personality is given by the law itself, as, for example, to the College of Cardinals; to others it is given by special decree of the competent superior. Who the competent superior is in each case must be seen in the different parts of the Code which deal with the various classes of moral persons. The Holy See erects cathedral and clerical collegiate chapters (Can. 392), consistorial benefices (Can. 1414), etc.; the Ordinary of the place may erect non-consistorial benefices, establish diocesan congregations. (Can. 482.)

214. (*b*) Institution. The decree of erection must, explicitly or implicitly but with sufficient clearness, confer upon the corporate or non-corporate body the prerogatives of legal personality. A simple approval would not suffice, as it is granted to and needed for merely collective persons.

(*c*) Object. The end of all particular societies or institutions in the Church, like that of the Church itself, to which it remains subordinated, must be religious or charitable, *i.e.* supernatural in itself or in its motive. A purely philanthropic object would not suffice for an ecclesiastical foundation.

(*d*) Elements. The constituent elements of each moral person are pointed out in the respective places; here it is simply stated in a general way that to constitute a moral collegiate person at least three physical persons are required. This is by ecclesiastical law and chiefly in order that the college be able to act as such and that it be possible to have a majority in a vote.

215. 4. *Juridical Status of Moral Persons.* (Can. 100, § 3.) Both corporate and non-corporate bodies are assimilated to minors, and the law extends to them the same protection as to persons under age, because, no doubt, the interests of institutions are liable to be neglected by administrators, and even in the case of collegiate persons what concerns the body does not usually receive the same attention as what touches individuals directly.

216. 5. *Mode of Acting of Moral Persons.* Non-collegiate persons can act only through administrators or representatives. Collegiate persons may also in some matters be represented by officials empowered to act in their name, but they may and regularly do act as a body, *collegialiter,* in a collegiate manner.

(*a*) Collegiate Procedure. In order that a decision taken by a moral body may have juridical value certain forms must be observed.

(i) Common or particular law may prescribe a special manner of proceeding in certain cases; thus the Code contains rules on elections in general (Can. 160-178) and the Const. *Vacante Sede Apostolica* (Pius X, Dec. 25, 1904) lays down still more specific regulations for papal elections in particular.

217. (ii) In the absence of any special legislation the following norm obtains:

In the first and second ballotings, for a juridically valid decision, the absolute majority of the votes cast is required, not counting the votes which are null. Who has the right, and who must be invited, to take part in the vote, is determined by law or particular statute for the various collegiate persons. Several of the rules regarding elections are applied by canonists to all collegiate proceedings. (Can. 162; Maroto, n.467; Reiffenstuel, Lib. III, Tit. XI.) In Roman law absolute majority meant two-thirds of the votes cast, but in canon law over one half is commonly considered as sufficient, *v.g.* eight out of fifteen. (I Monitore Ecclesiastico, Marzo, p. 90, Ap. p. 122, 1918.) The Decretals speak of the *major et sanior pars capituli* (c.i, III, xi); measures needed the support of the greater and better qualified part of the chapter to be passed. The present law does not mention the second condition, presuming it exists when the first one does.

When no absolute majority has been obtained either in the first or second voting, the relative majority will suffice in the third; thus, if out of fifteen votes four go to one candidate, five to another, and six to a third one, the six votes decide the election.

Should it happen that no relative majority is obtained in the third balloting, if *e.g.* one of the candidates had three votes and the other two six each, the president has the right to decide the matter.

If the president does not wish to use his privilege, another way of reaching a decision is provided by law, at least in the case of an election. Of the candidates who have the largest number of votes that one is considered elected who is the senior by ordination or by first religious profession or by age. The tests are applied in that order, supposing that there is occasion for it and need of it. Ordination is considered first, that is, the Orders received, so that a priest would be preferred to a deacon, and if they are of equal rank, the date of ordination. When the candidates are Religious, should ordination fail to determine the seniority because they received the same Orders, on the same day, the profession is taken into account, but it is the first one, whether temporary or perpetual, simple or solemn, the law making no distinction. The first test can not be applied when the candidates are not ecclesiastics, nor the second, when they are not Religious.

No special provision is made for the settlement of other matters than elections when three votings have failed to give even a relative majority in favor of any particular solution and the president refuses to decide. Nothing forbids a fourth or fifth balloting, but the result may remain the same.

(iii) In some special matters absolute majority is not sufficient for a legally valid decision, but unanimity is required. The principle was thus formulated in the 29th Rule of law: *quod omnes tangit, debet ab omnibus approbari* (V, xii, in Sexto). The modern legislator has added two words for the sake of greater precision; *quod omnes uti singulos tangit.* Measures which affect the members of a moral body individually must be approved by all. It has always been found difficult to determine what affects each member individually rather than as part of the body. Canonists give the example of compromise in election; as it deprives electors of the right which each one has to vote, only the consent of all can render it legitimate. (Can. 172.) Likewise to impose a new personal obligation, *v.g.* a personal contribution, on all members a unanimous vote would be necessary. (Reiffenstuel, vol. vi, p. 50.)

218. (*b*) Acts of Non-collegiate Persons and Non-collegiate Acts of Collegiate Persons. (Can. 101, § 3.)

For the acts of non-collegiate moral persons, such, for example, as pertain to the temporal administration of a parish or of a charitable institution, the Code refers us to the particular statutes or to the norms of the common law regarding such persons. The latter are given principally in the third book, which treats of ecclesiastical benefices, of schools, seminaries, and other pious institutions, and defines by whom they should be administered and in what manner. (Can. 1352-1371; 1476-1494; 1521-1528; 1649-1653.)

The actions of superiors who may, in certain matters, represent collegiate legal persons are regulated also by particular statutes or special norms of the common law.

219. 6. *Extinction of Moral Persons.* Of their nature moral persons are perpetual. In a collegiate body old members can be replaced by new ones and an institution lasts indefinitely.

They may be suppressed by the competent superior, that is, ordinarily, the one who has power to erect them. (Can. 494, 498, 699; 1470, 1494.)

They may also cease to exist, *de facto,* by destruction or by loss of all members, but as long as one member of a collegiate person remains the rights of the college rest with him; and in any case before a collegiate or non-collegiate person ceases to exist juridically it must have ceased *de facto* for a hundred years, otherwise it may be revived. Thus, if all the members of a chapter had died and not been replaced for fifty years, at the end of this period of time the chapter could be brought back to life again, with all its rights and privileges, by the appointment of the required number of canons.

III. INFLUENCE OF VIOLENCE, FEAR, DECEIT AND ERROR ON ACTS OF BOTH PHYSICAL AND MORAL PERSONS. (Can. 103, 104.)

C. 1-6, X, 1, 40; Maroto, n. 394; D'Annibale, I, n. 138.)

To have juridical value, an act must be human in the sense explained by moralists, and canon law may require besides that it be free from certain defects which, without destroying its moral character, lessen its independence and would, therefore, deprive it of at least some of its efficacy. The chief obstacles to the perfection of a juridical act are: violence, fear and deceit, error and ignorance.

220. 1. *Violence.* (*a*) Nature and divisions. Violence is defined as the "onset of force too great to be resisted." It is called absolute and physical or relative and moral according as resistance is really impossible or only very difficult.

(*b*) Effects. An act performed either by a physical or a moral person under extrinsic violence which can not be resisted has no juridical value and may be considered as non-existent. This is true even when no effort at resistance has been attempted because useless, provided this does not manifest willing acquiescence.

If resistance was possible, the act is not null on the ground of violence, but it may be at least voidable on account of fear.

221. 2. *Fear.* (*a*) Nature and divisions. Fear is a "perturbation of mind arising from present or future danger."

It is grave when the threatening evil is both imminent and serious. The evil may be serious absolutely, in itself and for all persons, with a few possible exceptions, *v.g.* danger of death, of perpetual imprisonment; or relatively only, for certain people, because of their disposition or of special circumstances.

If the evil is not a serious one or the danger is remote and easy to escape, the fear is called light. The fear of offending a superior, or reverential fear, is generally considered as light unless some other element be added to it, as if the superior's or parent's displeasure was to manifest itself by threats, blows, severe and repeated rebukes, etc. (D'Annibale, I, n. 138; Wernz, IV, n. 264; A. A. S., vol. iv, p. 671.)

Fear may also be *ab intrinseco* or *ab extrinseco,* due to a cause intrinsic or extrinsic to the person whom it affects. This distinction is variously explained by authors. (D'Annibale, l.c.; Pruemmer, Man. Theol. Mor., I, n. 68; Lehmkuhl, I, n. 84; Noldin, De Principiis, n. 49.) Practically fear may be considered as *ab intriseco* whenever not caused by a free agent distinct from the one who suffers the fear.

When caused by a distinct, free agent, fear may be just or unjust. It is unjust if it implies violation of a strict right, *i.e.* if the agent who causes it has no right to do so or to do it in that manner. A man has the right to threaten an offender with legal proceedings unless proper reparation be made, but not with acts of violence against his person or his property. In the latter case the fear thus caused would be substantially just, having for its object legitimate reparation, but it would be unjust as to the manner, *quoad modum.*

(*b*) Effects. (i) Fear which would so perturb the mind as to take away all deliberation and freedom would evidently, by natural law, deprive the act performed under its influence of all moral character and juridical value. On the other hand fear, absolutely and relatively light, is not taken into account in the external forum except possibly in penal matters as an attenuating circumstance.

222. (ii) An act performed under the influence of fear, yet freely, is valid by natural law (some authors would except such acts as religious profession, marriage consent, Wernz, IV, n. 267); but by positive law it is null and void, or at least voidable, if the fear is grave and unjust.

Thus grave and unjust fear renders invalid: votes in an election (Can. 169, §1); renunciation of office (Can. 185); admission into a novitiate (Can. 542); religious profession (Can. 572); marriage consent (Can. 1087); assistance of pastor at marriage (Can. 1095); vows (Can. 1307); remission of penalties (Can. 2238).

In all other cases in which law does not explicitly declare the act null *ipso facto* it is valid, but may be annulled by the court. The injured party may appeal to the competent judge to have it rescinded (Can. 1684-1686) or the judge may proceed *ex officio,* of his own accord, for the common good or the interest of individual souls.

That fear may have these effects, it should, according to some canonists, be substantially unjust (Maroto, n. 399); but according to others, injustice *quoad modum* suffices. (Wernz, IV, n. 265; Gasparri, De Matrimonio, n. 820.)

Again, some demand that it be inflicted for the purpose of extorting consent, but the present Code does not require this condition, explicitly or implicitly.

223. 3. *Deceit.* (*a*) In penal matters the term *dolus* is used in the sense of malice and defined as the deliberate will to violate the law" (Can. 2200); here it is taken in the usual sense of deceit, inducing others into error, ordinarily for the purpose of injuring them. Deceit affects the juridical value of an act only when it is its determining cause, not merely an accompanying circumstance.

(*b*) If the error into which the agent has been induced is a substantial one, the act performed under the influence of this deceit is invalid; otherwise it is valid, except in the cases specified by law, but it may be rescinded by the court, as has been said of the acts vitiated by grave and unjust fear.

224. 4. *Error.* (*a*) Nature and divisions. Error implies false judgment or assent of the mind to falsehood; ignorance is only an absence of knowledge and inadvertence an absence of attention or of actual, as distinct from, habitual knowledge. The effects of error and ignorance are often the same, but the legislator here deals directly only with error and treats of ignorance particularly in relation to laws (Can. 16) or to delinquencies and penalties. (Can. 2202, 2229.)

Error may be one of law or of fact, according as it bears on the law, its existence, nature, and extent, or on a fact or external object and its circumstances. Both may be substantial or accidental. An error about what constitutes the essential object of the marriage contract would be one of right and substantial (Can. 1082); if it was about the person with whom the marriage contract is made, it would still be substantial but of fact; it would be accidental if, for example, the party who is poor was thought to be wealthy.

The error may be substantial objectively, in itself, or only subjectively, in the intention of the agent who has attached his consent to a circumstance otherwise accidental. Thus, if a person has determined not to elect a candidate who does not possess a certain qualification, *v.g.* a theological degree not required by law, error about this qualification, which is a condition *sine qua non* of consent, would be, or amount to, substantial error.

(*b*) Effects. Objectively, or even only subjectively, substantial error, that is, error about what constitutes the substance of an act, or amounts to a condition *sine qua non* of consent, renders the act null and void.

Merely accidental error does not render the act performed under its influence invalid *ipso facto,* except by special provision of law, but it may give the right to an action in court for rescission of a contract.

It will be noted that this applies to contracts only, not to all acts, and that annulment can be pronounced solely under the conditions determined by law. (Can. 1684.)

IV. COUNSEL OR CONSENT REQUIRED FOR CERTAIN ACTS. (Can. 105.)

225. (*a*) Necessity. Ecclesiastical superiors, understanding by this term all who exercise any authority in the Church, are forbidden by law to act in some matters without the advice or consent of certain persons. Thus to permit the alienation of church property valued at between one thousand and thirty thousand francs an Ordinary must have the consent of the cathedral chapter or diocesan consultors, of the board of administration and of the interested parties; if the property does not exceed in value one thousand francs it suffices to consult the board of administration but the consent of the interested parties must be secured (Can. 1532, § 2, 3); pastors must be heard about the appointment of their assistants. (Can. 476, § 3.)

The necessity of such consent, which must not be presumed, is expressed in law by the clause *de consensu* or its equivalent; the words *de consilio capituli consultorum or audito capitulo, parocho,* etc., signify the obligation of getting advice or consulting.

When the consent of certain persons is required for an act and they have not been asked for it or have refused it, the act, if performed, is invalid.

If law only commands the superior to consult or hear other persons, he must, for the validity of the act, lay the matter before them and listen to their views; but he is not legally bound to follow their advice even if unanimous. It would not be prudent, however, to make light of an opinion which has the support of several councillors, and the legislator urges superiors not to go against it without proportionately grave reasons.

226. (*b*) Form. When consent or advice is to be obtained from only one or two persons this may be done in an informal way, orally or in writing, directly or through an intermediary; but if several persons have to be consulted together, either because they form a moral body, like a chapter, the diocesan board of administration, the council of superiors in Religious Orders, etc.; or because it is so ordained by common law or particular statutes, some formalities must be observed.

(i) The persons in question should all be duly convoked, otherwise the proceedings would be null or rescindable, as in the case of elections. (Can. 162.)

Legitimate custom, particular statutes, or special

indults may allow the sending of the vote or opinion, but regularly only those present at the meeting and assisting at the discussion of the subject can have a share in the decision. This is implied in the law and commonly held by canonists.

(ii) The superior should give the consultors an opportunity to express their views in all freedom, and they in turn ought to speak their mind with due reverence, in all sincerity and truthfulness.

(iii) Nothing is determined as to the form in which the consent or opinion should be expressed, whether orally or in writing, publicly or in secret. Particular statutes or the general principles of law regulating such matters will serve as guide. A clause prescribing the use of the secret ballot under pain of nullity was not retained in the final text of the law.

The superior may, if he thinks the matter of sufficient importance, impose upon all who took part in the deliberations the oath of secrecy.

V. PRECEDENCE AMONG PHYSICAL AND MORAL PERSONS. (Can. 106.)

(Decret., Lib. I, Tit. 33, De Majoritate et Obedientia; Ferraris, Prompta Bibliotheca, v. Praecedentia; Wernz, II, n. 160; Maroto, n. 477.)

227. Precedence as understood here means priority of rank, the right, *v.g.* to occupy a more honorable place at a public function, to cast a vote or sign a document before others, etc.

In every society there are members in more important positions than others; this difference must be recognized externally and some distinction granted to those higher in dignity. Moreover, unless some order be established confusion will soon follow and often controversies. Questions of precedence have given occasion to many a dispute. Hence the importance attached to them in all civilized communities. (Mackenzie; Observations upon the Laws and Customs of Nations as to Precedency; Edinburgh, 1680.) In 1539 an Act was passed at the instance of the King of England for the placing of the Lords in Parliament and ascertaining the relative rank of the members of the royal family, of the great officers of State, of the hierarchy, and of the peerage. Numerous other documents exist, of an earlier or later period, dealing with the same subject. With the diminution of court ceremonial in modern times, precedence does not need being regulated so minutely nor so strictly observed, but it can not be neglected altogether even in the most democratic society.

Still less could it be so in the Church, which possesses a hierarchy of divine origin and a most complete organization; which has always made profession of profound respect for authority and aims at perfect order in all things. Several of the ancient Councils remind the faithful of the special honors due to the clergy; they mark in detail the place every one should occupy in gatherings. (Nicaea, 325, c. 18; Mileva, 402; Bracara, 563, c. 6, 13; IV Toledo, c. 4; E. Martène, De Antiquis Ecclesiae Ritibus, Lib. III, c. 1, De Conciliorum Celebratione.)

The Council of Trent (Sess. XXV, c. 13, de Reg.) decreed that all controversies regarding precedence which often arise between ecclesiastical persons both secular and regular, principally at processions and funerals, to the scandal of the people, ought to be settled by the Ordinary of the place without possibility of appeal, at least in *suspensivo*.

Decretal legislation on the matter was contained chiefly, not exclusively, in the first book, title 33, *de*

Majoritate et Obedientia. The Congregation of Rites and that of Ceremonial have issued in modern times numerous decrees deciding particular cases and forming jurisprudence. (Decreta S. Rituum Cong., Romae, 1901, Index Generalis, Praecedentia.) The Congregation of Rites regulates precedence in liturgical functions and the Ceremonial Congregation regulates it among Cardinals and Legates sent by various nations to the Holy See. (Can. 253, 254.)

The Code sums up, modifies in some points, and completes the ancient legislation but only in its juridical aspect, without affecting liturgical rules. Here it gives the general principles; in treating of the different classes of persons all through this second book it defines in a more concrete manner their rights of precedence.

228. 1. *Rules Applying to All Persons.* (*a*) He who represents another derives precedence from him, whatever be his own personal dignity; thus a Legate of the Pope even if only a priest or a deacon would precede Bishops and Archbishops, not, however, Cardinals, unless he be a Cardinal himself. (Can. 269, § 2.)

In Councils and similar assemblies one who assists as procurator takes his seat after those of the same rank who are present personally; one representing an Archbishop would seat after the Archbishops, before the Bishops.

(*b*) A person who has authority over other persons, whether physical or moral, always enjoys precedence over them; right to command implies superiority and corresponding duty of obedience and reverence. A Vicar Capitular would take precedence of a Bishop residing in the diocese; a Bishop in his diocese takes precedence of visiting Archbishops except his Metropolitan (Can. 347); a Vicar-General has precedence over all ecclesiastics of the diocese, exception being made only for those who have the episcopal character. (Can. 370.)

Authority here is taken in a broad sense, including such power as that of superiors in religious communities or of pastors over their assistants.

229. 2. *Precedence Among Physical Persons.* Among ecclesiastical persons none of whom has authority over the other precedence is determined by:

(*a*) Rank, that is, the place which one occupies in the hierarchy of jurisdiction, as distinct from that of Orders, by reason of his authority, dignity, or canonical office. What place a certain office or dignity gives in that hierarchy is defined by special provision of law or particular decree, at least for some of them. Thus it is enacted that Cardinals precede all other prelates, even Patriarchs and Legates of the Holy See (Can. 239, n. 21); deans precede all priests in their districts (Can. 450); the pastor of the cathedral church precedes the other pastors of the diocese. (Can. 478.)

(*b*) Between persons of equal rank, precedence will be determined by the Order received, episcopate, priesthood, diaconate, etc.

(*c*) Should several persons of equal rank have the same Order, *v.g.* two resident Bishops, the next element to be considered is seniority of promotion to the rank, which for a Bishop means not election nor consecration, but preconization or solemn official promulgation of appointment in consistory. The following case was referred to the Congregation of Rites for settlement, April 15, 1904. The Right Rev. D. E. Dougherty, Bishop of Nueva Segovia in the Philippine Islands, had been consecrated in Rome in the

Church of Saints Peter and Paul on June 14, 1903, the ceremony beginning at 7 A. M.; the same day the Right Rev. F. Z. Rooker, Bishop of Jaro in the Philippine Islands, was consecrated also in Rome in the chapel of the American College, the ceremony beginning at 8 A. M.; the preconization of both took place in the consistory of June 22, 1903, but the name of the Right Rev. F. Z. Rooker was proclaimed first. Which of the two had precedence over the other? The Congregation answered: the one who was proposed and confirmed first in the consistory, and it referred to the decrees n. 270 Segobricen. March 21, 1609, and n. 1606 Terrulen. Nov. 26, 1677. (A.S.S. vol. 36, p. 629.)

(*d*) If two persons had been promoted at the same time, by one and the same act, or if no priority could be ascertained, seniority in Order would decide, unless the one who is junior by date of ordination had received his Order from the Sovereign Pontiff.

(*c*) A last means of deciding precedence when the two others have failed is the age of the persons.

Rite is never taken into account in this matter.

230. 3. *Precedence Among Moral Persons.* (*a*) Special laws establish the order of precedence among moral persons of different kind or rank; thus the secular clergy are given precedence over both clerical and lay religious bodies, clerical and religious organizations over the laical. (Can. 491.) Among Religious the order is: canons regular, monks, other regulars, papal congregations, diocesan congregations; among chapters: cathedral chapters, collegiate chapters *insignia,* collegiate chapters *non insignia.* (Can. 408); among pious lay associations: third orders, archconfraternities, confraternities, pious unions "primary," other pious unions. (Can. 701.)

(*b*) Between moral persons of the same kind and rank, precedence is determined by possession or priority in the place. Of two communities of monks, for example, of two collegiate chapters or confraternities, precedence belongs to the one which is actually in possession of it without its privilege being contested. If none is in possession the preference is given to the one which has been longest in the place. It may thus happen that in a locality the Dominicans have precedence over the Franciscans and in another the latter precede the former. This rule, formulated by Gregory XIII (Const. *Exposcit,* July 25, 1583) to settle questions of precedence between Mendicant Orders in processions, becomes now in the Code a general law applying to all moral persons and to all occasions. The privilege granted to Dominicans by several Popes to precede other Mendicant Orders and partially withdrawn by Gregory XIII, thus ceases to exist. (Praelectiones Juris Regularis, auctore F. Piato Montensi, vol. ii, n. 61-63; Blat, O P., o. c., p. 38.)

(*c*) Among the members of the same moral body precedence is regulated by the statutes of the organization and if these do not suffice by custom and the general principles of common law, that is, according to rank, Orders, age, etc.

4. *Power of Ordinaries in Matters of Precedence.* (*a*) The Ordinary of the place has authority to regulate precedence among his subjects, but he should be guided in this by the principles of common law and the customs of the diocese, taking into account every one's position and office.

231. (*b*) It is likewise for the Ordinary to settle all controversies regarding precedence and his jurisdiction extends even to exempt Religious if they assist in a body at a public function with other communities or organizations and the case is urgent; if, for example, religious communities one or several of which are exempt take part in a procession and the question arises which of them should precede the others, to preclude the possibility of those public disputes in which, according to ancient accounts, pious men would strike each other with the staffs of their banners and crosses, the Ordinary may or should decide at once, and from his decision there is no appeal *in suspensivo,* that is, it ought to be obeyed for the present, but recourse may be had afterwards to the competent superior, so that every one's rights be duly recognized.

5. Among the members of the pontifical household precedence is determined by special privileges, regulations, and traditions.

VI. GENERAL DIVISION OF PERSONS IN THE CHURCH. (Can. 107.)

232. There are three great classes of persons in the Church: the Clergy, the Laity and the Religious. The distinction between the clergy and the laity is of divine institution, inasmuch as Christ established in the Church a distinct hierarchy and priesthood, leaving the power of teaching, ruling, and exercizing the sacred functions not to all Christians, but to a few chosen ones, who thus form a divinely constituted body. (Mazella, De Religione et Ecclesia, Disputatio III, 7.)

By virtue of her own authority the Church has confided a share in those special powers to some men; these also belong to the clergy, but not by divine institution; for example, clerics who have received only tonsure or even, according to many canonists, clerics in minor Orders.

Both clerics and lay persons may dedicate themselves to a life of perfection by the three vows of poverty, chastity, and obedience; these are the Religious who, although they belong to either the clergy or laity, may nevertheless be considered as forming a distinct class because of their distinct privileges and obligations.

Hence the division of the second book of the Code into three parts, treating successively of the Clergy, the Religious, and the Laity. The first part has two sections, on the clergy in general and on the clergy in particular.

PART I

THE CLERGY

SECTION I

ON THE CLERGY IN GENERAL

(Can. 108-214.)

(Lib. I Decretalium; Conc. Trid. Sess. XXIII; Petavius, De Sacra Hierarchia; Haller, De Sacris Electionibus; Wernz, II; Thomassin, Ancienne et Nouvelle Discipline de l'Eglise, P. I; Bingham, Antiquities of the Christian Church; Maroto, n. 484; Blat, p. 41; Ferreres, Institutiones Canonicæ, n. 238.)

GENERAL NOTIONS. (Can. 108-110.)

233. 1. *Clergy.* The term *clerus* (lot, part, or portion falling to one by lot) was first applied to the whole Church or people of God as being the Lord's special possession or property (I Pet., v. 3), but soon it became appropriated to the ministers of religion as belonging to God in a most peculiar manner.

In a strict legal sense a cleric is one dedicated to the sacred ministry by the reception of tonsure. (Can. 108, §1.)

Under the former discipline, in favorable matters, the term *cleric* was commonly interpreted in a broad sense as including, for example, all Religious even women, whilst in odious matters it would not apply to Bishops, dignitaries, or regulars. (Wernz, II, n. 174.) In the present Code clerical privileges are explicitly extended to persons who without receiving tonsure are, however, consecrated to the divine service in a special manner (Can. 614, 680) and, on the other hand, exemption from some laws made for clerics is at times expressly granted to certain ecclesiastical dignitaries (Can. 2227, 1401, etc.), but unless there be some indication to the contrary the word *cleric* appears always to be taken in the strict legal sense.

234. 2. *Hierarchy.* (*a*) Nature. The sacred power left to the Church by Christ admits of, and is committed to the clergy in, various degrees; hence inequalities among clerics and subordination of one to another. This constitutes what writers have called the ecclesiastical hierarchy, a term which was popularized chiefly by the works falsely ascribed to St. Dionysius Areopagita (De Coelesti Hierarchia, De Ecclesiastica Hierarchia) and which serves to designate the powers themselves or the persons in whom they are vested.

(*b*) Kinds. A twofold power exists in the Church, the power of ruling the faithful, or power of jurisdiction, which is generally understood to include the power of teaching (Wernz, II, n. 2); and the power of Orders, or power of exercising the sacred functions, *i.e.* principally of offering the holy sacrifice and of administering the sacraments or sacramentals. Hence the two hierarchies closely related to but really different from each other.

The power of Orders has for its immediate object the sanctification of men; it is transmitted through the sacred rite of ordination, does not depend for its valid exercise on any human authority, can not be restricted, taken away, or lost once it has been obtained. The power of jurisdiction must also lead men to sanctity and eternal salvation, but this is rather its mediate object; it depends for its existence and valid exercise on canonical mission, can be restricted or taken away by ecclesiastical superiors and lost in other ways.

The power of Orders may exist in a person who possesses no jurisdiction, *v.g.* in a deacon, a priest, a titular Bishop. On the other hand, jurisdiction could be conferred on one who has not even received tonsure, and in itself it would not be impossible to elect to the Supreme Pontificate a layman, who would thereby become the head of the hierarchy of jurisdiction.

Ordinarily, however, and regularly jurisdiction is not granted to one who has not received at least tonsure, and the power of Orders is not lawfully exercised independently of the power of jurisdiction. (Wernz, II, n. 4.)

235. (*c*) Degrees. In the hierarchy of Orders there are, by divine ordinance, three degrees, the episcopate, the presbyterate, and the ministry or diaconate (Trent, Sess. XXIII, c. 6); more probably the subdiaconate and minor Orders, certainly tonsure, were instituted by the Church. (Gasparri, De Sacra

Ordinatione, n. 14, 33; Many, De Sacra Ordinatione, n. 3, 11.)

In the hierarchy of jurisdiction two degrees are of divine origin, the Supreme Pontificate and the episcopate. (Vatican, Sess. IV, c. 1-4.) The power of ruling and teaching was committed by Christ to Peter and the Apostles under him, and to their successors, the Roman Pontiff and the Bishops united to him. The offices of Cardinal, Patriarch, Primate, Metropolitan, and others do not belong to the essential constitution of the Church and are of ecclesiastical origin.

236. (*d*) Membership. The errors of ancient heretics, Arnold of Brescia in the twelfth century, Wycliff in the fourteenth, Huss in the fifteenth, Luther, Calvin, and Zwingli in the sixteenth, and of some modern writers like Hatch and Harnack, who maintain that to become member of the hierarchy of Orders or of jurisdiction the call or consent of the people or of civil rulers is necessary, have been condemned by the Church as contrary to the institution of Christ. (Trent, Sess. XXIII, c. 7.) To the faithful or to civil magistrates may be and has at times been granted, when deemed advisable, the privilege of manifesting their views or desires in regard to candidates for Orders or ecclesiastical offices, but this was a free concession always liable to be withdrawn and importing no real power. The intervention of the people or of civil rulers was never essential to the validity of the act, still less was it sufficient of itself. (Cavagnis, Institutiones Juris Publici Ecclesiastici, L. II.)

Membership in the hierarchy of Orders is obtained through the rite of ordination and in the hierarchy of jurisdiction through canonical mission or legitimate appointment, by which various degrees of power are transmitted.

As, however, the papal power is supreme it must come immediately from God Himself. By virtue of the divine institution of the primacy it passes to the one who, in the manner determined by the Church, has been chosen as successor of St. Peter and has accepted the election.

237. 3. *Prelacy.* A prelate in the strict canonical sense is a cleric, secular or Religious, who possesses ordinary jurisdiction in the external forum. Jurisdiction of the internal forum, sacramental or extra-sacramental, does not suffice; nor does delegated jurisdiction. But under the present law vicarious jurisdiction may be ordinary (Can. 197), as in the case of Vicars-General, Vicars Capitular, Vicars Apostolic, who are therefore prelates in the full sense of the term. A superior of a lay Religious Order who would not be a cleric could not be called a prelate even though his Order were exempt and he would enjoy ordinary jurisdiction over his subjects.

Some ecclesiastics, without possessing jurisdiction, receive from the Holy See the title of prelates as an honorary distinction. Their rights and privileges are determined by the regulations and traditions of the papal palace. (Can. 328; Pius X, *Inter Multiplices,* Feb. 21, 1905; Catholic Encyclopedia, Monsignor; J. A. Nainfa, S. S., Costumes of Prelates of the Catholic Church, Baltimore, 1909.)

238. 4. *Divisions of this First Section.* After these introductory notions on clerics and the hierarchies into which clerics are distributed follow the six titles which make up this section on the clergy in general and deal successively with the affiliation of clerics with a diocese, the rights and privileges of the clergy, their obligations, ecclesiastical offices and ecclesiastical jurisdiction which are regularly conferred only on clerics, and finally the loss of clerical prerogatives or, in a sense at least, of the clerical state.

TITLE I

AFFILIATION OF CLERICS WITH, OR INCARDINATION IN, A DIOCESE

(Can. 111-117.)

239. 1. *Nature.* Every member of the Church is connected by domicile, quasi-domicile, or habitation with some diocese whose Ordinary has authority over him, but he may change his residence and consequently his diocese when he pleases.

Clerics who are set apart for the divine service must have assigned to them the field in which they are to labor and find their support. It may be a certain territory like a diocese, an institution or a moral body like a Religious Order. The bond which unites a cleric to his diocese or community is called affiliation or incardination, but the latter term is usually reserved to affiliation with a diocese. The Code treats here of incardination in this restricted sense; affiliation with Religious Orders is mentioned only incidentally, as the subject belongs to the second part of this book, on Religious.

240. 2. *Necessity.* The Council of Arles (314, c. 2, 21) forbids clerics to leave the place in which they were ordained under pain of suspension. The practice introduced in some regions by ecclesiastics to pass from one church to another is condemned by the Council of Nicaea (325, c. 15) as contrary to rule. It must, therefore, have been an ancient custom, dating perhaps from apostolic times, to ordain clerics for a specified church. This became a formal law in the Council of Chalcedon (451, c. 6), which decreed that no one should be ordained priest, deacon, or cleric in an absolute manner, but should be attached to some church in the city or in the country, or to the oratory of a martyr or to a monastery. The ordinations had to be local as opposed to absolute. (Van Espen, Comm. in Can., T. IV, p. 239.) Thus, it was expected, no more clerics would be promoted than were necessary; each one would have a definite occupation and be sure of a decent maintenance instead of wandering about in idleness and being compelled to engage in unbecoming occupations for a living.

History mentions some illustrious examples of absolute ordinations; St. Jerome remained a monk and returned to his solitude after receiving the priesthood (Ep. 61 ad Pammachium); St. Paulinus consented to receive Orders (Barcelona, 392) only on condition that he would not be attached to any church. (Ep. 1 ad Severum, n. 10, Migne, Pat. Lat., t. 61, col. 159.) According to Theodoretus, the Bishop of Antioch Flavianus ordained absolutely the famous Syrian monk Macedonius, and Sozomen relates the same thing of two or three other anchorites of Edessa. (Hist. Ecc., lib. VI, c. 34.) These cases, however, seem to have been rare in the ancient Church. They grew more numerous in the Middle Ages after the institution of non-residential benefices and the introduction of personal patrimony as a canonical title for ordination. (Benedict XIV, De Synodo, L. XI, c. 2 ff.) Abuses followed against which Synods protested apparently without much success. (Placentia, 1095, c. 15.) They continued unabated till the Council of Trent, which deemed it necessary to renew the prescriptions of Chalcedon and decreed that no one in future should be ordained without being attached to that church or pious place for the necessity or utility of which he is promoted. (Sess. XXIII, c. 16, de Ref.)

241. By this legislation as well as by that of Nicaea and Chalcedon, a cleric must be attached to a particular church or pious place; incardination in a diocese is not mentioned as yet. In modern times, however, particularly after the changes in ecclesiastical organization brought about in several countries by the Revolution of the eighteenth century, it was found impossible to assign a special church to each cleric from the moment of his first ordination, and the custom gradually prevailed almost everywhere of incardinating in the diocese. (Benedict XIV, l. c., n. 9; Gasparri, De Sacra Ordinatione, n. 582, 583.)

Numerous decisions of Roman Congregations since the beginning of the last century have given to this practice implicit sanction and virtually force of law. Under the Tridentine discipline a cleric who had not been attached to a church or pious place would not be considered as really incardinated and remained free to leave the diocese. (In Arim., 5 Dec., 1574; in Terr., 19 Feb., 1628.) Recent decrees, on the contrary, recognize the Bishop's right in such cases to retain a priest if he is needed, provided a fair maintenance be assured him. (In Nuc. 5, Sept., 1818; in Amer., 14 Dec., 1822; in Reat., 26 Jan., 1833; Bouix, De Episcopo, P. V, c. 24; Bargilliat, Praelectiones Juris Canonici, 1893, n. 607; Irish Ecclesiastical Record, April, 1918, p. 300.)

The present law affirms again the necessity for all clerics of affiliation or incardination and explicitly declares that unattached, *vagi,* acephali ecclesiastics are not admitted. But, taking into account present conditions and confirming the discipline introduced by custom, it prescribes affiliation with a diocese or Religious Order, not with a particular church. Every cleric, therefore, must be under the authority of a Bishop or superior and he remains so even if he does not reside within the territory placed under the authority of this prelate.

242. 3. *Initial Affiliation or Incardination.* A person enters the clerical state by the reception of tonsure; it is then, consequently, that he must become affiliated with, or incardinated in, a diocese. He is incardinated in the diocese for the service of which he is promoted. When a Bishop ordains a subject of his diocese for the service of another diocese, as Can. 969 allows, the cleric becomes attached to the diocese for the service of which he is ordained, not to the diocese of his proper Bishop or ordaining prelate. (Pont. Comm., Aug. 17, 1919.)

243. 4. *Transfer of Affiliation or Excardination and Incardination. A.* Former Discipline. In the ancient Church, down to the eleventh or twelfth century, a cleric was attached to a diocese principally by ordination; domicile or origin had little importance. (Thomassin, P. II, L. I, c. 1-6.) A Bishop was strictly forbidden to ordain a cleric who had already received Orders from another Bishop. Only with the permission of the prelate who had ordained him might he then pass to another church (Chalcedon, 451, c. 20, 23; Angers, c. 1; I Tours, 461, c. 11, 12); but with the introduction of absolute ordinations and particularly after the decrees of Clement IV and Boniface VIII officially recognizing that one may become the subject of a Bishop for the purpose of ordination by reason of his origin, domicile, or benefice, and that any one can be ordained legitimately by his proper Bishop, the bond of a previous ordination ceased to be considered as conferring so exclusive a right. (C. 1, 3, l. I, Tit. IX, in Sexto; Thomassin, l. c., c. 7.) "Variation" became permitted, that is, a cleric having received an Order from one Bishop might leave him and receive the other Orders from another prelate who was his proper Bishop by another title.

Clerics were also transferred from one diocese to another by mutual agreement. This was done regularly in a formal manner and in writing; according to some canonists, under the old legislation, oral, implicit, or equivalent incardination was also valid, provided there was no doubt about the intention of the Ordinaries concerned, on the part of one to dismiss, on the part of the other to accept, the cleric perpetually and unconditionally. (A. S. S., vol. XXXIX, In Viterbiensi, p. 211.) The value of such transfer, however, was not admitted by all (Reiffenstuel, Lib. III, Tit. 29, n. 11; Ferraris, v. Testimoniales, n. 16; A. S. S., l. c., p. 492); in fact, some doubted that even a formal excardination gave to a Bishop the right to ordain a cleric unless he became his subject by complying with the requirements of the Const. *Speculatores*. (Many, l. c., n. 67; Gasparri, n. 864, 891.) In some places implicit or presumed incardination had the force of law by particular legislation. Thus the Third Plenary Council of Baltimore provides that a Bishop intending to attach to his diocese a priest who has been duly released by his own Ordinary may try him for three or five years, and at the end of this period the priest is presumed to be incardinated if no explicit declaration to the contrary is made. (N. 62-66.)

244. The decree *A primis* (S. C. Conc., Jul. 20,

1898) put an end to controversies on this point by enacting that incardination had to be effected in writing, and prescribing in detail the formalities to be observed. Excardination was not permitted without just cause and it became effective only when incardination in another diocese followed. The incardinating Ordinary was to secure all necessary information on the subject he adopted and the latter was to promise under oath to remain and labor permanently in the new diocese; both excardination and incardination had to be perpetual and absolute. (A. A. S., vol. IV, p. 249; V, p. 34; IX, p. 18; Canoniste Contemporain, Mai, 1912, p. 335; Mars, 1913, p. 167; Eccl. Review, April, 1913, p. 465.) Special care was recommended in the incardination of subjects of different tongue and nationality. These provisions were to hold, all things to the contrary notwithstanding, and a few years later it was explicitly declared for the United States that whilst the decree had no retroactive effect it abrogated for the future the enactment of the Baltimore Council regarding presumed incardinations. (Sept. 15, 1906; A. S. S., vol. XXXIX, p. 489, 498.)

A subsequent decree (Nov. 24, 1906) explained on what conditions a Bishop could transfer his claims over one of his lay subjects to another Bishop, who thus became the proper Bishop for ordination. As a layman is not incardinated he can not, strictly speaking, be excardinated, but this manner of transferring him from the jurisdiction of one Ordinary to that of another for the purpose of ordination was very similar to, and had the same effect as, the excardination and incardination of a cleric. It had been practiced for a long time in many countries and now received official sanction. (Many, l. c., 67; Canoniste, Dec. 1906, p. 705, 727; Jan. 1907, p. 12; A. S. S., l. c., p. 498, 600.)

By order of Pope Pius X the Congregation of the Council published again, Sept 7, 1909, a decree of Nov. 14, 1903 (A. S. S., vol. I, p. 692) containing special regulations on the transfer of clerics from Europe to the United States or from any part of the world to the Philippines. (Nouvelle Revue Théologique, 1904, p. 221; 1909, p. 754.)

245. *B.* Present Law. Under the present law it is, as it was in the ancient Church, principally by ordination that the relation of cleric to Bishop is determined and there does not seem to be room for "variation." When one has been ordained for a diocese he can not pass to another without being dismissed from the first. Excardination or canonical transfer of laymen is not mentioned here. For the excardination of clerics the Code renews the precriptions of the decree *A primis* with some important modifications.

1°. Modes of transfer or of excardination and incardination. Transfer of affiliation may now be effected in three ways:

(*a*) By formal letters. Regularly, in order that a cleric's affiliation may be validly transferred from one diocese to another, he must obtain from his own Ordinary letters signed by him of absolute and perpetual excardination and from the Ordinary of the diocese to which he wishes to become attached letters signed by him of absolute and perpetual incardination. These were the conditions required by the decree *A primis,* likewise under pain of nullity of the transaction.

The Ordinary who has power to issue these letters is the Bishop of the place or Prelate Nullius, not the Vicar-General, except by special mandate. The Vicar Capitular can grant them with the consent of the chapter when the see has been vacant for a whole year. Formerly Vicars-General and Vicars Capitular enjoyed the same power as the Bishop in regard to incardination. In regard to excardination their power had the same limitations as at present.

246. (*b*) By reception of a residential benefice. Besides formal, the Code admits implicit or equivalent, excardinations and incardinations, which had been abrogated by the decree *A primis.*

A cleric who, with the written consent of his Ordinary or his written permission to leave the diocese forever, receives from the Ordinary of another diocese a residential benefice, becomes by the very fact incardinated in that other diocese. Under the present law a parish is considered as a benefice in the strict sense of the term, even if it is not endowed and all its revenues are derived from the offerings of the people. (Can. 1410.) It is clearly a residential benefice.

The permission needed is that of accepting a certain benefice in another diocese or, in general, of leaving the diocese. In both cases it must be written. The permission to leave the diocese must be perpetual, but it is not explicitly stated that it must be absolute. Nor is it explicitly required that the permission to accept a benefice be either absolute or perpetual.

These permissions being equivalent to excardination, it must be concluded that they may be granted only by the superiors who have power to grant formal excardination itself. The incardination which follows is effected by the conferring of the benefice, therefore by the superior who is competent to make the appointment as defined by law for the various benefices.

247. (*c*) By religious profession. The Religious who takes perpetual vows, whether simple or solemn, loses *ipso facto* the diocese he had in the world (Can. 585) and becomes attached to the Order or community in which he makes his profession. This is not excardination proper unless the Religious be a cleric; nor does the reception of tonsure or minor Orders before perpetual profession (Can. 964, 3°) suffice for incardination in the community. (Maroto, n. 495.)

If afterwards the professed Religious who was thus excardinated leaves the Order he can be received and incardinated in a diocese on the conditions and with the formalities laid down in another part of the Code. (Can. 641, 672.)

248. 2°. Conditions for the lawfulness of excardination and incardination.

(*a*) Excardination should not be granted without just cause, of which the excardinating Ordinary is the natural judge. Although the text of the present law might seem to make this a condition for its validity, more probably it is required only for its lawfulness, as under the decree *A primis.* (Blat, p. 49; Maroto, p. 471.)

(*b*) An Ordinary should not incardinate a cleric of another diocese unless the necessity or utility of his own diocese demands it, and whenever such a transfer is effected care must be taken to observe the canonical prescriptions regarding the title for ordination. If the old one is lost another must be substituted.

(*c*) The incardinating Ordinary must have an authentic document proving that excardination has been duly secured. Oral testimony does not suffice for the lawfulness of the act which, however, would be valid as long as the excardination had been really granted.

(*d*) Opportune testimony, written or oral, regarding the birth, life, morals, and studies of the cleric in question should also be obtained, under secrecy if necessary, from the excardinating Curia, particularly for the incardination of subjects of a different language and nationality. The excardinating Ordinary is bound in conscience to see that the testimony is in conformity with the truth.

(*e*) The cleric must declare under oath, in presence of the incardinating Ordinary or of his delegate, that he intends to become attached to the new diocese in accordance with canonical rule. Nothing indicates that this oath is now necessary for the validity. The last clause implies that the incardinated cleric will belong to the new diocese and be under the jurisdiction of his new Ordinary in the same manner as the other members of the clergy.

(*f*) Once the incardination is completed the Ordinary who has issued the letter of excardination should be informed of the fact as soon as possible, in order that he may know that the dismissed cleric has ceased to belong to him, as excardination takes effect only when incardination follows.

These rules apply directly and strictly to formal excardination and incardination; from their very nature, some of them can not concern transfers of affiliation effected implicitly or equivalently.

TITLE II

RIGHTS AND PRIVILEGES OF CLERICS.

(Can. 118-123.)

(Comment. on Decret. L. I, tit. 15, 33; L. II, tit. 2; L. III, tit. 49; L. V, tit. 39; Wernz, II, n. 157 sq; Cavagnis, Institutiones Juris Publici Ecclesiastici, P. II, n. 105 sq; Thomassin, P. III, L. I, c. 33; Bingham, B. V, c. 2, 3.)

No very clearly marked difference exists between the rights and the privileges granted by the common law to clerics; the rights recognized to them partake of the nature of favors or privileges, and their privileges imply rights or a moral power of doing, exacting, or obtaining certain things; there is, however, a foundation for the distinction suggested in the heading of this title. Clerics have a real right to special respect and reverence and an exclusive right to power of Order and jurisdiction, as also to ecclesiastical benefices and pensions; they enjoy the privilege of a special court, of exemption from personal burdens, and of sufficient support in case of insolvency. The so-called privilege of the canon is less a privilege than a protection extended by the Church to the person of clerics against injuries which are a violation of their strict rights. The present law maintains it in this sense.

249. 1. *Exclusive Right to Obtain the Power of Order and of Jurisdiction, Ecclesiastical Benefices and Pensions.* 1°. Only those who have already received tonsure may legitimately, in the present discipline of the Church, be promoted to Orders either major or minor. The permission given at times to laymen to exercise functions of minor Orders does not imply communication of any powers. In no case, however, does the validity of an ordination depend on previous reception of tonsure.

2°. The general law of the Church forbids the conferring upon laymen of ecclesiastical jurisdiction, benefices, or pensions. In the past benefices have been given to lay members of certain Orders, particularly military Orders, but these were exceptions which can be made only by the supreme authority. Appointment of a layman to even a simple benefice by a superior of lower rank would be invalid. (Maroto, n. 504.)

It is a disputed question among canonists whether women are excluded from the exercise of ecclesiastical jurisdiction by divine or only by ecclesiastical right; in practice the exclusion is absolute. (Maroto, n. 576.)

250. 2. *Right of Clerics to Special Reverence and Respect.* (Can. 119.) 1°. Because of the position which the clergy occupy in the Church, all the faithful, whatever be their rank, should entertain for them sentiments of sincere reverence, which will be manifested in various ways according to circumstances of time, place, persons, etc. The same honors are not paid to a priest as to a Bishop; in liturgical functions clerics precede all lay persons, but it is not necessarily so in a civil ceremony; an ecclesiastic would not expect the same kind of deference from a public magistrate as from a private citizen. The Council of Trent, however, strongly urges Bishops not to yield too readily to temporal princes and to maintain the dignity of their high office. (Sess. XXV, de Ref., c. 27.)

2°. These rights of the clergy were readily recognized in the early Church by the faithful and by the State itself after the conversion of the emperors. Councils describe in detail the marks of respect which should be showed to ministers of religion. (II

Macon, 585, c. 15.) But in the course of time, principally after the Barbarian invasions, a change took place in the attitude of the people towards them. Attacks upon their persons grew so frequent that new measures had to be taken for their defence. Severe penances were imposed upon the offenders and even separation from the Church pronounced against them in particularly grave cases. (Synod. in Villa Theodonis, 821; Mayence, 888, c. 7.)

When, in the eleventh century, in order to lessen the evils resulting from the frequent wars of the times, Popes and Councils established the Peace of God and the Truce of God, they extended their special protection to clerics and Religious, who suffered particularly from those disorders. The abuses continued, and Urban II, in the Lateran Council of 1097, decreed that a major excommunication would be incurred by any one laying violent hands on ecclesiastics. Innocent II renewed this penalty in the Council of Clermont (1130) and in the Council of Rheims (1135) he promulgated it again in the Canon *Si quis suadente diabolo,* which several Councils and Popes confirmed afterwards. (Lateran, 1139, Trent.) These canonical enactments have been considered as constituting for clerics the privilege called of personal inviolability, privilege of the canon *Si quis,* or simply privilege of the canon.

The present law only declares in this place that acts of violence or real injuries against clerics add the malice of sacrilege to that of injustice. The punishments attached to them are defined in the fifth book of the Code. (Can. 2343; Penal Legislation, n. 288.) As formerly Religious share this privilege with clerics. (Can. 2343, § 4; 614, 488, 680.)

251. 3. *Privilege of the Court.* (Can. 120.) 1°.

Origin. St. Paul rebukes the Corinthians for bringing their disputes before pagan judges. (I Cor. vi. 1.) Still more did it seem repugnant to the Christian sense that priests and Bishops should appear before laymen to be judged by them. Hence the decrees of early Councils prescribing that ecclesiastical causes be referred to the Bishop's tribunal. (III Carthage, 397, c. 9; Chalcedon, 451, c. 9; Agde, 506, c. 32; III Toledo, 589, c. 3.) Christian emperors gradually recognized, in part at least, the legitimacy of these demands. A Constitution of 355 had granted to Bishops immunity from the jurisdiction of civil courts in criminal matters; by the end of the fourth century the concession had been extended to all clerics by custom or jurisprudence, and the Theodosian Code sanctioned it. (R. Genestal, Les Origines du Privilège Clérical, Paris, 1908.) Abolished by Julian, it was restored, then abolished again, and restored once more in the Justinian Code.

In the Frankish and Germanic kingdoms only the purely ecclesiastical matters were at first withdrawn from the jurisdiction of secular courts, then the civil and lesser criminal causes of clerics, until finally the principle of the exclusive competence of ecclesiastical judges in any clerical case whatsoever was admitted in the law of Christian nations as laid down in the canons of the Church. This did not come in England till the days of the Norman kings.

Ecclesiastical courts have lost much of their importance in modern times; in some countries, by mutual agreement between the Holy See and the civil power, their jurisdiction is limited to purely ecclesiastical matters. In other places the same restrictions are placed upon them by the State, but the Church does not renounce her claims. The privilege of the court is of divine right or, as more commonly held, based on divine right and formally established by ecclesiastical authority, so that while it may be modified in its applications and its exercise partially suspended, it can not be given up altogether. (Schmalzgrueber, L. II, Tit. 2, n. 98; Gennari, Consultations Canoniques, IV; Cavagnis, l. c., n. 115.)

252. 2°. Present Law. (*a*) In all civil as well as criminal causes clerics ought to be brought before ecclesiastical courts, unless other provisions have been made for particular places or unless permission has been obtained to proceed otherwise.

The privilege holds for all causes, whether civil or criminal, real or personal. (Wernz, V, 300; Maroto, n. 515.)

It is granted to all clerics without any other condition than the reception of tonsure, and also to Religious. (Can. 614.)

To be brought before a court *conveniri* is commonly understood in the sense of being summoned as a defendant, not as a simple witness. (Maroto, n. 515; Blat, p. 54; Ferreres, Institutiones Canonicae, vol. i, n. 255.) The privilege of personal immunity may exempt an ecclesiastic from appearing as witness. (Penal Legislation, n. 274.)

The law explicitly admits that there may exist in some places legitimate provisions by which the privilege of the court ceases to be in full force. This may be the result of concordats, formal concessions by the proper authority, or even custom. In the United States such a custom has been in existence for many years, allowing laymen to have their controversies with ecclesiastics decided by lay judges; this does not hold in the case of an ecclesiastic suing another. (Eccl. Rev., Sept., 1912, p. 313.)

253. (*b*) When no special provisions have been made for a particular country, clerics may be brought before secular judges by permission from the proper authority.

The proper authority to grant it is the Holy See if suit is to be brought against Cardinals, Papal Legates—which term includes Apostolic Delegates (Can. 267)—Bishops, even titular ones, Abbots, Prelates Nullius, superiors-general of papal institutes (Can. 488, 3°), or higher officials of the Roman Curia in reference to matters pertaining to their office. In all other cases it may be granted by the Ordinary of the place in which the case is to be tried, not the Ordinary of the parties, even when Religious are concerned.

No reason is required for obtaining that permission; the legislator rather warns Ordinaries not to refuse it without just and grave cause, especially when the plaintiff is a lay person, and most particularly when they have tried in vain to bring the parties to a satisfactory agreement.

(*c*) Should an ecclesiastic be summoned to appear before lay judges without the required permission, he should regularly refuse to obey and not cooperate in the violation of law. In cases of necessity, to avoid greater evils, he may go to court, but he ought to notify the Ordinary from whom permission should have been obtained.

Penalties against offenders are enacted in Can. 2341. (Penal Legislation, n. 276.)

254. 4. *Privilege of Personal Immunity or Exemption from Certain Public Burdens and Offices.* (Can. 121; Wernz, II, n. 166; Thomassin, o. c., P. III, L. I, c. 33 ff.)

(*a*) Origin. The first Christian emperors exempted the clergy from all civil offices both personal and predial, that is, connected with men's estates; from those which were called honorable, such as the municipal or curial offices, as well as from the ones called mean and sordid, *munera sordida,* in order, it was said, that clerics might not be "hindered in the performance of divine service by any sacrilegious distractions." (Bingham, o. c., Book I. c. iii, n. 12.) Thus exemption was granted them from military service, guardianships, trusteeships, etc.; from various taxes, the poll tax, the recruit tax, the road tax, and others. (Smith & Cheetham, Dictionary of Christian Antiquities, Immunities, ii, iii.)

In the Middle Ages clerical immunity as defined by canonists was generally respected by princes. The Church insisted in a special manner on exemption from military obligations in those days of incessant wars without, however, refusing to contribute to the defence of the country. Bishops assumed the burden, when needed, of supplying and equipping a contingent of troops, each one according to his resources. Some of them marched at the head of their militia, but this was usually not demanded of them by secular rulers and canon law did not approve of it. (Thomassin, l. c., c. 40-47.)

The Council of Trent, after declaring that ecclesiastical immunity is founded on divine law and canonical sanctions (Sess. XXV, c. 20), admonishes princes to observe what Councils and Roman Pontiffs have ordained on this subject.

Down to the present day Popes have likewise maintained the principle of immunity for clerics, but in its application they have made numerous concessions either formally in concordats or implicitly by tacit acceptance of customs or legislation which curtail the privilege in various ways. (Syllabus of Pius IX, Prop. XXX, XXXIII; Leo XIII, Epist. ad Card. Nina, Aug. 27, 1878.)

255. (*b*) Present Law. "All clerics are exempt from military service and from functions and public civil offices unbecoming to the clerical state."

There is no mention here of exemption from taxes formerly implied in the privilege of immunity, but only from personal obligations and offices; and not from all, but only from such as are not in keeping with the character of the clerical state, particularly from military service.

Under the former discipline ecclesiastical students were understood to be exempt from military service even though they had not yet received tonsure (Wernz, II, n. 168) and some canonists would interpret the present law in the same sense (Maroto, n. 521, Can. 6, 2°); the Code, however, speaks only of clerics here and formally extends the privilege afterwards to Religious and novices, but to no others. (Can. 614, 680.)

Which obligations or services should be considered as foreign to the clerical state the legislator does not state, as much depends on circumstances. In general they are those which take an ecclesiastic away from his duties, which would interfere with the sanctity of his calling, or are looked upon commonly as base and unbecoming to cultured people, *e.g.* the office of judge in secular courts, of mayor, of postmaster, of bailiff, constable, of trustee, guardian, etc., and all those which canonical law forbids to ecclesiastics. (Can. 113-115.)

No special penalty is attached to violation of personal immunity.

256. 5. *Privilege of Competency.* (*a*) Ancient

canonists usually based this privilege on a decision of Gregory IX in the case of a cleric named Odoardus, who had been excommunicated by his Ordinary for not satisfying his creditors (c. 3, X, III, 23); the cleric appealed to the Pope, who declared that if he was really unable to pay his debts he should be freed from the censure, provided he would promise to pay them should he ever be able to do so. Commentators explained these words as implying that an insolvent cleric should not in any way be molested for his debts. Then arguing from the Roman law, which did not permit creditors to attach the entire salary of a soldier, and from the unfitness of a cleric being reduced to the necessity of begging or engaging in sordid occupations, they concluded that in case of insolvency an ecclesiastic should not be molested for retaining what he needs for a decent support, on condition that he has acted in good faith, that his debts are personal ones, and that he will pay them should he some day have the means.

(*b*) The Code now formally sanctions the discipline which custom had introduced and enacts that clerics who are forced to pay debts should not be deprived of what they need for a decent living.

How much they need is left to the prudence of the ecclesiastical judge to decide, as no general rule can be given which would apply to all places and times.

It must always be understood that the obligation of paying the debts is not extinguished, but only suspended until circumstances are more favorable.

Other conditions required by ancient canonists for the application of this privilege are not mentioned by the present law and may be considered as abrogated. As these cases are ordinarily taken to the secular courts, in practice clerics will be able to benefit by this concession of the Church in the measure only in which it is made also by the State.

257. 6. *Loss of Clerical Privileges.* (Can. 123.) (*a*) A cleric can not renounce his privileges, for they are not granted for him individually and for his own personal advantage, but rather for the body and for the good of religion.

(*b*) He may lose them. There are only two ways at present in which any of the clerical privileges can be lost: by reduction or return of the cleric or Religious to the lay state and by perpetual privation of the right to wear the ecclesiastical dress. When and how this reduction is effected and this privation pronounced will be found in another part of the Code. (Can. 211-214; 640, 648, 2304.)

(*c*) If the penalty is remitted or the cleric reinstated and received again among the clergy the privileges revive. (Can. 212.)

TITLE III

ON THE OBLIGATIONS OF CLERICS.

(Can. 124-144.)

(Decret. L. III, Tit. 1, 2, 3, 41, 51; Wernz, II, n. 174 sq.; Blat, p. 72 sq.; Maroto, n. 529 sq.; Thomassin, P. I, L. III; P. III, L. III; Bingham, Book VI.)

In the Decretal Collections the legislation on this subject was found chiefly in the first and last titles of the third book, "De Vita et Honestate Clericorum, Ne Clerici vel Monachi Saecularibus Negotiis se Immisceant." Many of the modern Councils had also a chapter on the life of the clergy. The Code sums up here the ancient prescriptions, adapts them to present conditions, and adds a few important ones concerning especially the personal life of clerics and the means of promoting among them piety and learning.

After laying down the general principle that clerics are bound to a high degree of sanctity, the legislator treats successively of their positive and of their negative obligations. The positive obligations (Can. 124-136) pertain to the exercises of the spiritual life, the practice of obedience, study, chastity, community life, recitation of the Divine Office, and clerical dress. The negative obligations or prohibitions (Can. 137-144) have reference mainly to the various occupations or amusements which ought to be avoided as dangerous, unbecoming, or little in keeping with the character of the clerical vocation.

I. GENERAL PRINCIPLE. (Can. 124.)

258. Clerics are bound to a higher degree of internal and external sanctity than ordinary laymen, to whom they owe the example of all virtues.

The necessity of this eminent holiness in the clergy has been proclaimed repeatedly since the time of Our Lord and of the Apostles to the present day in numberless official documents, in the early Synods, in the canonical Collections, in the Councils of modern times, general and particular, in the Constitutions of the Popes. The most august assemblies and the highest authorities in the Church have thought it their duty to enact laws regulating every aspect of a cleric's activity, the prayers he should say, the occupations he may engage in, the dress he must wear, the amusements and recreations he ought to avoid. (C. 3, D. LXI; c. 5, C. VI, q. 1; Trent, Sess. XIV., de Ref., proemium; Sess. XXII, de Ref., c. 1; Sess. XXIII, de Ref., c. 11, 13; Sess. XXV, de Ref., c. 1, 14; Benedictus XIII, *In supremo,* Sept. 23, 1724; Pius IX, *Nostis et nobiscum,* Dec. 8, 1849; Leo XIII, *Pergrata nobis,* Sept. 14, 1886; Pius X, *E supremi,* Oct. 4, 1903; *Pieni l'animo,* Jul. 28, 1906; *Haerent animo,* Aug. 4, 1908; Benedictus XV, *Ad beatissimi,* Nov. 1, 1914.)

From the general obligation to sanctity imposed upon clerics by their very vocation flow the more particular obligations which form the object of the canons that follow. These, then, must be binding on all ecclesiastics, even or principally on those who occupy higher positions in the hierarchy, and also on Religious, unless the contrary be clear from the context. (Can. 592, 679.) The obligations special to certain offices, dignities, etc., are dealt with in other parts of the Code.

Ecclesiastical law is concerned directly with external acts and hence the rules given here pertain immediately to external conduct, but indirectly they affect also and are calculated to promote inward holiness, without which external sanctity would be of little value.

II. POSITIVE OBLIGATIONS. (Can. 125-136.)

259. 1. *Exercises of Piety.* (Can. 125.) 1°. After affirming the necessity of holiness in the clergy, the legislator warns Ordinaries to take care that clerics under their charge employ the necessary means to attain it. How they can obtain this and what sanctions they may use must depend on circumstances and is left to their prudent judgment.

2°. The means specified by law are: (*a*) Frequent confession, that is, for Religious and seminarians (Can. 595, 1367) weekly confession; for secular priests, weekly or fortnightly confession whenever conditions permit it. No time is determined for them, as had first been intended, because it seemed impossible to have the same rule for all.

(*b*) Daily meditation and visit to the Blessed Sacrament for about half an hour and a quarter of an hour respectively, according to common interpretation and practice.

(*c*) Daily recitation of the Rosary or of about five decades and examination of conscience. Daily communion is recommended to all (Can. 863) and needed no mention here. (Cf. Can. 595, 1367.)

260. 3°. The canon under consideration concerns directly Ordinaries, and by it these exercises do not become obligatory for clerics, as the recitation of the Divine Office, for example, is by Can. 135 (cf. Can. 805, 1365), but the ecclesiastical legislator practically pronounces them the regularly necessary means to the sanctity demanded of clerics by divine law. They thus for the first time receive official recognition in the common law of the Church.

This is partly at least the result of the development in Catholic piety which has taken place in the last three centuries. To take meditation in particular, whilst pious souls in all ages have reflected on eternal truths, formal meditation, if we understand by this the present practice of setting aside every day a certain time for the methodical consideration of a definite spiritual subject, may be called a modern devotion. The rules of St. Pachomius, St. Basil, St. Benedict, St. Bruno do not speak of it, nor the primitive rule of St. Francis or of St. Dominic. Recent studies on the sources of the Exercises of St. Ignatius, on the Brothers of the common life, and on some early Franciscan writers, have shown that it commenced to be taught and practiced in the fifteenth century. Still, St. Ignatius himself did not prescribe it; custom rendered it obligatory under his immediate successors. (Watrigant, Quelques Promoteurs de la Meditation Méthodique au Quinziéme Siécle, Enghien, 1919.) About that same time new Orders were founded which all assigned a place to meditation in their rule, as has ever been done since. The founders of seminaries, St. Charles Borromeo, St. Vincent de Paul, Father Olier, looked upon it as one of the most important factors in clerical training; St. Francis de Sales, in his "Introduction to a Devout Life," teaches its methods and recommends it to pious persons of the world; ascetic writers are unanimous in recognizing its utility and moral necessity for true spiritual life. Rome refuses to approve any Order which does not give one hour every day to mental prayer (Normae secundum quas S. Congregatio Episcoporum et Regularium Procedere solet in Approbandis Institutis Votorum Simplicium, n. 154; June 28, 1901), and Pius X more recently declared that "no priest can omit meditation without being guilty of serious negligence. (Exhortation to the Catholic Clergy, Aug. 4, 1908.)

Some of the other religious practices now endorsed by the Code had gone through the same development as meditation and during about the same period. New social conditions since the sixteenth century called for greater outward activity on the part of the clergy, for more personal, more intense piety, more independent of external support. "As the European mind became more subjective, the reign of mental prayer was spread." (Faber, Growth in Holiness. The True Idea of Devotion, p. 408.) When changes in the forms of devotion correspond to a general need and are, besides, approved by the Church, it is impossible not to see in them the action of the Holy Spirit and providential indications which could not safely be neglected. (Cardinal

Mercier, Conferences delivered to his Seminarians, London, 1910, p. 103; Etudes, 20 Juillet, 1909, p. 187; Recrutement Sacerdotal, Juillet, 1914, p. 272; F. Naval, Theologiae Asceticae et Mysticae Cursus, n. 63, Marietti, Rome, 1920.)

261. 2. *Spiritual Retreat.* (Can. 126.) 1°. What has been said of formal meditation and the manner in which it became in modern times one of the essential exercises of a devout life applies in large measure to retreats. Ascetic writers of the Middle Ages make no reference to them nor do the rules of Religious Orders; the first known enactment concerning them is found in the Fourth Council of Milan, presided over by St. Charles Borromeo in 1576. Even in the seventeenth century they are still often spoken of as of recent institution.

2°. In the eighteenth and particularly the nineteenth century various local Synods prescribe them at various intervals for the secular clergy. (III Baltimore, n. 75; Maynooth, n. 198; Collectio Lacensis, T. vi, p. 49, 200, 268, 815.) Several Bishops in the Vatican Council desired that they be made obligatory by common law every year or every two years, but it did not seem possible to demand so much of all secular priests indiscriminately and the votum finally adopted left it for Ordinaries to see that their clergy spend a certain number of days in retreat every three or four years in a house suitable for that purpose.

262. 3°. Under the present law all secular priests ought to make a retreat at least every third year for a length of time to be determined by the proper Ordinary in some pious or religious house to be designated by the same Ordinary. No one should exempt himself from the retreat, except in a particular case, for a just cause, and with the express permission of the Bishop.

(*a*) It is a strict obligation introduced now for the first time by common law and imposed directly on the clergy.

(*b*) The law is binding on all secular priests; this includes also canons, honorary prelates, and other lower dignitaries, but probably not Bishops or prelates having ordinary jurisdiction. Special provisions are made elsewhere for Religious (Can. 595, 679) and for seminarians. (Can. 1367, 4°.)

(*c*) It had been proposed to prescribe at least five full days, but as in some cases this might work a real hardship, the duration of the retreat was left to be determined by the Ordinary; nor is it explicitly required, as it is for seminarians, that the time be continuous.

(*d*) It is also for the Ordinary to designate the place in which the retreat shall be made. He should naturally choose some religious house or pious institution conveniently situated and adapted for the purpose.

(*e*) Ordinaries are given power to dispense from this law, but only in particular cases and for a just cause. A grave cause is not required. The dispensation should not be presumed but must be granted explicitly.

263. 3. *Canonical Obedience.* (Can. 127; Decret. L. I, Tit. 33, De Majoritate et Obedientia; Wernz, II, n. 190; Maroto, n. 552.)

1°. General Duty of Respect and Obedience. (*a*) All Christians owe to their Bishop reverence and obedience. From the days of St. Clement of Rome (xxi, 6) and St. Ignatius of Antioch (A Phila., vi) Fathers, Councils, and Pontiffs have always insisted on submission to and union with the Bishop as essential to the life and prosperity of the Church.

(*b*) This duty is particularly binding on clerics, who are dedicated to the service of the Church under the direction of the Bishop. It is binding in a most special manner on priests, because of the formal and solemn promise they make on the day of their ordination. The practice to demand this promise from priests existed as early as the fifth century; St. Leo refers to it in one of his letters (C. 3, X, I, 33). It is explicitly prescribed by the Eleventh Council of Toledo (675, c. 10). Often the promise had to be in writing.

(*c*) This promise is not equivalent to the vow of Religious; it is made to a man, not to God, and imposes an obligation of fidelity not of religion, confirming in a solemn manner the obligation existing already by divine and ecclesiastical law. It extends to everything that the Bishop legitimately ordains for the good of the diocese, and the Bishop's ordinances are legitimate whenever they tend to promote the interests of God and of souls and are not contrary to canonical prescriptions. (Claeys Bouaert, De Canonica Cleri Secularis Obedientia, Louvain, 1904.)

264. 2°. Special Duty to Accept Ecclesiastical Offices. (Can. 128.) (*a*) In the beginning priests and inferior clerics lived with the Bishop or close to him and were sent by him, as circumstances demanded, to attend to the needs of the faithful in or outside the episcopal city.

When independent parishes were established they usually had their own clergy ordained for them and permanently attached to them. (Lesetre, La Paroisse, p. 27, 35, Paris, 1906.) In the course of the ninth, tenth and eleventh centuries the system of benefices became prevalent in most countries; whoever possessed a benefice was bound and could be compelled to fulfil the duties of the corresponding office, but his obligation did not seem to go beyond this. In the thirteenth century it was even allowed to ordain clerics without benefice, *titulo patrimonii,* and as these received no ecclesiastical support they claimed absolute exemption from any ecclesiastical service.

The Council of Trent decreed (Sess. XXIII, de Ref., c. 16) that henceforth no one should be ordained except for the service of some special church or pious place, but there continued to be unattached clerics, and the Congregation declared on several occasions that they could not be compelled by their Bishop to accept a function, assist at processions, or take part in similar services. (S. C. of the Council, May 8, 1627, in Panormitana; Sept. 9, 1628; Ap. 15, 1628; Ap. 26, 1636.) It was admitted, on the other hand, that ecclesiastics attached to a church could be compelled to accept and discharge in it certain functions (In Ancon., Feb. 14, 1609), and Benedict XIII, by the Const. *In supremo,* Sept. 23, 1724, empowered and directed Bishops to assign to all independent clerics some church and duties to be discharged therein. (Gennari, Consultations Canoniques, Consultation 69.)

So far, however, there is question in the Roman decisions of subordinate services only, but during the nineteenth century, owing to the changes which had taken place in the organization of dioceses and the scarcity of priests, Bishops had to refer to Rome cases of ecclesiastics who refused the burden of the care of souls. Some of the decisions seem to give

Ordinaries in such cases a delegated and limited power to exact and compel obedience (Tolos. May 9, 1884; Forojulien. Jan. 31, 1891); others imply that Bishops have that power and may legitimately use it under certain conditions. (Urbevet., May 10, 1766; Trid. Aug. 18, 1860; Calven. March 28, 1890; S. J. de Maur., Aug. 6, 1910; A. A. S., 1910, p. 911; Nouvelle Revue Théologique, Mars 1911, p. 155 ff.) It is in this second sense that the question is explicitly settled in the new law. In fact, if priests were free to refuse the pastoral office at the present time, their promise of obedience would be little more than a vain formality and Bishops would be unable to provide for the needs of dioceses.

265. (*b*) Clerics are bound to accept and faithfully discharge the functions entrusted to them by their Bishop if in the estimation of the Ordinary the needs of the diocese demand it, unless they have a legitimate excuse.

The terms of the law are general and imply that Ordinaries may appoint to such functions as those of catechist, teacher, chaplain, as well as to the pastoral office.

The rights of Ordinaries are not absolute, however, in this matter; it is only in cases of necessity that they can compel one of their subjects to accept an office. The necessity need not be very grave, nor is it explicitly required that it be grave; still, mere utility would not suffice. The Ordinary is the judge of this necessity, but there may be an appeal from his decision.

What would be a sufficient excuse for refusing the appointment is not said and will depend on many circumstances. Here also the Ordinary is the best judge. (Forojul. Jan. 31, 1891; Mauriana, Aug. 7, 1910.)

This law applies to all ecclesiastics, even to those who have been ordained with the patrimonial title. Those who have been ordained *ad titulum servitii Ecclesiae* depend more entirely on their Ordinary and more may be demanded of them.

4. *Study.* (Can. 129-131; T. B. Scannell, The Priest's Studies, London, 1908; J. B. Hogan, S. S., Clerical Studies, Boston, 1898; Moussard, Le Prêtre et la Vie d'Etudes, Paris, 1890.)

266. 1°. General Obligation. (*a*) The law explicitly and solemnly warns ecclesiastics not to stop studying once they have received the priestly ordination. Numerous Councils have proclaimed the necessity of learning and therefore of study for the clergy. (Carthage, 813, c. 1, 16, 20; IV Toledo, 633, c. 25; Mayence, 813, c. 10; III Lateran, 1179, c. 3; IV Lateran, 1215, c. 26.)

In modern times that duty of study for priests has been affirmed still more emphatically and more frequently by both Synods and Pontiffs. (Utrecht, 1865, Tit. ix., i; Toulouse, 1850, Tit. iv, c. 6; Collectio Lacensis, vol. v, p. 910; Encyclicals of Gregory XVI, May 11, 1844; Pius IX, Nov. 9, 1846; Dec. 8, 1849; Leo XIII, several.) Priests must study, they say, in order not to forget what they have learned, to acquire a more complete knowledge of the sacred sciences, to be able to defend the truth against the attacks of enemies, to be safe guides of souls and reliable spiritual physicians, to do honor to the Church and to the priesthood, to avoid idleness.

(*b*) A priest must study first and principally the ecclesiastical sciences; he is not asked, however, to confine his attention exclusively to them. Several

Councils positively encourage him to cultivate profane sciences, particularly those which have been used against the Church. (Spoleto, 1949, Tit. ix, Coll. Lac., vol. vi, p. 760.)

(*c*) In religious matters, priests should not depart from the solid, traditional, and commonly received teachings, "avoiding the profane novelties of words and oppositions of knowledge falsely so called." (I Tim. vi. 20.)

267. 2°. Junior Clergy Examinations. After completing their course of studies, all priests, even such as might have a parochial or canonical benefice, shall, unless they be exempted by the Ordinary for a just cause, undergo every year for at least three years an examination in the various branches of the sacred sciences designated beforehand, according to the form prescribed by the Ordinary.

In making the appointments to ecclesiastical offices or benefices, the preference shall be given, everything else being equal, to those who have been more successful in these examinations. (Can. 130.)

(*a*) Examinations for young priests after their ordination had been established for some time in many places by particular Councils or diocesan regulations. The Council of Toulouse, 1850, prescribes them for six years (Tit. iv, n. 6); the Council of Urbino for a few years (Tit. vi, n. 144; Coll. Lac. vol. vi. p. 48); by the Third Plenary Council of Baltimore, 1884, they are obligatory for five years. (N. 186.) Now by common law, secular priests have to undergo them for at least three years and Religious for five. (Can. 590.) Their purpose is primarily to encourage study but also to find out who are the ecclesiastics of the diocese best qualified for the more important positions.

(*b*) All are bound to take these examinations whatever may be their position, talent, or previous studies. The Ordinary alone can grant exemption and he is cautioned not to do so except for just, it is not said grave, reasons. In the case of Religious the law itself exempts those who teach theology, canon law, or scholastic philosophy.

268. (*c*) The matter of the examinations is not determined in detail by law; this is left to the Ordinary, who will fix beforehand, leaving sufficient time to prepare, the subjects on which the candidates are to be interrogated. The Baltimore Council mentions: Holy Scripture, Dogmatic and Moral Theology, Ecclesiastical History and Liturgy, to which may be added Ascetic Theology, Homiletics, Sociology, Philosophy and, some say, Latin. The nature and form of the examinations are likewise determined by the Ordinary and the examiners selected by him.

(*d*) These examinations must have a sanction and the legislator demands that success obtained in them be taken into account in making the appointments to ecclesiastical offices or dignities. Other qualifications are necessary, but learning has always been considered as a most important one.

The Baltimore Council requires that examinations omitted without proper permission or found insufficient be taken or repeated at the end of the five year period.

3°. Ecclesiastical Conferences. (Can. 131.) (Wernz, II, n. 867 ff; Thomassin, o. c., P. II, L. III, c. 74, x; 76, i, ii, iii; Péchenard, Etude Historique sur les Conférences Ecclésiastiques, Paris.)

269. (i) It is not enough for ecclesiastics to apply themselves to study during the first years of their priesthood; Benedict XIV speaks of priests who after being excellent confessors at the beginning of their ministry came, through neglect of study, to be wanting in the essential knowledge of their theology. (Inst. xxxiii, n. 4; III Plen. Coun. Balt., n. 189.) Hence the necessity here also of some supervision.

(*a*) Early Councils direct Bishops, when parish priests meet for the Synod or the Litany, to examine them on the manner of ruling parishes or of administering the sacraments. (IV Toledo, 633, c. 26; VI Arles, 813, c. 4.)

The archdeacons, archpriests, and rural deans are to hold monthly meetings with the clergy under their care and give them instructions on the manner of administering the sacraments and other duties. (London, 1237, c. 11, 20.)

Atton, Bishop of Vercelli in the second part of the tenth century, orders all the priests and clerics of every district to come together once a month and discuss questions pertaining to faith, the sacraments, and the various ecclesiastical duties. (Spicileg., T. VIII, p. 12; Capit. Attonis, c. 26, 27.) These meetings were usually held on the first day of the month and for this reason called Kalends. They existed as early as the ninth century in the diocese of Rheims, and Bishop Hincmar admonishes his clergy not to transform them into occasions for banquets but to be satisfied with a light collation, *et singulos biberes accipiant, maxime autem ultra tertiam vicem poculum ibi non contingant.* (Ibid. T. I, p. 714.) One of the questions which St. Ulderic, Bishop of Augsburg (d. 973), asks of his archpriests and deans in Synod is whether they hold regularly the monthly meetings according to the tradition of their predecessors. (Surius, 4 Jul., c. vi.)

270. (*b*) Towards the end of the sixteenth century these assemblies had lost much of their importance; some Councils reduce them to two or three a year (Rouen, 1581, Rheims, 1583) and in some places they seem to disappear entirely. But about that time they are reorganized in Italy with a more intellectual character by St. Charles Borromeo. In his first Council of Milan it was decreed that each diocese would be divided into districts over each of which would preside a vicar forane or dean. It would be the duty of the vicars to call a meeting of the clergy in their district once a month and discuss with them cases of conscience, reserved cases, the Constitutions, Councils, and Synods.

The example of Milan was followed by other Churches. (Aix, 1585; Toulouse, 1590; c. 6; Aquileia, 1595, c. 17.) Benedict XIII, in the Roman Council of 1723, strongly recommends the establishment of ecclesiastical conferences where they do not exist; and the Congregation of the Council declared that all pastors and all priests having faculties to hear confessions would be bound to attend them. (Aug. 30, 1732.)

In the United States the Second Plenary Council of Baltimore recommended and the Third prescribed the ecclesiastical conferences. (N. 68; 189.)

The Const. *Romanos Pontifices* given for England and Scotland, May 8, 1881, and extended to the United States, Sept. 25, 1885, declares that "all rectors of missions are bound by their office to assist at the conferences of the clergy and, moreover, it commands vicars and other religious men holding ordinary missionary faculties and living in residences or small mission houses to do the same."

271. (ii) By the present legislation the conferences of the clergy become an institution of the common law.

(*a*) They are to be held in the episcopal city and in every deanery several times a year; it is for the Ordinary to determine the exact number of times. In religious houses there must be one every month. (Can. 591.) The Council of Baltimore prescribes at least four a year in cities and two in country places.

(*b*) The main object of these conferences is to discuss questions of moral theology and liturgy; any exercises calculated to promote study and piety among the clergy may be added. The canon regarding conferences for Religious mentions also a sermon on a dogmatic subject or cognate doctrines. In some places the program includes questions of Scripture, Church History, Ascetic and Pastoral Theology, Canon Law, a pious exhortation, and Benediction of the Blessed Sacrament.

(*c*) If in some districts it was found difficult for the clergy to come together they might treat the proposed questions in writing and send their manuscript as directed by the Ordinary.

(*d*) Unless express exemption has been obtained beforehand from the Ordinary, the conferences ought to be attended or, if there can be no meeting, the written solution of the cases ought to be sent in, by all secular priests and by all Religious having charge of souls; and also by all such Religious as hold faculties to hear confessions from the Ordinary of the place unless they have in their houses the conferences prescribed for them. (Can. 591.)

(*e*) Benedict XIII gives the following directions regarding the manner of conducting clerical conferences: there is a president and a secretary appointed by the Bishop; the meetings are held in church, they begin with the recitation of the *Veni Creator Spiritus,* a prayer to the Blessed Virgin, and *Actiones nostras;* the secretary has the list of all who should be present and notes down the absentees; at the beginning of the meeting the president explains for a quarter of an hour a chapter of the Provincial Council or Diocesan Synod; then the discussion begins. Each question is treated by the one whom lot has designated for it; all ought to be ready. After the discussion the president or one of the members of the conference appointed by him sums up the whole argument. A quarter of an hour is devoted to the sacred rites and another to mental prayer. Some times the president shall draw the name of the one who is to give the meditation aloud in order that all may acquire practice in so important and so necessary an exercise. (Thomassin, vol. v, p. 370.)

5. *Celibacy.* (Can. 132.) (A. de Roskovany, Coelibatus et Breviarium, Pestini, 1861; Wernz, II, n. 196 ff.; The Catholic Encyclopedia, Celibacy; Dictionnaire d'Archéologie Chrétienne et de Liturgie, Célibat; Dictionnaire de Théologie Catholique, Vacant-Mangenot, Paris, Célibat; Hefele-Leclercq, Histoire des Conciles, T. II, p. 1321; E. Vacandard, Etudes de Critique et d'Histoire Religieuse, Paris, 1905, Les Origines du Célibat Ecclésiastique.)

272. 1°. Former Discipline. (*a*) Celibacy was counselled as more perfect by St. Paul (I Cor. vii, 7-8) and practiced by many of the clergy from the beginning (Tertullian, De Exhortatione Castitatis, c. XIII), particularly by those in major Orders; but there is no clear proof that it was obligatory during the first three centuries. The first legislation we have on the matter is that of the Council of Elvira, which imposes celibacy upon Bishops, priests, and deacons. (300, c. 33.) If the subject was at all discussed in the Council of Nicaea, as the historian Socrates affirms, no positive decision was taken. The next Council to deal with it was one held at Rome in 386 or 387; it passed an edict forbidding priests and deacons to have intercourse with their wives. Pope Siricius communicated this decree to the Bishops of Spain and of Africa, asking them to have it enforced and threatening the disobedient with severe punishment. (P. L., T. 56, col. 558-562, 728-730.) Pope Innocent I wrote in the same sense to Victricius of Rouen and Exuperius of Toulouse. (Ibid., col. 501, 523, 524.) Councils of Carthage likewise forbid priests and deacons who are married to use their marriage right after their ordination. (390, 401, c. 2, 3.) A Council of Toledo (400, c. 1) excludes from all promotion clerics in major Orders who live with their wives.

By the middle of the fifth century the law of clerical celibacy had obtained general recognition in the West. St. Leo the Great even extended its obligation to the subdeacons, who had hitherto been exempt; this, however, remained for a time a merely local provision. Pope Zachary in the eighth century explicitly allowed each Church to retain its custom on this point. Unity of discipline was to be fully attained only in the twelfth century.

In the East the Council of Neocaesarea, in 315, forbids priests to contract a new marriage under pain of deposition. The Council of Ancyra (314, c. 10) forbids deacons themselves to marry unless they reserved that right at their ordination. This legislation, completed by the Council of Trullo (692, c. 13), constitutes the law for most of the Oriental Churches to the present day; priests and deacons may take a wife before ordination, not after.

273. (*b*) The law of clerical celibacy seems to have been faithfully observed during the sixth and seventh centuries, but in the eighth ecclesiastical writers often denounce infractions. (Bonifacii, Epist. 49, Migne, P. L., T. 89, col. 745.) In Spain, King Witiza takes upon himself to abrogate the law as impossible of enforcement. The Councils of the Carolingian period, supported by the princes, succeeded, at least partially, in correcting the abuses. Unfortunately the disruption of Charlemagne's empire opened the door to new and greater disorders.

To some the condition of the clergy in the tenth and eleventh centuries seemed without remedy, but God gave then to His Church a series of Pontiffs whose zeal and energy overcame all obstacles. In numerous Councils St. Leo IX (Rome, 1050), St. Gregory VII (Rome, 1074, c. 11-20), Urban II (Melfi, 1089, c. 12; Clermont, 1095, c. 9, 10, 25), Calixtus II (Rheims, 1119, c. 5; Lateran, 1123, c. 7, 21), with untiring energy attacked vice and prosecuted offenders, until after a long struggle, in spite of obstinate resistance, with the co-operation of Provincial Synods and of the faithful themselves, they had at last restored the discipline of clerical celibacy. (O. Delarc, St. Grégoire et la Réforme de l'Eglise au Onziéme Siécle, Paris, 1889; Heffele-Leclercq, Histoire des Conciles, T. V. P. II.) The law attained its full development and efficacy when Callistus II (Lateran, 1123, c. 7, 21) and more explicitly Innocent II (Lateran, 1139, c. 7) declared that marriages contracted by priests, deacons and subdeacons were not only illicit, but also invalid, and to be treated as sacrilegious concubinages.

Abuses did not disappear entirely, but the fight continued against them, as the repeated decrees of Particular Councils clearly prove. (Cognac, 1260, c. 10; London, 1268, c. 8; Cologne, 1280, c. 2; Valladolid, 1322, c. 7; Aquileia, 1339, c. 10; Prague, 1355, c. 22, etc.) At times the enforcement of the law appeared again so difficult that the suggestion to abrogate or mitigate it was made by men otherwise esteemed for their piety and regularity of life, by Durandus the Younger in the Council of Vienna, 1311, by Cardinal Zarabella in the Council of Constance, 1414-1418; by Emperor Sigismond in the Council of Basel (Sess. 23, Jan. 23, 1435) and by others. The Church refused all concessions.

In the Renaissance period, disorders had become very common in certain countries. One of the first things done by the pseudo-reformers and one of the causes of their success was to allow priests to marry. When the Council of Trent met, the Emperor, the Duke of Bavaria, and the Duke of Brunswick proposed that, as a means of stopping the spread of heresy and of restoring peace in Europe, the law of clerical celibacy be abrogated. (Pallavicini, Histoire du Concile de Trente, l. XIV, c. XIII, n. 8; l. XV, c. v, n. 9; l. XVII, c. 4, n. 8 ff.; Theiner, Acta Genuina SS. Conc. Trid., T. II, p. 39.) A special commission took up the question and discussed it under all its aspects for thirteen sittings, beginning Feb. 10, 1563. As a result the Council pronounced formal condemnation against those who maintain that clerics in major Orders can marry validly. (Sess. XXIV, c. 9.)

Manifestations of more or less open opposition to the law of clerical celibacy have not been unknown in modern times. By an Encyclical of August 15,

1831, Gregory XVI condemned an association formed in Württemberg and Baden for the purpose of carrying on agitation against it. More recently Benedict XV pronounced anathema against the leaders of a similar movement in Bohemia (Jan. 3, 15, 1920; A. A. S., xii, 33, 37) and declared that the Church would never abrogate or mitigate this law.

274. 2°. Present Legislation. It confirms the former discipline and sanctions a slight change which had been introduced by custom.

(*a*) Clerics in major Orders remain forbidden to marry and so bound to practice chastity that by offending against this virtue they become guilty also of sacrilege. Exception is made for those who received Orders under the influence of a grave fear. (Can. 214.)

(*b*) This obligation is not of divine but only ecclesiastical right; according to some it is imposed upon the subdeacon by the law of the Church. According to others it arises from a vow conditionally commanded by the Church and taken, at least implicitly, by the subdeacon when he accepts ordination. Others again consider it as an effect of both an ecclesiastical precept and a vow. (Wernz, II, n. 201; IV, n. 393.) Whatever be the theory adopted, and the Code does not really settle the old controversy, it must be admitted that the obligation of celibacy for the clergy is one of religion, and that any sin against it contains the malice of sacrilege, as has been declared by the legislator. It must be admitted, likewise, that the obligation extends to both internal and external acts, and that it would be contracted even if, at the moment of ordination, the subdeacon had no thought or intention of making a vow. If one, however, received major Orders without having any knowledge of the obligation of chastity connected with them, which is hardly possible at present, and would not be admitted without proofs, his case would be similar to that of one ordained in infancy or under the influence of fear. (Can. 214.)

275. (*c*) Although some Particular Councils seem to have demanded of clerics in minor Orders the practice of chastity, the common law always permitted marriage to them (Chal. 451, c. 14; Epaon, 517, c. 37), but those who took advantage of the permission lost, under the ancient decretal law, all the privileges of the clerical state. Boniface VIII (l, III, 2, in Sexto) and later on again the Council of Trent mitigated somewhat the rigor of this discipline by granting to such clerics some at least of the advantages of the *privilegium fori* and *canonis.* It was, however, under conditions which could very seldom if ever be verified at the present time, so that the concession had become of little avail. The new law enacts therefore without any distinction that clerics in minor Orders contracting marriage return by the very fact to the lay state and lose all clerical privileges; an exception is made only in favor of clerics whose marriage would be null because of an impediment of fear.

(*d*) A married man may not lawfully receive major Orders as long as his wife lives. (Can. 987.) Should he receive them with a dispensation from the Holy See he would contract the same obligation to chastity as other clerics, so that children born to him after the ordination would, by canonical law, be illegitimate. If he is promoted to major Orders without the required dispensation, even in good faith, the Church forbids him to use the powers thus illegally obtained.

(*e*) Dispensation from the law of celibacy can be granted by the Pope and by him alone or his delegate. It is granted sometimes, for grave reasons, to subdeacons or deacons. It has been granted in a few cases to priests, for reasons of common good, as was done in England under Mary Tudor for the termination of the Anglican schism and in France, after the Revolution, to facilitate the reorganization of the Church. It is not granted to priests for reasons of a private character and the condition in any case is that those thus allowed to live in the married state will not exercise any of the sacred functions. There is no authentic example of a Bishop receiving such a dispensation.

6. *Cohabitation with and Frequentation of Women.* (Can. 133.) (Wernz, II, n. 205; Hefele-Leclercq, Histoire des Conciles, T. I, p. 201, 536; T. II, p. 463; Revue d'Histoire Ecclésiastique, Louvain, 1905, T. VII, p. 58-62; Bingham, o. c. B. VI, c. 2, n. 13; Smith & Cheethan, Dictionary of Christian Antiquities, Subintroductae.)

276. 1°. The Church demands of her clerics to avoid not only what is evil or positively dangerous to them, but also frequently what has the appearance of evil or might give scandal to others.

(*a*) Ancient Councils often refer to a class of women called *agapetae, subintroductae,* or sisters, usually consecrated virgins who, on the plea of spiritual relationship, resided in the houses of the clerics. This practice soon became the occasion of disorders and scandals against which ecclesiastical authorities repeatedly directed denunciations. The Council of Elvira (300, c. 27) forbids clerics to have any females residing with them except a sister or a daughter, and even these ought to be consecrated virgins.

The Council of Nicaea (325, c. 3), according to the Coptic version, allows clerics to have in their house only their mother, sister, or aunt, whose natural relationship would disarm all suspicion. Similar enactments are met with in numerous other Synods. (Carthage, 348, c. 3, 4; Arles, 452, c. 3; Lerida, 524, c. 15; Seville, 590, c. 3; Toledo, 527, c. 3; 633, c. 42; Agde, 506, 1011; Lyons, 583, c. 1.) These texts do not always agree as to the relations who may be permitted to reside with clerics, but nearly all exclude strangers absolutely. Some Councils go so far as to exclude even near relatives, the mother and sisters not excepted. (Nantes, 658, c. 3; Friuli, 796, c. 4; Mayence, 888, c. 10.) These, however, are particular prescriptions which do not represent the general discipline of the Church at any period of its development.

277. (*b*) Gratian inserted in his Decree the third canon of the Council of Nicaea according to the version of Dionysius Exiguus, which allows clerics to have with them their mother, sister, or aunt, and also other women provided these be above suspicion; but by decretal law all strangers remained excluded (c. 16, D. xxxii.; c. 1, 9, X, ii, 2), and particular Councils or canonists defined that the relationship which rendered cohabitation lawful did not go beyond the second degree of consanguinity or affinity.

(*c*) In practice an interpretation of the law based on the more lenient version of the Nicene Council gradually prevailed. With some hesitation at first, ecclesiastics were authorized to have women, other than their near relations, do the housework for them, provided they would be of blameless character and of mature age. A special permission was required for this in some places, in others a tax had to be paid.

The age demanded varies between thirty and fifty, generally it is forty. (Wernz, II, n. 206; Benedict XIV, Institutiones Ecclesiasticae, Institutio 82, 83; De Synodo Dioecesana, l. xii, c. 12, n. 14 sq.)

(*d*) Modern Councils and diocesan Synods take it for granted that clerics may have women in their service, but they contain numerous regulations regarding the age, character, and other qualifications or circumstances that have to be considered in order to remove all danger or occasion of suspicions. (III Plen. Coun. Balt., n. 81; Coll. Lac. v. Castitas.)

278. 2° The new Code insists again on the obligation for clerics to avoid cohabitation with, or, in general, frequentation of, women who are not above suspicion.

(*a*) It permits cohabitation with relations without determining what must be the degree of relationship; it mentions the mother, sister, and aunt, but the enumeration is not given as complete. The natural bond, whether of blood relationship or of affinity, must be such as to preclude all danger of suspicion. When is this condition fulfilled depends on many circumstances; ordinarily the relationship should not go beyond the second degree, according to ancient canonists.

(*b*) As to strangers, in order that their presence in a priest's house may not give rise to unfavorable criticism or cause scandal, two things principally are required: a good moral character and mature age. What constitutes the *aetas provectior,* or canonical age, the common law does not define; particular Councils or diocesan regulations may do so.

(*c*) The Ordinary has also power to decide in individual cases whether cohabitation or frequentation is permissible, whether it ought not to be discontinued even though no material violation of the law can be proved.

A legal presumption of concubinage would exist against a cleric disregarding the admonitions of the Ordinary in this matter.

7. *Life in Common.* (Can. 134.) (E. Amort, Vetus Disciplina Canonicorum Saecularium et Regularium, Venetiis, 1747; Thomassin, o. c., P. I, l. iii, c. 2-12; Dom P. Benoit, La Vie des Clercs dans les Siécles Passés, Paris, 1914; Dictionnaire d'Archéologie Chrétienne et de Liturgie, Chanoines; Revue du Clergé Francais, 15 Decembre, 1917, p. 481 ff.)

279. 1°. It has often been felt that isolation is a great cause of weakness for the secular clergy and hence various plans have been devised to procure for them the advantages of community life.

(*a*) The Apostles formed with Our Lord a community or rather family during the time of their training, but soon after Pentecost they separated and little is known of their subsequent relations with one another or with their immediate disciples. The letters of St. Clement of Rome and of St. Ignatius of Antioch testify to the close union prevailing in their day between Bishop and clergy, but they give no details about the internal organization of the churches. What ancient writers tell us of the monthly distributions made to clerics in various proportions according to their rank does not point to a community life which, in fact, would not be possible in times of persecution. (St. Cypr., l. iv, Epist. 5; l. v, Epist. 24; l. v, c. 28.)

(*b*) St. Eusebius of Vercelli (d. 371), according to St. Ambrose, was the first Bishop of the West who attempted to unite monastic observances with clerical duties. Having visited the monasteries of the East and conceived a great admiration for the mode of life of the cenobites, he wished to introduce a similar discipline among his clergy. He gathered them around him and gave them a rule which included most of the practices of the strictest asceticism, poverty, fasting, abstinence, manual labor, the singing of the office, etc. (St. Ambrose, Epist. 63, 81, Serm. 89.) The burden proved a heavy one and St. Eusebius does not seem to have had many followers.

St. Augustine met with greater success. After his conversion he had spent several years in a monastery with a few disciples at Tagaste and then at Hippo. (Possidius, Vita S. Augustini, c. 3; P. L., T. 32, col. 30.) On being raised to the Episcopate he decided to have his clergy live with him in the episcopal residence. All had to join his community who would be ordained; they renounced private property, had everything in common, and led as regular a life as the duties of the ministry permitted. Any one who after accepting these conditions did not continue faithfully was deprived of his rank. Fearing, however, lest by this severity he would make hypocrites, Augustine mitigated his rule on this point and allowed those who desired to have personal property and enjoy greater freedom to leave the community and go as clerics where they pleased, but they would be erased from the list of his own clergy.

The community of Hippo gave to the Church of Africa numerous Bishops who in turn established similar organizations in their respective dioceses; their example was imitated by other prelates, so that common life had become fairly general among the African clergy when the Vandal invasions and persecutions brought ruin to this as to so many other Christian institutions.

280. (*c*) In the sixth and seventh centuries we find in some regions, particularly in Gaul and in Spain, the clergy of the episcopal city grouped around the Bishop and the archpriest. According to the Second Council of Tours (567, c. 12, 13), the Bishop must always have with him, even in his room, *in cella,* his priests, deacons, and other clerics, as guardians of his virtue and reputation. They alone are to serve him, and they have the authority to expel all women from the episcopal residence.

In order to remove all occasion of nefarious suspicion or slanderous talk, says the Fourth Council of Toledo (633, c. 22, 23), Bishops shall have persons of good reputation living with them, *in conclavi,* as witnesses of their virtue. Priests and deacons shall reside with the Bishop, and if there are any who can not do so because of old age or infirmities they may live in private dwellings, but they too must have witnesses of their good conduct. The social conditions brought about by the Barbarian invasions rendered these measures of prudence necessary.

Other Councils speak of the common table for ecclesiastics, of reading during their meals to avoid idle conversation (III Toledo, 589, c. 7). St. Gregory when sending St. Augustine to England recommends to him the establishment among his clergy of the common life and renouncement of private property, in accordance with the ancient practice. (Beda, l. 1, c. 27.)

(*d*) By the end of the seventh century very few ecclesiastical communities remained even where they had once flourished, and the evils of isolation reappeared in many places. A Council of Vernon (755, c. 11), deploring the existing disorders and confessing its inability to remedy them at once, decrees at least that henceforth clerics shall not live like private persons, but shall all either retire to a monastery or place themselves under the Bishop's authority and observe the canonical rule.

One of the difficulties had always been to reconcile the exigencies of community life with the demands of the pastoral office. To be practicable the canonical rule, as it was called, had to be adapted to these special conditions. St. Chrodegand, Bishop of Metz, undertook this work in 763. The rule which he drew up for the clergy of his diocese resembled in many respects that of Religious Orders, but it differed from it in several important points. It imposed common dwelling, common table and dormitory, the singing of the Office and manual labor, each one, for example, taking his turn for a week in the kitchen, but it left more independence and did not exact renouncement to all personal property. (Labbe & Cossart, Sacrosancta Concilia, T. VII, col. 1444.)

King Pepin and after him Charlemagne in their zeal for Church reform gave St. Chrodegand's rule the full support of their authority and with the co-operation of several Councils extended its prescriptions to all the clerics of their dominion. (Capit. of Aix-la-Chapelle in 789, c. 72, 73, 77; Capit. of 801, c. 37; 805, c. 9; 813; c. 4; Labbe & Cossart, T. VII, col. 1184 ff.; Councils of 813 at Tours, c. 23; Rheims, c. 8, 23, 25; Mayence, 9; Chalons-sur-Saone, Arles, etc.)

Continuing the same policy, Louis the Pious in 817 called a meeting of Bishops at Aix-la-Chapelle and asked them to take new measures for the enforcement of discipline among the clergy. The Bishops willingly acceded to his desires although, they say, most of them lived with their subordinates in accordance with the canons. A new collection of rules, not essentially different from that of Metz, was prepared and submitted to the assembly for approval. The emperor approved it also, gave it the force of law in his territory and sent a copy of it to all Metropolitans, urging them to see that it was observed by those concerned.

Like the documents previously referred to, this rule speaks of canons rather than of clerics, but that name, reserved at first to the clergy of the episcopal city, had gradually come to be applied to all ecclesiastics attached to, and on the roll or canon of, some church, and to be practically synonymous with cleric as opposed to monk. (Clermont, 535, c. 15; Aix-la-Chapelle, 789, c. 72, 77, 93.) The canonical rule was intended for the whole clergy of the diocese.

Community life must have been difficult if not impossible outside of cathedral or collegiate churches and perhaps of the more important centers in the country; hence the necessity of numerous exceptions. But wherever circumstances permitted, it seems to have been generally observed, at least within the limits of the empire, during the ninth century, although the repeated enactments of Councils on the subject may imply that obedience was not perfect. (Rome, 827, c. 7, 10; Meaux, 835, c. 53; Pavia, 876, c. 8.) It disappeared almost entirely in the confusion and disorders of the iron age.

281. (*e*) The Popes of the eleventh century, Nicholas II, Alexander II, St. Gregory VII, tried to restore this community life as one of the most efficacious remedies against the great evils of the day, simony and unchastity. (Rome, 1059, c. 4.) They succeeded only partially and temporarily; by the end of the twelfth century little of it remained among the parochial clergy. Those who chose to live under rule formed communities of canons regular, the others were called canons secular or secular priests.

In the seventeenth century, B. Holzhauser of Augsburg, Bavaria, established a society of secular priests who would lead a community life even in parishes where there would be only two or three together. Innocent XI approved his Institute (*Creditae nobis,* Jun. 7, 1680), but it did not last to the end of the eighteenth century. Similar attempts in other places met with varying degrees of success. The S. Cong. of the Propaganda in an Instruction of Oct. 18, 1883, highly commends the Vicars Apostolic in the Far East for their efforts to maintain some community life among their missionaries.

282. 2°. The present law praises and encourages life in common for clerics and asks that, as far as possible, it be continued wherever it exists already. Without imposing a formal obligation of establishing it where it does not exist, the legislator clearly manifests the wish that this be done when circumstances permit it and in the measure in which they permit it.

8. *The Divine Office.* (Can. 135.) (Roskovany, o. c.; Thomassin, o. c., P. I, L. II, c. 71-78; Baumer, Histoire du Bréviaire, Paris, 1905; Duchesne, Christian Worship, 1905, c. xvi; Batiffol, History of the Roman Breviary, 1893; The Catholic Encyclopedia, Breviary.)

283. 1°. Custom introduced the obligation for the clergy to recite the Divine Office and written law sanctioned it afterwards.

(*a*) The early developments of the discipline and the origin of the various parts of the Breviary remain still obscure. The Apostles and first Christians retained the ancient Jewish custom of devoting to prayer certain hours of the day, and we see them for a time repairing to the Temple at the traditional moment with other pious Israelites. (Acts, ii, 15; iii, 1; x, 3, 9, 30.) They had, besides, chiefly on the evening of the Sabbath, their special reunions in private houses. The greater part of the night would be spent in the chanting of psalms, reading of Scriptures or instructions, and on Sunday morning the Sacred Synaxis or Holy Eucharist was celebrated. (Pliny, Epist. x, 97.) Our present evening, night, and morning service, or Vespers, Matins, and Lauds, seem to be only divisions of the original night service or vigil. At first only the feast of the Resurrection, then every Sunday, the station days, and the feasts of the great martyrs were preceded by a vigil, in which both the people and clergy took part.

(*b*) In the fourth century, when Christians had become more numerous, fervor decreased and the masses commenced to neglect public services, but the more important communities possessed by that time a body of devout persons, the *ascetae,* who gave themselves to a life of prayer and introduced the practice of the daily vigil. They had it first privately in their houses, then publicly in the newly erected basilicas. Their example had to be followed by the clergy; in the fifth century the vigil was held daily in the principal churches of Rome, the *Tituli Presbyterales,* by the clerics attached to them. A Council of Vannes (465, c. 14) decrees that a city cleric who absents himself from Matins without valid excuse should be deprived of communion for a week. The same negligence, in case of obstinacy, is punished with deposition by a Council held under Pope Martin about the year 572. (Dist. xcii, c. 9.) A law of Emperor Justinian in the sixth century commands all clerics to sing the morning and evening service in their churches. When the *ascetae* had withdrawn into monasteries and the faithful had ceased to attend regularly, the whole burden of the celebration of the Divine Office fell on the clergy.

(*c*) From the eighth century on this was principally, although not exclusively, the duty of clerics living in common. (1, X, III, 41; Tours, 567, c. 18; Coyaca, 1050, c. 6.) When the canonical communities became fewer and the Divine Office ceased to be sung publicly outside of cathedral, collegiate, or conventual churches, clerics remained bound to recite it in private. In the Council of London, 1213, Archbishop Langton authorizes his clergy to say the Office in a low tone of voice; and a Council of Treves (1227, c. 9) orders priests when they travel to have a copy of the Breviary with them that they may recite it.

(*d*) About this time also a distinction is made between clerics in regard to the obligation of reciting the Office. A Council of Pennefiel (1301, c. 1) mentions as bound only those who have received sacred Orders or who possess an ecclesiastical benefice. In general, however, Councils and the Decretals themselves have nothing definite concerning the gravity and the extent of this obligation. (9, X, III, 41; Clem. III, 14.) It certainly existed for beneficed clerics at the time of the Fifth Lateran Council, which explicitly confirms it. (Sess. IX, Const. Leon. X, *Supernae,* § 38, 5 Maii, 1514.) For clerics in sacred Orders who have no benefice the obligation rested till the publication of the Code on custom or local legislation, not on any general decree.

284. 2°. The present law formally enacts that

clerics in sacred Orders are bound to recite the canonical hours.

(*a*) The obligation begins with the hour corresponding to the time of the ordination; it would not be contracted by a subdeacon who would be forced to receive Orders. (Can. 214.) It ceases if the cleric returns to the lay state legitimately (Can. 135, 213) but not if he is suspended or excommunicated.

In another part of the Code the same obligation is imposed on beneficed clerics (Can. 1475) and on some Religious. (Can. 610.)

(*b*) The Office must be recited every day, entirely according to the form approved for the Church to which the cleric belongs. Private recitation suffices provided it remains an external prayer.

9. *Clerical Dress and External Appearance.* (Can. 136.) (Decret. Lib. III, Tit. I; Thomassin, P. I, L. II, c. 38-57; Wernz, II, n. 175 ff.; Bingham, B. VI, c. iv, 15.)

285. 1°. Dress. (*a*) During the first four or five centuries the dress of clerics did not differ from that of the laity either in form or in color but only, if at all, in modesty and simplicity. Pope Celestine (428) sharply reproved Bishops who made themselves conspicuous by retaining after their elevation to the Episcopate the pallium of the monks.

About the sixth century the laity commonly adopted the short tunic, trousers, and cloak of the Teutonic invaders, but the clergy retained the long tunic and toga of the Romans. Councils of that period forbid them to wear the dress of the Barbarians, which is almost synonymous with secular dress (Agde, 506, c. 20; Matiscon, 581, c. 5; C. Germ. 742, c. 7); they recommend that richness or brilliancy of colors as well as slovenliness and impropriety be avoided. (Nicaea, 787, c. 15; Aix, 816, c. 124.) The Fourth Lateran Council (1215) summed up, completed, and solemnly promulgated these regulations, which in their new form passed into the canons of numerous local Synods and with some further modifications into the *Corpus Juris.* (15, X, III, 1; 2, Clem. III, 1.) Thus gradually the plain, long, closed tunic, the *vestis talaris,* or cassock, became by custom and positive law the distinctive dress of the clergy. At first it was generally white, then of sombre colors; the Fourth Lateran Council asks that it be not red or green. Councils in the fifteenth and sixteenth centuries prescribed black, which has prevailed since. (Milan, c. 1563, c. 17, 23.)

Although the habit does not make the monk, says the Council of Trent, clerics ought by the modesty of their dress make manifest the goodness of their moral character; and it condemns those ecclesiastics who wear a secular dress even in public; beneficed clerics and all in sacred Orders must wear the dress suited to their order and dignity according to the prescriptions of the Ordinary, under pain of suspension and even of privation of office in case of relapse. (Sess. XIV, c. 6, de Ref.) Sixtus V (Const. *Cum Sacrosanctum,* 9 Jan., 1589) went a step farther and decreed that the *vestis talaris* should be the proper ecclesiastical dress everywhere. This, however, canonists interpreted as referring only to the habit required for ecclesiastical functions; outside of these it remained lawful for ecclesiastics to wear a shorter dress where the custom existed. (Benedict XIV, De Synodo, L. xi, c. 8; Coll. Lac., passim, v. Sacerdotes, Clerici.) The Postulatum presented by some Bishops in the Vatican Council demanding that the Const. of Sixtus V be applied literally remained without effect.

(*b*) The present law prescribes the clerical dress for all clerics and not simply for those who are in sacred Orders or who possess a benefice. The form and color of the dress are to be determined by legitimate customs and diocesan regulations. In English-speaking countries generally the clerical dress consists, in the church and house, of the cassock and Roman collar; outside of the house, of the Roman collar and black suit with coat of proper length, *i.e.* reaching *infra genua* according to the Second, *ad genua* according to the Third, Plenary Council of Baltimore. (N. 77; cf. IV Westminster, ii, 12-14.)

286. 2°. Wearing of the hair. Synods have numerous ordinances on this subject, especially since the fifth century.

(*a*) In the *Statuta Ecclesiae Antiqua* it is decreed that clerics ought not to let their hair or beards grow. (N. 44.) According to another reading of this canon, they were neither to let their hair grow nor to shave their beards. The first Council of St. Patrick (456, c. 6, 10) ordains that the hair of the clergy shall be shorn according to the Roman fashion and that any one letting his hair grow shall be excluded from the church. Clerics who wear long hair shall be shorn by the archdeacon, even against their will, says the Council of Agde (506, c. 20); they shall not officiate with long, but rather closely-cut, hair and open ears. (Braga, 572, c. 11; Toledo, 633, c. 41; Trullo, 692, c. 21.) Two Roman Councils (721, c. 17; 743, c. 8) pronounce anathema against clerics who allow their hair to grow. Clerics, writes St. Jerome, should neither have their heads shaven like the priests of Isis and Serapis nor let their hair grow to an extravagant length like barbarians and soldiers, but the hair should be just so long as to cover the head. (In Ezech., c. 44.) In another place he denounces monks who indulge in beards like goats and ringlets like women. (Epist. 18, ad Eustochium.)

(*b*) The new Code has no formal provision on this point; it only recommends simplicity and modesty.

287. 3°. The clerical crown. (*a*) The practice of wearing the clerical crown or tonsure began among the secular clergy in the sixth century and perhaps in the fifth in some places. (Thomassin, l. c., 37.) The Fourth Council of Toledo (639, c. 4) decreed that clerics should cut the hair on the top of the head and leave only a crown around it. Similar prescriptions become frequent after the tenth century; in the fifteenth the crown had been very much reduced in size and in the sixteenth ecclesiastics no longer wore it in several countries. The Council of Trent and the Provincial Synods which followed it restored the ancient discipline throughout the Catholic world.

In England tonsure has not been worn since the Reformation and in the United States it has never been in use.

(*b*) By the present law all clerics are bound to wear the tonsure unless the custom of the country be against it.

288. 4°. Wearing of the beard. (*a*) In the ninth century it was a distinctive mark of the Latin clergy to shave their beards, as can be seen from the controversy with the Greeks on that point. This had been the general custom for some time, perhaps since the fifth century. It continued so till the sixteenth, when the contrary custom prevailed in spite of the opposition of several Councils and Pontiffs.

(Lateran, 1512-1517.) Ecclesiastics wore the beard till the end of the seventeenth or the beginning of the eighteenth century. The ancient discipline restored about that time has been maintained to the present day. Some ecclesiastics made an attempt in the last century to reintroduce the custom of wearing the beard; Pius IX, in a letter to the Archbishop of Munich (1863), condemned the movement as an innovation not even tacitly approved by the Holy See and, therefore, illegitimate. Several Particular Councils published the Letter and on the same occasion renewed the provisions of ancient canons. (II Plen. Balt., n. 151; IV Westminst., xi, 13; Ami du Clergé, 19, Jan., 1905, p. 56 ff.)

(*b*) The new Code contains no special enactment on this matter. Some interpreted at once its silence as implying withdrawal of former prohibitions which, a few thought, Bishops had no longer authority to maintain.

Interrogated by the Bishop of Breslau on the soundness of this view, the S. Cong. of the Council rejected it as unfounded and declared that the existing discipline remained unchanged. (Jan. 10, 1920; A. A. S., 2 Feb., 1920, p. 43.)

The principle that "disciplinary laws formerly in force and not renewed implicitly or explicitly in the Code cease to bind" (Can. 6, 60) applies to laws, not to customs, and to universal, permanent laws, not to particular, temporary ones. (Can. 20, 22.) The prohibition for the secular clergy to wear the beard is the result of custom or of particular law, not of any real, general decree. If one existed it could be only of a provisional character, since it must be conditioned on the customs of the country, which vary with time and place. (Nouvelle Revue Théologique, Juillet, 1920, p. 407.)

289. 5°. Ring. Clerics should not wear a ring unless authorized to do so by law or apostolic privilege.

Those authorized by law are: the Sovereign Pontiff, Cardinals, Bishops, Abbots, Prothonotaries, canons of cathedral churches, doctors in theology and canon law. Doctors, titular Prothonotaries, canons, and even Abbots who have not been blessed, may not wear it when saying Mass. (Cong. of Rites, March 9, 1894.)

6°. Sanctions. Clerics who of their own authority, without legitimate cause, put off the clerical dress or do not wear the tonsure should be warned by the Ordinary. Should the admonition remain without effect for a whole month clerics in minor Orders forfeit the clerical state (Can. 136, 3); those in sacred Orders should be suspended from the Orders received and even deposed if they continue for three months longer in their obstinacy. (Can. 2379.)

III. NEGATIVE OBLIGATIONS OF CLERICS, OR THINGS FORBIDDEN TO THEM. (Can. 137-144.)

(Thomassin, P. III, L. III, c. 42; Bingham, B. IV, c. 4; Wernz, II, n. 211 ff.)

290. 1. *Standing as Surety.* (Can. 137.) A cleric is forbidden to give bail even on his own personal property without consulting the Ordinary; he should not assume responsibility for another person's obligations without great caution, and as the honor of the clergy may be involved Bishops have the right to exercise some supervision over such transactions.

(*a*) The Apostolic Canons pronounce deposition against any cleric becoming surety (c. 20; cf. Apost.

Const., ii, 6) and Emperor Justinian confirmed the prohibition, "lest clerics should be distracted from their sacred functions." (Novel. 123, c. 6.) In the Decretals the law against clerics being sureties and bondsmen is absolute (1, X, III, 22), but custom had allowed some exceptions.

(*b*) The present law mentions no exceptions, but the prohibition itself is conditional; bail is not to be given without consulting the Ordinary of the place. This concerns secular clerics, for Religious there are other regulations.

The advice of the Ordinary is required, not necessarily his consent, but his consent too would no doubt be necessary even for the validity of the act if bail was given on ecclesiastical property, for this is a species of alienation. The Ordinary ought to be consulted even when bail is to be given on personal property, as the canon explicitly states, or when it is to be given in favor of fellow clerics or of pious institutions, since the legislator makes no distinctions and there is no reason for exceptions, but the contract would more probably be valid without this formality when ecclesiastical property is not pledged.

291. 2. *Occupations and Amusements Unbecoming the Ecclesiastical State.* (Can. 138.) The Church has always asked clerics to abstain from many things which, although not unlawful in themselves, do not befit one consecrated to the service of the altar. What should be considered as improper for ecclesiastics depends much on circumstances and public sentiment, and legislation on this subject usually reflects the spirit as well as the tendencies of the age.

Early Synods often forbid clerics to play at dice (Elvira, 305, c. 79), to enter taverns, or assist at scenic spectacles (Laodicea, 343, c. 24, 54), to attend nuptial banquets. (Agde, 506, c. 19.) When the sons of the Germanic invaders have entered the sanctuary and monasteries in large numbers, decrees against hunting, bearing arms, following the armies, and engaging in actual warfare appear frequently in the Acts of Councils (Agde, 506, c. 55; Epaon, 517, c. 4; Conc. Germ., 742, c. 2; Soissons, 744, 3); and in the Middle Ages it is found necessary to enact penalties against clerics who become comedians, jesters or clowns, and buffoons, *qui se joculatores seu goliardos aut buffones faciunt.* (12, X, III, 1; 1, II, 1, in Sexto; 1, II, 14, in Clement.)

The new Code, after affirming again the obligation for the clergy to avoid all that is unbecoming their vocation, explicitly renews with some modifications the ancient prohibitions in regard to five things:

292. 1°. Unbecoming Arts or Professions. Canonists give as examples of these the profession or trade of public actor, innkeeper, butcher, executioner, and in general all occupations looked upon by the public as of a sordid, mean nature and engaged in only by a low class of people.

2°. Games of Chance. (*a*) The Apostolic Canons (c. 41, 42) threaten with excommunication or degradation clergy or laity who play with dice, and Councils are hardly less severe. (Elvira, c. 79; Trullo, c. 50.) Emperor Justinian decreed suspension with seclusion in a monastery for three years against any ecclesiastic of whatever rank he might be who played or even merely assisted at games of chance. (Novel. 123, c. 10.) Later Synods contain similar provisions. (IV Lateran, 1215, c. 16; Salzburg, 1420, c. 4.) The Council of Sens (1485, Art.

ii, c. 8) condemns dicing absolutely, but playing at such games as checkers it considers only a light offence, provided this be not done publicly and frequently.

In modern Councils a distinction has been clearly and explicitly made between games depending exclusively on chance and those depending partially at least on skill; the latter are usually not prohibited, provided they be played with moderation and without scandal. The First Provincial Council of Baltimore had forbidden cards, but the Congregation found this too severe and the decree was modified. (Collectio Lac. vol. iii, col. 24, 31; col. 443, 784.)

(*b*) The new law strictly forbids games of chance played for money and somewhat habitually; games which depend principally on skill and are played only occasionally, for the sake of recreation, not for money, or for small sums, would not come under this rule. Local legislation may be stricter if special circumstances demand it.

293. 3°. Carrying Arms. (*a*) The First Council of Macon (581, c. 5) provides that any ecclesiastic found carrying arms or wearing an unbecoming dress shall be imprisoned and kept for thirty days on bread and water; and the Fourth Council of Toledo (633, c. 44) decrees that clerics who have willingly borne arms in a revolt shall lose their rank and be sent for discipline to a monastery. Clerics carrying arms are deprived of their office by several Synods. (Meaux, 8455, c. 37; Tours, 1060, c. 7; London, 1175, 11.) The Council of Leptines (743, c.) allows some priests to accompany the armies, but they must not bear arms; this applies also to prelates who by their feudal tenure are bound to send soldiers from their lands and may lead them to battle. (Soissons, 744, c. 3.)

The multiplication of these prohibitions shows to what extent the clergy had been influenced by the warlike spirit of the age. They refer primarily to military arms intended for use against man, not to weapons carried for the purpose of shooting game; moreover, Councils explicitly allow clerics to carry arms on their journeys when the roads are unsafe and they fear aggression.

(*b*) Under the present law it remains forbidden regularly for ecclesiastics to carry arms except when they need them for their own protection.

294. 4°. Hunting. (*a*) The Council of Agde (506, c. 55) punishes with excommunication Bishops and priests who keep hawks and hounds for the chase; a multitude of Synods contains similar provisions forbidding all ecclesiastics and monks to hunt with hounds, hawks, and falcons. (Epaon, 517, c. 44; Soissons, 744, c. 3; Tours, 813, c. 8; Chalons, 813, c. 9; Montpellier, 1214, c. 7, 14; Albi, 1254, c. 50; Salzburg, 1420, c. 4.) Bishops who kept dogs under the pretence that they were necessary for the protection of their house are reminded by the Council of Macon (585, c. 13) that "not barks but hymns, not bites but good works, are the proper protection of a Bishop's house, which ought to welcome and not repel men, and not subject any who came for the relief of their sorrows to the risk of being torn by dogs." St. Ferreolus, Bishop of Uzes (558), allows his monks to set dogs at the wild animals which waste their crops, but only that they may drive them away, not that they may catch them, for, he says, hunting and hawking dissipate the mind.

Looking on or being present at the fighting or hunting of wild animals in the amphitheatre is also strictly forbidden by Councils (Trullo, 692, c. 24, 51), and hunting is so often mentioned in such connection with dances and dramatic performances that it may be presumed that theatrical sports are referred to in these texts. (Tours, 813, c. 8; Chalons, 813, c. 9.)

From this a few canonists had concluded that all condemnations of hunting in Councils were intended, at least originally, for the sports of the amphitheatre not for hunting as we understand it generally. (Berardi, Jus Ecclesiasticum Universum, vol. i, p. i; G. Sebastianelli, Praelectiones Juris Canonici, de Personis, n. 43.) Others, on the contrary, arguing from some texts which forbid hunting without qualification, pronounced all forms of this recreation unlawful. (Benedict XIV, De Synodo, L. XI, c. x, n. 8; Thomassin, l. c. 42, iv.) Others, again, seeing that canons usually deal with hunting in which hounds, hawks, etc., are needed made a distinction between the *venatio* which they call *clamorosa* and the *venatio quieta,* the former one alone being condemned in these texts. (1, 2, X, V, 24, de Clerico Venatore.) The Council of Trent seemed implicitly to confirm this view when it commanded ecclesiastics to abstain from forbidden hunting. (Sess. XXIV, de Ref., c. xii.)

(*b*) The Code practically accepts the distinction when it gives as a rule to clerics not to indulge in any form of hunting, that is, not to make a habit of it or devote much time to it and to abstain absolutely from the *venatio clamorosa.* As it does not define the canonical meaning of this expression, we have to go for its interpretation to canonists. They generally call *venatio clamorosa* the one which is attended with great noise and tumult caused by the presence of numerous dogs, falcons, horsemen, etc.; and *quieta* that which is carried on quietly, with snares and nets or even with a gun and one or two dogs. (Lehmkuhl, Theologia Moralis, II, n. 615; Irish Ecclesiastical Record, 1918, p. 478.)

295. 5°. Entering Taverns. (*a*) The Apostolic Canons forbid ecclesiastics to enter public houses except in cases of necessity when they are travelling. (Can. 54, D. 44, c. 2.) Several Councils have repeated this prohibition, often in the same terms. (Laodicea, 341-381, c. 24; Frankfort; II Rheims, IV Lateran, 15, X, III, 1; Salzburg, 1274, c. 12.) Obedience was not perfect and punishments had to be inflicted. Hincmar of Rheims threatens his clergy to grant the faithful the permission which they have asked, to seize the horse or cloak of their pastor if they catch him in a tavern. (Thomassin, c. 45, ix.)

(*b*) Under the present common law ecclesiastics must not enter taverns or places of that character except in cases of necessity or for a just cause approved by the Ordinary of the place.

No permission is required when there is a real necessity; in other cases it should regularly be obtained, or at least the reason should be such that the approval of the Ordinary may prudently be presumed.

Particular legislation may determine more in detail what should be considered as a case of necessity or a just cause for going into a restaurant, inn, or other public house. It is supposed that these places are otherwise respectable and that they can be visited without scandal.

296. 3. *Employments Foreign to the Clerical State.* (Can. 139.) 1°. "No man being a soldier to God," says St. Paul, "entangleth himself with secular business." (II Tim. ii. 4.) In order that the clergy might not be distracted or taken away from their spiritual work, Constantine exempted them from the ordinary municipal duties, and the Church forbade them to seek or accept public offices as soon as, persecution having ceased and pagan legislation abrogated, they manifested inclinations to do so. (Sardica, 343, c. 8.) The Apostolic Canons threaten with deposition or degradation Bishops, priests, and deacons who busy themselves in any secular administrations. (C. 7, 81, 83.) The rule that clerics and monks should not meddle in secular affairs has been repeatedly promulgated, especially during the Middle Ages, when perhaps the temptation was stronger and infractions more frequent. (Vernon, 755, c. 16; Aix-la-Chapelle, 789, c. 22; Friuli, 796, c. 5; Mayence, 813, c. 14.)

Ecclesiastics are forbidden in particular to be tutors or guardians (Carthage; St. Cyprian, Epist. 66; Chalc., 451, c. 3) except to near relations, and this concession is not always made; to plead at the bar in civil courts unless it be in their own case or in that of their church or of the poor (III Lateran, 1179, c. 12; London, 1102, c. 8); to hold the office of notary, assessor or judge in civil courts (Avranches, 1172, c. 12), at least in criminal cases (London, 1175, c. 3); to study or practice civil law or medicine and surgery. (Clermont, 1130, c. 5; Rheims, 1131, c. 6; II Lateran, 1139, c. 9; Tours, 1163, c. 8; c. 10, X, III, 50.)

Necessity or charity often obliged the Church to depart from the strictness of these rules. The Fourth Council of Toledo (633, c. 31) allows ecclesiastics to assist in the administration of justice when requested by the king (C. 29, C, XXIII. q. 8), and such requests were frequent after the laity had left learning and culture almost entirely to clerics and monks. For a time, says a writer, the Church supplied the State with its principal officials. By the force of circumstances Bishops found themselves temporal princes, counsellors of kings, and ministers of State. Clerics seem to be particularly numerous in courts of justice, and Councils of the thirteenth century implicitly authorize them to serve as judges, procurators, or advocates, provided they do not take part in trials which may result in the effusion of blood. (London, 1266, c. 7; Paris, 1213, p. i, c. 6.)

297. 2°. The present Code lays it down again as a general principle that ecclesiastics must abstain from those employments which, although not unbecoming, are not in the line of their work, and it specifies certain occupations which they may not engage in without the permission of the Holy See or of their Ordinary.

(*a*) Without apostolic indult they must not: (i) practice medicine or surgery. The prohibition certainly affects now all clerics and Religious, even missionaries, and those who may have done medical work before ordination.

The rule is the same for medicine and surgery.

Practice, *exercere,* implies something habitual, done *ex professo,* usually for the purpose of gain; a person would not be practicing medicine because he would give medical assistance once in passing, accidentally in an emergency; nor probably if he prescribed only for members of his family, nor if he simply recommended ordinary, common remedies. Apparently homeopathy, naturopathy, etc., do not come under this law, but they may be forbidden by particular statutes. (Maroto, l. c., n. 567; Wernz, II, n. 222.)

(ii) They may not act as notaries public except in ecclesiastical courts. Formerly clerics in minor Orders were not forbidden to hold that office in the civil, whilst those in major Orders and regulars were excluded from it even in ecclesiastical courts.

(iii) They must not seek or accept public offices which involve the exercise of lay jurisdiction or administration, such as the offices of President of the Republic, governor, judge, mayor; president or treasurer of a lay association.

298. (*b*) Without the permission of their Ordinary, that is, their Bishop or superior, ecclesiastics and Religious should not: (i) undertake the administration of property belonging to lay persons or accept private secular offices that impose the obligation of rendering an account; they may not, then, be tutors or guardians, and the exception in favor of near relations is not explicitly made here as in ancient canons; neither may they act as presidents, secretaries, or treasurers of banks, cooperative associations, savings banks, and similar organizations, even though these be of a purely benevolent character. To hold these offices clerics needed the permission of the Holy See, by a decree of the Consistorial Cong., Nov. 10, 1910; that of the Ordinary suffices at present, as provided in this canon and declared by the Commission of Interpretation, June 3, 1918. (Nouvelle Revue Théologique, Fév. 1911, p. 86.) For the administration of ecclesiastical property no special permission is necessary.

(ii) They should not exercise the office of procurator or advocate in secular courts unless their own cause or the cause of the church in which they have an office or benefice be in question. The cause of their near relations may probably be considered as their own. Ancient canons permitted them also to take up the causes of poor persons, but this provision has not been maintained, because it left a door open to abuses.

Clerics are not forbidden any longer to act as advocates in ecclesiastical courts.

299. (iii) Unless forced to do so, they are not to take any part, not even to give testimony, in criminal cases in lay courts when a grave personal penalty may be inflicted or is demanded by the prosecution. When summoned by legitimate authority there is for them necessity to appear, and permission is not required for this, although it might be proper to notify the Ordinary. A moral necessity would exist also, according to some, if they had something to say for the defendant.

(*c*) Without the permission of the Holy See or that of the Ordinary they must not seek or accept membership in the legislative assemblies, as senators, deputies, or representatives.

In some countries, by special decree, permission from the Holy See is required, *v.g.* in Italy, France, Bosnia-Herzegovina. Where no such provision exists the candidate must have the consent of his Ordinary and that of the Ordinary of the district which he is to represent.

300. 4. *Amusements: Spectacles, Dances, and Other Exhibitions.* (Can. 140.) 1°. Christians found the public amusements tainted with the depravity which infected all heathen society. Ancient writers speak of "the mad excitement of the circus, the impurity of the theatre, the luxury of the play, the barbarity of the arena, and the cruelty of the amphitheatre," of the obscene love songs and lascivious dances which it was customary to have at nuptial and other convivial entertainments (Agde, 506, c. 39; Braga, 610); hence the apparent severity of the rules laid down for the clergy by Councils. They are not to assist at any spectacles in theatres or at nuptial celebrations. (Laodicea, 341, c. 53, 54.) The Council in Trullo (692, c. 24, 51, 72) forbids them to be present at dances, horse-races, or any scenic amusements. Later Synods renewed these absolute prohibitions even in modern times. (Bordeaux, 1583, 21; Avignon, 1594; IV Westminster, 1873, n. 9; Baltimore, 1884, n. 79; Maynooth, 1900, n. 180.) In others, only unbecoming spectacles and comedies are condemned. (Tours, Chalons, 813, c. 7, 9.)

The Council of Mexico (1585, L. III, Tit. v) states that by a decree of Pius V clerics in major Orders who assist at bull-fights incur excommunication and may be also punished by the Ordinary.

301. 2°. The Code gives on this subject a general rule, which will admit of very different applications according to times, places, and other circumstances.

It provides that ecclesiastics should not assist, particularly in public theatres, at plays, dances, or other performances, *pompis,* which would be unbecoming or at which they could not be present without scandal.

(*a*) The word *spectacula* comprises all theatrical representations and likewise such exhibitions as horse-races, bull-fights, prize-fights, etc., at least if it is taken in its most general sense; in particular decrees it may have a more restricted meaning.

All balls and dances, whether held in private houses or public halls, may come under this law.

By "pomps" are understood other celebrations, festivities, entertainments of various kinds.

(*b*) These amusements become prohibited, by common law, only when they are in themselves unbecoming or when for some reason people would be scandalized if clerics assisted at them. This will more readily be the case if they are held in a public theatre, not necessarily, however, nor exclusively.

(*c*) When in some places theatrical or other amusements are ordinarily of such character that ecclesiastics could seldom or never assist at them without impropriety or scandal, local Ordinaries or Synods may issue against them general and absolute prohibitions, as was done, for example, in the United States against horse-races and theatres (III Baltimore, 1884, n. 79), in England against public dances and scenic spectacles in theatres (IV Westminster, Decretum XI, n. 9), in Ireland against public horse-races, circuses, and theatrical exhibitions including operas (Maynooth, 1900, n. 180), in Rome against cinematographic representations. (Ordin. of Vicariate, July 15, 1909, A. A. S., 1909, p. 600.)

By a decree of the Consistorial Congregation, universal in its application although enacted in view of local abuses, all clergymen, secular as well as regular, are strictly forbidden to promote or favor dances or balls, even should these be held to help and support a good and pious cause; they are, besides, prohibited to attend such dances if arranged by laymen. (March 31, 1916; A. A. S. 1916, p. 147; 1918, p. 17.)

5. *Military Service.* (Can. 141.) (Thomassin, o. c., P. III, L. I, c. 40, 45-47: O. Havard, Le Prêtre-Soldat dans l'Histoire, Paris, 1919.)

302. 1°. Early Christians looked with some distrust upon the profession of arms as scarcely compatible with the Christian calling, because of the superstitious obligations connected with it and also of the necessity it might place one in of shedding human blood. Some ecclesiastical writers positively condemned it (Tertullian, De Idol. c. 19, P. L., t. i., col. 768; Clement of Alexandria, Paedag. L. III, c. 11, P. G., t. viii, col. 625; Lactantius, Inst. Div., L. V, c. 18, P. L., t. vi, co., 604), but others, without denying its dangers, held it lawful in itself, and in practice many of the faithful must have adopted this view, since Tertullian himself could write, even though with some exaggeration, "we fill your camps, we man your fleets, and serve in your armies." (Apol., c. 37, 42.)

With the publication of the Milan Edict conditions changed and the chief objections no longer existed. (St. Augustine, Epist. 48, P. L., t. xxxiii, col. 186.) The Council of Arles (314, c. 3) pronounced anathema against those who threw down their arms in time of peace, probably alleging their Christian character as an excuse for evading the duties of citizenship. (Vacandard, Etudes de Critique et d'Histoire, 2e série, p. 129 ff; Smith, Dictionary, Military service.)

For clerics, military service always was prohibited. Such of them as engaged in warfare incurred excommunication. (Chalc. 451, c. 7; Tours, 461, c. 5.) Of St. Germain of Auxerre it is related that on one occasion he took command of the Briton troops and defeated the Picts and Scots, but the only weapons he used were prayer and praise. (Bede, H. E., i, 20.) We read of other holy prelates marching at the head of armies against barbarians or heretics, guiding and encouraging them. All, it is true, were not satisfied with giving moral assistance.

St. Gregory of Tours speaks of two who wore armor and slew many men with their own hands in battle (Hist. Franc., iv, 43), and St. Boniface, writing to Pope Zachary, asks his advice about certain Bishops who fought armed and shed blood; the answer came back: let them be deposed.

It was not apparently at this time an unusual thing to find large numbers of clerics and monks in the camps. Bede chronicles the slaughter in the year 613 of twelve hundred monks of Bangor who had assembled at Westchester to help the army of the Britons with their prayers. (ii, 2.) Charlemagne in one of his Capitularies (800, c. 91, 103) declares that, acting on the advice of the Pope, Bishops, and priests, he has resolved to amend his ways and not allow any longer in his armies more than two or three Bishops and a few priests, who will not bear arms but attend exclusively to the spiritual needs of the soldiers.

Bishops had, however, to contribute their share to the defence of the empire, which they did willingly (Cressy, 858, c. 6), with the Pope's approval, but soon they commenced again, perhaps at the request of the emperor, to accompany or lead their troops personally to battle and many of their clergy followed their example. (Vernon, 844, c. 8; Meaux, 845, c. 47.) Hincmar of Rheims writes to Pope Nicholas that he and his fellow Bishops can not attend a Synod because they must go with the king against the Britons and Normans, according to the custom of the kingdom. William the Conqueror had with him when he invaded England two Bishops and numerous clerics and monks. The Popes temporarily tolerated this practice and they had themselves to take part in not a few military expeditions. It was always understood that ecclesiastics should abstain from actually mingling in the fight (Rheims, 1049, c. 6; Coyac, 1050, c. 3), except possibly in cases of very grave public necessity (2, X, III, 49; Wernz, II, n. 225, iv), but the temptation proved too strong for some and these injunctions were occasionally violated on various pleas. (Baronius, an. 1010, n. 3.)

The Church obtained exemption from the obligations of supplying troops for the common defence, in the fourteenth century, in France and a little later in other countries; from this moment it became easier for the Roman Pontiffs to keep the clergy from following armies to the field.

303. 2°. The Code, maintaining the ancient discipline, forbids clerics to volunteer for military service or to enter the army of their own accord. Where they are compelled to do so by civil legislation they submit to necessity and they may, with the permission of their Ordinary, anticipate the period of service in order sooner to be free from military obligations.

It forbids them also to give assistance under whatever form in intestine or civil wars and in disturbances of the public order. In its original form this canon had "in intestine wars or political contentions"; the second clause was modified lest it should be concluded that the clergy may not have any share in the political or social activities of the country.

Clerics in minor Orders who, in violation of this law, freely and of their own authority join the army, forfeit by that very fact their clerical state.

6. *Commercial Trading.* (Can. 142.) (Decret. L. III, Tit. 50; Thomassin, P. III, L. III, c. 17-21; Wernz, II, n. 216 ff.; Maroto, n. 572.)

304. 1°. In ancient canonical texts the term

negotium, negotiatio is often used in the sense of trade in general and handicraft, as well as in the more restricted meaning of commercial trading; hence some uncertainty about the real import of a few enactments. It is clear, nevertheless, that whilst clerics, particularly those in minor Orders who might have a family to support, were allowed to work for a living at honorable trades or even to carry on a small business, Synods uniformly forbade them to engage in strictly commercial enterprises for filthy lucre's sake. (Statuta Ecclesiae Antiqua, 48-52; c. 1, 2, 9, 10, D. 88; c. 3, 4, D. 91.) The Council of Elvira (300, c. 19) warns Bishops, priests, and deacons not to leave their stations for the sake of trade and not to go around the provinces seeking lucrative markets. St. Jerome writes to Nepotian: "A clergyman who engages in business and rises from poverty to wealth avoid as you would the plague." (On Clerical Life.) After the fifth century prohibitions against trading become still more severe and absolute without excluding the possibility of exceptions in cases of necessity. (Tarragona, 516, c. 2; Orleans, 538, c. 27; Mayence, 813, c. 14; London, 1175, c. 10; Lateran, 1216, c. 15, 16; Cologne, 1260, c. 2; Arles, 1275, c. 14, 15; 1, X, III, 50; Trent, Sess. XXII, de Ref., c. 1.)

By the Const. *Ex debito* (Feb. 22, 1633) of Urban VIII and the Const. *Sollicitudo* (Jan. 17, 1639) of Clement XI, missionaries in the East Indies and in America who personally or through agents, in their name or that of their church, buy and sell for gain, even only once, incur an excommunication from which they can not be absolved till the acquired gain has been returned. Although the censure was not contained in the Const. *Apostolicae Sedis,* the Cong.

Prop. Fide declared in 1872 that it continued in force. (Collectanea, n. 351, 352.) According to some theologians it did not affect the native clergy or had gone into desuetude in the United States before the publication of the Code. (Putzer, Commentarium in Facultates Apostolicas, 1898, n. 140; Genicot, Theologiae Moralis Institutiones, 1902, II, n. 612; Sabetti, Theologia Moralis, 1898, n. 1015.)

305. 2°. Under the present discipline ecclesiastics are forbidden as before to engage in trading, personally or through others, whether for their own benefit or for that of others.

(*a*) Canonists distinguish various forms of trading: domestic trading, or buying supplies for one's own household and selling what may be left over with some profit; politic trading, *i.e.* buying supplies for a large community such as a town or an army and selling to individuals with or without profit; artificial lucrative trading, which consists in buying commodities and selling them at a higher price after they have been notably changed by personal or hired labor; lucrative trading strictly so called, which consists in buying commodities with the intention of selling them at a higher price without changing their nature.

Only trading proper comes under this law, that is, according to the common interpretation of canonists, lucrative trading strictly so called, *v.g.* dealing in stocks, and artificial lucrative trading when the change in the commodity has been obtained through paid labor, for example, buying material and having it manufactured by hired workmen. Politic trading is likewise forbidden, if not by this law, at least by the previous one, as an occupation foreign to the ecclesiastical state.

Buying commodities for consumption is not trading, nor selling the product of one's land or animals or industry.

(*b*) As the Church forbids clerics to trade through others, canonists have asked themselves whether this implies prohibition to invest in shares or stock of industrial or commercial companies. Several distinctions have been made and different answers given to the question. Without entering into the details of the controversy, it will suffice to say that the prohibition is at least doubtful, *dubio juris,* and therefore not binding.

In its original form, the present canon contained the positive statement that such prohibition did not exist, but the legislator has deemed it advisable to abstain from giving a formal decision, which under different circumstances might have to be modified.

It would not be lawful to hold stock if this meant joint responsibility in the administration of the society.

(*c*) Exceptions to this law are admitted in cases of necessity, if a cleric has no other way of supporting himself or his near relations than to engage in some honest business, but whenever possible permission should be obtained from the Holy See or at least from the Ordinary.

The same authorization may be granted for reasons of great utility, as when commercial transactions can not be interrupted without serious loss, *v.g.* in the case of a cleric inheriting a large store which he can not dispose of for some time.

306. 7. *Absence from the Diocese.* (Can. 143, 144.) 1°. The Council of Trent, renewing ancient prescriptions, decreed that only those clerics should be ordained whose services were necessary or useful to a certain church; to this church they would become attached and they should not leave it without the Ordinary's permission. (Sess. XXIII, c. 16, de Ref.)

At present, ecclesiastics when they are ordained do not necessarily receive a benefice or office and are not assigned to a special church, yet they become affiliated with a diocese and are placed under the authority of its Ordinary. They must remain at the disposition of this Ordinary and ready to render the services which may be asked of them. Therefore, they must habitually reside in the diocese, even if they have no office or benefice, and not leave it for a notable period of time without the consent, at least reasonably presumed, of their superior. This is particularly true of those who have been ordained *ad titulum servitii ecclesiae* or *Missionis,* but applies also to those ordained *ad titulum patrimonii.*

Two months would probably be a notable period of time for which a permission would be needed, unless custom or statutes rule otherwise. Presumed permission suffices, but there must be a reasonable foundation for the presumption. Generally, if the absence is to be a very long one, the Ordinary will expect to be notified if this can be done conveniently.

The Ordinary can evidently refuse the permission; he should not do so without reasonable cause, and he has to provide for the support of clerics whom he thus retains in his diocese.

307. 2°. An ecclesiastic who, with his Ordinary's permission, has gone into another diocese without losing affiliation with his own, may be called back for a just cause, but care should be taken that no undue hardship be imposed upon the cleric concerned or upon the diocese which received him.

An Ordinary may command an outside cleric to leave his diocese or refuse him permission to remain any longer, if he has a just reason to do so, unless he had conferred upon him a benefice, which act would imply permission to reside in the place until the benefice is lost.

TITLE IV

ON ECCLESIASTICAL OFFICES

(Can. 145-195.)

PRELIMINARY NOTIONS

308. 1. After ordination clerics are usually given some definite work to do in the diocese or functions to exercise; hence, after treating of the rights and obligations of the clergy in general, the Code naturally passes to the question of appointments to ecclesiastical offices.

Office, in canon law, is so closely related to benefice that some canonists consider them as one and the same thing under two different aspects, office designating directly a sacred function to which has been attached a perpetual right to a certain compensation, and benefice designating directly the right itself but indirectly also the spiritual function. Consequently, they often treat of office and benefice at the same time and generally under the heading benefice. There exists, however, a real difference between the two, and one may be found without the other, as in the case of a canonry to which no prebend is attached. This led some modern authors to distinguish them more carefully and to study them separately.

The legislator, following this plan, deals with ecclesiastical offices here in the book *De Personis* and in the section on clerics in general, leaving the question of benefices for the third book, *De Rebus;* a benefice is something in itself temporal. When an office has a benefice attached to it, as is frequently the case, it comes also under the laws which govern benefices. (Can. 146.) Likewise, much of what is said of erection, division, suppression, etc., of benefices applies at least indirectly to offices but more directly to benefices, and for this reason has been reserved for the third book.

Here we find only the general principles on acquisition and loss of offices.

309. 2. Nature of Ecclesiastical Offices. (Can. 145.) An ecclesiastical office, in the broad sense of the term, is defined as a function exercised for a spiritual end in conformity with canonical rules; thus we speak of the office of sacristan, chanter, chaplain, episcopal secretary, etc.

In the strict sense an ecclesiastical office is a function established by divine or ecclesiastical authority, permanent in character, to be conferred in the form prescribed by canons and implying some participation of ecclesiastical power either of Order or of jurisdiction. It supposes therefore:

(*a*) A function spiritual in its end, origin, or object.

(*b*) Divine or at least ecclesiastical institution. The episcopal office is of divine, the office of Metropolitan or Vicar-General of ecclesiastical, origin.

(*c*) Objective if not subjective perpetuity. The office itself must be of a permanent character and not established temporarily and to meet an accidental emergency. The understanding must be that when one holder loses it another one has to be appointed, provided the same conditions exist; the office of Vicar Capitular is perpetual in this conditional sense. Subjective perpetuity is not required and the holder may be removable, as is the case with the office of Vicar-General.

(*d*) Canonical provision. Appointment to an ecclesiastical office must be made in accordance with the laws of the Church.

(*e*) Ecclesiastical power either of Order or of jurisdiction, whether of the internal forum, as in the office of pastor and of canon penitentiary; or of the external forum, as in the office of Bishop.

In law the term office is taken in the strict sense, unless the contrary be evident from the context.

Chapter I

Appointment to Ecclesiastical Offices

(Can. 147-182.)

(Wernz, II, n. 284 ff.; Cavagnis, Institutiones Juris Publici Ecclesiastici, P. II; Thomassin, o. c., P. II, L. i, ii, iii; Maroto, n. 583 ff.)

GENERAL NOTIONS. (Can. 147-151.)

310. 1. *Nature.* Canonical appointment or canonical provision is defined as the conferring of an office, by the proper ecclesiastical authority, and in accordance with canonical prescriptions.

Three conditions are, then, required for a canonical provision: that a real office be conferred, that this be done by the proper authority, and that it be done in the manner prescribed by Church law.

Who has authority to appoint to the various ecclesiastical offices, what is prescribed as to the mode of appointment in each case, the qualifications of the appointee, and other conditions, will be explained in detail when treating of these offices in particular; here only general principles are given.

2. *Necessity.* No one can obtain an ecclesiastical office except by canonical appointment or provision.

In every society, the offices are distributed by those in whom the social powers are vested. In the Church, which is a complete and independent society, the appointment to offices must belong exclusively to the representatives of the ecclesiastical power and must be made in accordance with the laws laid down by the ecclesiastical authority.

This exclusive and independent power of the Church has been denied in practice, if not always in theory, by many civil rulers, who, at various times, have tried to interfere in ecclesiastical appointments, from the days of the Byzantine and German emperors to our own day. The Popes, whilst granting at times even to laymen some share in the choice of the candidates, have always maintained the exclusive right of the ecclesiastical authority to confer the offices, as we see, for example, in the quarrel about investitures in the eleventh and twelfth centuries.

311. 3. *Modes of Canonical Provision.* Appointment to ecclesiastical offices may be, according to the manner in which the candidates are designated and the offices conferred, by free collation, presentation or nomination and investiture, election and confirmation, postulation and acceptation, simple election followed by acceptation.

(*a*) It is by free collation or appointment when the ecclesiastical superior who confers the office has also the designation of the appointee.

(*b*) By presentation or nomination and investiture, when the candidate is presented by one having the right of patronage or nominated by a person to whom this privilege has been granted, as is done at times in concordats, and receives the investiture from the ecclesiastical superior.

(*c*) By election and confirmation, when the candidate is designated by the vote of an electoral body to whom this right belongs and confirmed by the proper superior, as when chapters elected Bishops who received confirmation from the Holy See.

(*d*) By postulation and acceptation, when electors ask for the appointment of a candidate whom they can not elect because of some canonical impediment and the superior who regularly confirms the election accedes to their request.

(*e*) By simple election, when no confirmation is necessary, as, for example, the election of the Pope or of superiors general of Religious Orders, which does not have to be confirmed but takes effect as soon as accepted.

In English-speaking countries appointment to nearly all secular offices is by free collation.

The Code deals with investiture in connection with benefices and the right of patronage (1448-1471); in this part it gives the general rules which govern free appointment, election, and postulation.

312. 4. *Conditions for Canonical Provision.* 1°. Fitness of the Appointee. A candidate who has been designated, by whomsoever it may be, for an ecclesiastical office, whether it was by election, postulation, presentation or nomination, must not be confirmed, admitted, or invested till he has been found qualified by his own Ordinary.

This rule is binding on all ecclesiastical superiors, the Pope alone excepted.

The Ordinary of the candidate pronounces on his fitness even though he may not be the one who makes the appointment, unless the appointment be made by the Holy See.

He ascertains the fitness of the candidate by means of an examination if the law calls for one in the case or the nature of the office demands it; otherwise he may form his judgment in the manner which he deems best.

313. 2°. Vacancy of the Office. An office is vacant *de jure* when no one has a legal title to it, even though an intruder may be in actual possession of it. Offices become vacant by resignation, privation, removal, transfer, lapse of time, or death of the holder. (Can. 183.)

An office is vacant *de facto* when no one actually fills it although some one may have a legal claim to it, *v.g.* a see from which the legitimate Bishop is exiled. It is vacant both *de facto* and *de jure* if no one holds it or claims it.

(*a*) Appointment to an office not vacant *de jure* is null and void and it remains null even if the vacancy occurs afterwards.

Nor has the promise of an office not vacant any juridical effect, whoever may have made it and in whatever form.

Those appointments or promises have been reproved from the beginning as liable to become the source of abuses, yet exceptions were permitted under the form of coadjutorships with right of succession or of *gratiae expectativae.* In the latter Middle Ages principally the Popes not infrequently granted to ecclesiastics letters or rescripts declaring that the bearer was entitled to a benefice as soon as one would become vacant. This practice caused much dissatisfaction against the Roman Court, and Alexander III decreed its suppression (Lateran, 1179; 2, X, III,

8), as did afterwards Boniface VIII (2, 3, III, 7, in Sexto), and again the Council of Trent (Sess. XXIV, de Ref., c. 19; XXV, c. 7, 21), but abuses continued until the Revolution of the eighteenth century.

Boniface VIII forbade the promises of benefices not vacant, whether determined or undetermined, and likewise promises of the first vacant benefice or even general promises to appoint to a benefice at the first opportunity when none is vacant at the time. The present law is also absolute, without, however, going into the same details in regard to promises.

The Council of Trent allowed some exceptions and reserved the right of the Pope; the present Code mentions no exception or reservation, but the Pope can always dispense from an ecclesiastical law.

The prohibition is under pain of nullity and, therefore, no coadjutor with right of succession can validly be appointed to any office except by the Holy See.

(*b*) Appointment to an office vacant by right, although not in fact because an illegitimate possessor holds it, is valid and lawful on two conditions: the *de facto* possession must be juridically declared illegitimate and mention of this must be made in the letter of appointment.

ARTICLE I

ON FREE APPOINTMENT OR COLLATION.

(Can. 152-159.)

Although the provisions of this article concern directly free appointments, most of them are formulated in general terms and apply to all forms of appointments; the context shows when they must be understood in a more restricted sense.

314. 1. *Notion of Free Collation.* Appointments

are said to be canonically free when the superior who confers the offices designates also the candidates, even though he may have to choose among the candidates approved in a concursus or recommended by a third party, provided some choice be left to him; they are likewise considered as free although they may need approval or ratification.

2. *Power of Ordinaries to Make Appointments.* The Ordinary of the place, Bishop, Abbot, or Prelate Nullius, Vicar and Prefect Apostolic, is presumed to have power to make all canonical appointments in his territory unless in particular cases there be some proof that his authority has been restricted. Common law reserves to the Pope the appointment to dignities in cathedral or collegiate churches, to benefices which have been left vacant by Roman prelates or monsignors, etc. (Can. 396, 1435); he may reserve other appointments to himself for special reasons. Private persons may possess the right of presentation to certain offices and benefices, but all these are only exceptions not to be admitted without proof; regularly the Ordinary of the place appoints freely to all secular offices in his territory.

What is said here of local Ordinaries does not necessarily apply to Administrators Apostolic (Can. 315) nor to Coadjutor Bishops. (Can. 351.) The powers of a Vicar Capitular or Administrator during the vacancy of the see are limited in many respects. (Can. 445, 455.)

Vicars-General can not appoint to ecclesiastical offices without special mandate.

315. 3. *Qualifications of Appointees.* 1°. No one is eligible for an ecclesiastical office, by common law, unless he be a cleric, as clerics alone can possess power of Order or of jurisdiction in the Church.

(Can. 118, 145.) The Pope could make exceptions to this rule, but no other superior.

2°. The priesthood is required generally for all offices which imply care of souls in the external or the internal forum and specifically for the office of Cardinal (Can. 232), Bishop (Can. 331), Abbot or Prelate Nullius (Can. 320), Vicar Capitular (Can. 434), Vicar-General (Can. 367), Synodal Judge (Can. 1574), Vicar Forane (Can. 445), diocesan consultor (Can. 423), pastor, (Can. 453), rector of a church (Can. 479), and a few others. Appointment of one who is not a priest to any office to which is attached the care of souls would be null. (Can. 154, 434, 453.) This sanctions a change introduced by almost universal practice in the ancient legislation.

3°. Appointees must possess, besides, all the qualifications required for each individual office by common or particular law or by the law of foundation. The Code enumerates the qualifications demanded by common law when dealing with the various offices. They pertain to the age of candidates, their learning, virtue, freedom from censures, disabilities, etc.

4°. Nor does it suffice to choose for an ecclesiastical office one who has all the necessary qualifications; the Church commands to give the preference to the one who, all things being taken into account, possesses them in the highest degree, and to avoid acception of persons, that is, not to be influenced in such choices by considerations which have nothing to do with the fitness of the candidate, *v.g.* relationship, friendship, etc. Passing over a worthier candidate would not, however, as long as the appointee be really worthy, render the appointment null *ipso facto,* nor even rescindable, at least as a general rule and more probably. It is explicitly enacted that confirmation or investiture can not be refused to one duly elected or presented provided he be found worthy, *idoneus.* (Can. 177, 1466.)

5°. Some qualifications are demanded, by general or particular law or by the law of foundation, for the validity of the appointment. Those for which this is not specified are simply conditions for lawfulness and their absence would not render the appointment null but only rescindable. It may be annulled by sentence of the legitimate superior.

316. 4. *Time of Appointment.* (Can. 155.) In some cases the law fixes a special period of time within which certain offices ought to be filled. Patrons have four months to present their candidates (Can. 1457) and two more months are allowed for the investiture. (Can. 1467.) Elections must be made within three months.

When there is no time determined by special ordinance six months may be taken to make the appointment but not more. These six months are reckoned from the day knowledge of the vacancy has been obtained. The law calls them *menses utiles,* which implies that they do not run if the superior is prevented from exercising his right. (Can. 35.) In accordance with the prescriptions of Canon 34, § 3, they should be taken as they stand in the calendar, not counting the first day.

The Code authorizes Ordinaries to take a longer time for appointments to pastorates if in their estimation circumstances of places and persons render this course advisable. (Can. 458.)

An appointment which has not been made in due time passes by way of devolution to a higher authority. (Can. 161, 178, 274, 1°, 432, § 2.)

317. 5. *Incompatible Offices.* (Can. 156.) 1°. Notion. Canon law holds incompatible offices the duties of which can not ordinarily be properly discharged by a single person, because, for example, each one requires residence or the presence of the holder in a distinct place, or his whole attention and time. Thus the legislator explicitly declares that a Bishop should not have two dioceses to rule (Can. 394) or a pastor two parishes (Can. 460); that the same ecclesiastic should not have two residential benefices, or the offices of Vicar-General and of Canon Penitentiary or pastor (Can. 367, 3), of judge and notary in the same cause. (Can. 1585.)

The objection of incompatibility would not exist if one of the offices was held only temporarily, as if a Bishop or pastor had the administration of a second diocese or parish only for a time; nor if the two offices have been permanently united. Benefices are incompatible when one suffices for the support of the holder. (Maroto, n. 595.)

318. 2°. Former legislation. The Church began to legislate against the abuses of the plurality or cumulation of offices as early as the Council of Chalcedon. (451, c. 10; Thomassin, o. c., P. II, L. 3.) Relatively rare in the fifth century, these abuses became more frequent with the organization of benefices, in the sixth and seventh centuries, still more so in the eleventh and then again at the time of the Great Schism. They continued in spite of the decrees enacted against them by Popes and Councils, particularly by St. Gregory VII, Alexander III (Lateran, 1179, c. 13), Innocent III (Lateran, 1215, c. 29), Boniface VIII, John XXII, the Council of Trent (Sess. VII, de Ref., c. 4, 5, Sess. XXIV, de Ref., c. 17), Urban VIII, and Clement XI, (Wernz, II.

n. 317 ff.) In modern times they have been much rarer, since the spoliation of ecclesiastical benefices at the end of the eighteenth century.

319. 3°. The present law renews the ancient prohibitions, absolutely forbidding the conferring upon the same person of two incompatible benefices; it does not, like the fourth Lateran Council, mention the possibility of an exception in favor of the *sublimes et litteratae personae,* without, however, excluding it.

A cleric loses *ipso facto* the offices he holds if he accepts and obtains pacific or uncontested possession of another which is incompatible with the former (Can. 188); if he attempts to retain the former also he loses both. (Can. 2396.)

The Holy See can dispense from this law, but the intention of doing so must not be admitted without proof. Should the Pope confer an office upon a cleric who holds one incompatible with it the appointment would be considered as due to a mistake and therefore null, unless in asking for the second office the petitioner mentioned the one he had already, or unless in the appointment such derogatory clauses are used as to manifest the intention of making an exception to the general rule; it must, then, be clear that the Holy See intends to confer on the same cleric two incompatible offices or that it is willing to confer upon him a certain office even if he had already another regularly incompatible with it.

6. *Exclusion of Relations from Certain Appointments.* (Can. 157.)

320. 1°. In their desire to confer on their relations or friends offices the appointment to which is in their power, ecclesiastical superiors have been tempted at times too readily to accept the resignation of the actual incumbent or to pronounce sentences of privation without sufficient cause. At other times it was the incumbent himself who would volunteer to resign with the implicit or explicit understanding that the office would go to his own relations or friends. These practices savored of favoritism or nepotism, even if they did not contain formal injustice, and they tended to introduce hereditary succession in ecclesiastical benefices; several Popes condemned them, particularly Pius IV (*Cupientes,* Oct. 11, 1560, § 1) and Pius V (*Quanta Ecclesiae,* Ap. 1, 1568, § 5.)

2°. The Code confirms substantially their rulings and enacts that when an office becomes vacant by resignation or a sentence of privation the superior who accepted the resignation or pronounced the sentence of privation can not validly confer that office on his own relations by blood or marriage to the second degree inclusively nor on his familiars. He can not confer it either on the relations or familiars of the person who resigned it.

In order that the law may apply, the office must have become vacant in one of the two ways specified in this canon. The prohibition concerns the Ordinary who accepted the resignation or pronounced privation, not others.

It deals with appointment proper, not, *v.g.* presentation or election, and the persons excluded are the Ordinary's relations whether by blood or by marriage to the second degree, not beyond, and his familiars, as also the relations in the same degree and the familiars of the person who resigned the office; there is no mention here of the one who was deprived of it.

By familiars of the Ordinary canonists generally

understand persons who live with, serve, and are supported by, him.

Appointments made in violation of this law would be invalid.

321. 7. *Appointments by Way of Devolution.* (Can. 158.) When the superior who regularly should appoint to an office is unable or neglects to do so, his right passes by devolution to higher authority. Thus the Metropolitan supplements the inability or negligence of the chapter in the election of a Vicar Capitular (Can. 274, 3; 432, 2) and the Holy See that of local Ordinaries who leave benefices vacant for more than six months. (Can. 1432, 3.)

But the law explicitly declares that by this act the extraordinary appointer does not acquire any new power over the appointee and that the latter's juridical status, his right and obligations, remain the same as if he had received his office in the ordinary way.

322. 8. *Written Record of Appointments.* (Can. 159.) Appointments to ecclesiastical offices may be made orally, but a record of them must be kept in writing in order to have an authentic proof of the transaction when needed; for example, when a Bishop takes possession of his diocese he must present the Apostolic letters. (Can. 334, § 3.)

Neglect of the formality prescribed by this canon would not invalidate the appointment.

ARTICLE II

ON ELECTION. (Can. 160-178.)

(Decret. L. I, Tit. vi, De Electione et Electi Potestate; Wernz, II, n. 352 ff.; Ojetti, Synopsis Rerum Moralium et Juris Pontificii, Electio; Thomassin, o. c., P. II, L. II; The Catholic Encyclopedia, Election; Dictionnaire de Théologie Catholique, Elections; Maroto, o. c., n. 607 ff.; Blat, o. c., p. 39 ff.)

323. 1. *General Notions.* 1°. To elect, in general, means to choose; in a juridical sense election implies designation of one person for a certain office or function, whatever be the manner of proceeding, whether it be by election proper or by postulation, presentation, nomination, recommendation, petition, or free collation.

In the strict sense, a canonical election, as distinct from other modes of appointment to offices, is the canonical calling of a fit person to a vacant ecclesiastical office or benefice, by the votes of the lawful electors.

2°. The successors of St. Peter have always been designated by election; the same method prevailed for a long time in the appointment of Bishops. Under decretal law they were elected by cathedral chapters; hence, in the *Corpus Juris,* the importance of the title, *De Electione et Electi Potestate,* which concerned chiefly episcopal elections, and the detailed commentaries given of it by ancient canonists. In the fourteenth century chapters lost their prerogative and the appointment of Bishops became, by the second Rule of the Apostolic Chancery, one of the major matters reserved by the Holy See.

Under the present discipline it is by election, ordinarily, that superiors or dignitaries are appointed in Religious Orders or communities, both of men and of women, in cathedral and collegiate chapters; in confraternities and various associations approved by ecclesiastical authority. (Can. 506, 507, 715.) Vicars Capitular are elected by chapters (Can. 432); in the United States it is the diocesan consultors, provided they be five or six in number, who elect the Administrator during the vacancy of the see. (Consist. Cong., Feb. 22, 1919.) Some form of election is required also for the appointment of synodal examiners and parish priest consultors (Can. 385, 386), and of synodal judges. (Can. 1574.)

3°. The Const. *Vacante Sede Apostolica* (Dec. 25, 1904) defines the manner of proceeding in the election of the Pope. Other ecclesiastical elections are governed by the rules laid down in this title. Should there exist, in regard to certain offices, special statutes enacted by legitimate authority, they must be observed also.

324. 2. *Time Allowed for Elections.* (Can. 161.) An electoral college has three months to fill a vacancy, unless ruled otherwise by special provision (Can. 432) or particular statutes; thus the election of a Vicar Capitular must be made within eight days whilst in Religious Orders some offices may be permitted to remain vacant for a half year.

The time is *tempus utile* in the sense explained above and does not run while not usable; it is computed from the day the vacancy becomes known.

If the election is not made within the time prescribed the electors lose their prerogative and the appointment to the office devolves upon the superior who regularly would confirm the election or the one whom law empowers to supply the negligence or incapacity of the college. The Metropolitan appoints the Vicar Capitular when the chapter fails to elect one in due time. (Can. 432.)

325. 3. *Convocation of Electors.* (Can. 162.) 1°. Particular constitutions or customs often determine the superior who is to issue the summons as well as the precise time, the place and other circumstances of the election; in the absence of such special rulings this is done by the head of the collegiate body or by the highest dignitary. He chooses a suitable place and fixes the day, hour, and other details of the proceedings, allowing reasonable time for all to come.

2°. Law may demand in some cases that each elector be summoned personally; even then it is enough to send the letter of convocation to the person's place of domicile, quasi-domicile, or actual residence.

When the summons does not have to be personal it may be served by way of general edict and inserted in the official paper, or posted in some public place, or made known in some other effective way.

3°. All who have a right to vote must be convoked; ancient canonists added, provided they can conveniently come, but no such restriction is expressed or implied in the present law, and as long as an elector can be reached, morally speaking, he should be invited, leaving it to his discretion to accept the invitation or decline it.

Should one of the electors be overlooked or not called in due time and consequently not take part in the proceedings, his absence would not *ipso facto* nullify the election, but he would have the right to ask that it be annulled, and the superior could not refuse to do so, even should the election have been already confirmed, if the omission of invitation and consequent absence were proved, provided he would put in his claim within three days from the moment he heard of the election. It must be juridically established that he sent his petition within that period of time although it may have reached the superior later.

If more than one third of the electors were thus neglected and deprived of their right to vote, the election would be invalid *ipso facto* and subsequent approval by the injured persons would not give value to it. But in this case also, if the uninvited electors do come and exercise their right the mere omission of convocation has no juridical effect on the election.

4°. Electors should be convoked soon after the vacancy of the office to be filled, so that they may complete the election before the time allowed for it elapses. The election may be held or at least prepared for before the vacancy occurs when the tenure of the office is only temporary; but if the incumbent was appointed for life convocation of electors before the vacancy would be without juridical effect.

326. 4. *Actual Electors.* (Can. 163, 164, 168.) All the formalities of convocation having been duly complied with, the proceedings for the election may begin on the appointed day and hour; there is no obligation of waiting for the electors who have not yet come even if it be without any fault of their own. Those will take actual part in the election who fulfill the following conditions:

1°. Personal presence. (*a*) The Code explicitly excludes voting by letter and also voting by proxy, which had been forbidden by the Council of Trent (Sess. XXV, de Reg., c. 6) in the elections of regulars. The Holy See may permit exceptions to this general rule, by way of particular law, statute, or privilege, not inferior legislators. Contrary customs are not expressly reproved and can therefore be retained or introduced on the usual conditions (Can. 5); contrary laws have been abrogated. (Can. 6, 1°.)

The right of election belongs to the electors present exclusively, even if they are only a small minority; strictly speaking one would suffice by common law, but particular statutes often require more.

(*b*) An elector actually present in the house but unable on account of sickness to repair to the room or hall in which the election is held remains nevertheless entitled to his vote; the tellers go and get it from him in writing. He is considered as equivalently present, but to benefit by this concession of the legislator he must be present in the building itself, not merely in the neighborhood and prevented from joining the other electors by the condition of his health, as distinctly specified, not by other causes.

(*c*) Should one of the electors present be personally entitled to a vote on a twofold ground, *v.g.* as irremovable rector and as diocesan consultor, he would not for that reason have two votes; but if he served as proxy in cases in which it may be permitted he would have the right to cast two votes, one in his own name and the other in the name of the person whom he represents.

327. 2°. Membership in the moral body or college which has the right of election. In a chapter all the canons usually enjoy the right of voting, but in religious communities and other societies all the members do not necessarily take part in elections; particular legislation determines which belong to the electoral body.

Formerly the regular electors had authority, provided every one consented, to admit an outsider, once in passing, to share in their prerogative; outsiders could acquire the right of voting by custom and prescription or be given it in the law of foundation.

Under the present discipline an election would be null *ipso facto* if one who is not a member of the electoral college was allowed to take part in it. Previously acquired privileges are not abrogated, however, but for the future the Holy See alone can grant new ones, and they will not be obtained by custom which can be but a series of invalid acts.

3°. Freedom from legal disabilities. To exercise their right electors must be in a condition to elicit a juridical act; natural and ecclesiastical law exclude several classes of persons:

(*a*) All who do not possess the use of reason, whatever be the cause, *v.g.* infants, the demented, etc.

(*b*) Children under the age of puberty, *i.e.* girls under twelve and boys under fourteen.

(*c*) Persons under censure, *i.e.* under excommunication, suspension, or personal interdict; those who have incurred the *infamia juris* or loss of good name pronounced by law against certain offences. (Can. 2293; Penal Legislation, n. 161 ff.) Censure and infamy produce this effect only when they have been inflicted by sentence of the judge, condemnatory or declaratory.

(*d*) Those who have become affiliated with a heretical or schismatical sect either by enrolling their names on the official books of the sect or making public profession, in word or deed, of allegiance to it.

(*e*) Electors who have been deprived of "active voice" or right of voting, either by sentence of the judge or by law, general or particular, which attaches this penalty to certain offences, *v.g.* to simony. (Can. 2392, 2°.)

If any one of these persons is admitted to take part in the election, his vote is null and void, but the election itself is not invalid except in two cases: when it is certain that this vote completed the majority which would not have been obtained without it, and when the electors have knowingly admitted one excommunicated by condemnatory or declaratory sentence.

5. *Conditions for the Validity of Votes.* (Can. 166, 169, 170.)

328. 1°. Exclusion of all lay interference. The mere material presence of a layman would not vitiate an ecclesiastical election, but what the Church does not tolerate is the intervention, under whatever form, of lay persons, particularly of civil authorities, in violation of its right to complete independence in these matters; thus an election would be invalid if lay persons would assume direction of it, act as presiding officers, tellers, secretaries; use threats, importunities, promises, deceit, etc., to influence the votes. (Maroto, n. 655.)

2°. Freedom. Absolute violence and substantial error take away all freedom and hence render a vote null by the very law of nature. It is pronounced null by canon law when the elector is compelled by grave fear or deceit, directly or indirectly, to choose a certain candidate or one of several, *v.g.* one of three presented to him, James, Peter, or Artemon.

The fear must be grave and the deceit real; they must have a determining effect on the vote, whether this had been intended or not. Want of freedom due to other causes than the ones mentioned here would not render canonically void a naturally valid vote.

329. 3°. Required Form. Ecclesiastical law demands that the vote be:

(*a*) Secret. In order to secure greater independence and remove occasions of intrigue, partisanship, and other disorders, none of the electors should know for whom the others are voting. A vote which becomes known is null by the very fact. This condition of strict secrecy concerns only the act of voting;

a person is free to announce beforehand whom he intends to favor and he may make it known afterwards without losing his vote. However, the Council of Trent (Sess. XXV, c. 6), prescribing secrecy in the elections of regulars, commanded that it be maintained even after the publication of the results, and this would seem to be the intention of the present legislator, who orders the immediate burning of the ballots.

(*b*) Certain. There must not be any doubt as to the candidate voted for.

(*c*) Determined. Alternative suffrages are null, as if one said I vote for Andrew or for James; the choice must be made by the elector himself and not left to others.

(*d*) Absolute. The vote must not be conditional nor should special obligations be imposed on the candidate, his powers restricted, etc. These conditions or stipulations do not, however, endanger the validity of the vote, unless they constitute extrinsic additions; for if they are implied in the vote itself or contained in the law they have no real effect, as, *v.g.* voting for N. on condition that he is eligible or with the understanding that he will ask for confirmation in due time. They must, moreover, be attached to the vote itself; those which precede the election are considered as non-existing and no obligation arises from them.

(*e*) A special condition for the validity of a vote in ecclesiastical elections is that it be not cast for the voter himself.

330. 6. *The Scrutiny or Balloting.* (Can. 171; 42, X, I, 6.) 1°. Appointment of scrutators or tellers. In an election by scrutiny at least two tellers are required to collect or receive the votes. They must be appointed immediately before the election unless they be designated beforehand by particular statutes, which would *v.g.* reserve that office to the senior or to the junior member of the college. They are chosen by secret ballot and taken from the college itself, unless a special provision of the law or particular constitutions call for outsiders. (Can. 506, 2.) The tellers and the presiding officer, if he is one of the electors, promise under oath to discharge their duty faithfully and keep the proceedings secret, even after the election.

2°. Voting. There are various ways in which electors may manifest their will, by word of mouth or in writing, by printed ballot or manuscript notes. At present the printed ballot is generally preferred, but regard should be had to particular rules or customs.

Whatever be the system adopted, the tellers must see that the votes remain secret, that they be cast with proper diligence, one after the other, not several at the same time, in the order of precedence.

331. 3°. Counting and examination of the votes. When all the votes have been collected the tellers count them in presence of the presiding officer in the manner prescribed by the constitutions of the college or by custom, and compare the number of the ballots with that of the voters.

Should the ballots prove more numerous than the electors there is no need of going any further, the election is null and must be begun over again. Nothing is said of the case in which the votes cast would be fewer than the electors; this would be taken to show that some of the latter have renounced their privilege, which under the present law is ordinarily not forbidden and would not affect the value of the proceedings, although ancient canonists found in it another cause for nullity.

After counting the ballots the tellers examine them and announce the results, stating how many votes each candidate received.

4°. Burning of the ballots. After each scrutiny or after each session, if there have been several scrutinies in one session, the ballots must be burned, not simply thrown away or torn, in order by this complete destruction to protect more effectively the secrecy of the vote. The same rule applies to any written note or document containing the same indications as the ballots.

5°. Written record of the proceedings. A complete account of the election must be accurately written down by the acting secretary, signed at least by the secretary himself, the presiding officer, and the tellers, and preserved carefully in the archives of the college.

332. 7. *Compromise.* (Can. 172, 173.) 1°. Nature and lawfulness. The common law authorizes electors, except in cases for which there exist special legitimate provisions to the contrary, to transfer their right of electing to one or several persons called *compromissarii,* who, for that time, not habitually, act in the name and place of the college; but, in accordance with the principle that what touches all the members of a corporate body individually must be approved by all (Can. 101, 2°), the consent given by the electors to this transaction or compromise must be unanimous. It must, moreover, be expressed in writing to avoid misunderstandings and uncertainties and remove possible occasions for future disputes. Unanimity, however, is demanded only on the compromise itself; its accidental circumstances may be decided by the usual majority of votes, *v.g.* that the *compromissarii* must act within a week, that they must elect one of the chapter, etc.

333. 2°. The *Compromissarii.* There may be one or several of them; they may be taken from the college or outside, provided they possess the proper qualifications for the office. *Compromissarii* for a clerical college must have the sacerdotal character. The Code contains no prescriptions on the mode of appointment.

3°. Scope of Compromise. (*a*) Various conditions may be attached to a compromise; as long as they do not contravene the common law they must, for the validity of the election, be observed faithfully. Those which militate against the law are not taken into account. In the absence of any condition the *compromissarii* follow the general legal enactments on elections.

(*b*) To the *compromissarii* always applies the rule that no candidate can be elected by his own suffrage; hence if there is only one *compromissarius* he cannot be elected; if several, they can choose one of their number but none can accede to the votes cast for himself or add his own vote to those given him by the others and be thereby elected. The present law seems stricter on this point than the former one. (33, X, I, 6.)

4°. Cessation of Compromise. The compromise ceases and the right of electing returns to the college in three ways:

(*a*) By recall. Electors can withdraw their consent to a compromise when they choose, provided the latter has not yet taken effect and it takes effect legally at the moment the *compromissarii* commence to treat formally of the person to be elected.

(*b*) By non-fulfilment of conditions, whether through the fault of the *compromissarii* or not, as if they failed, for whatever reason, to make the election within the set time, or did not proceed in the manner stipulated, or elected a candidate devoid of qualifications demanded by law or by the college.

(*c*) By completion of the election, whether valid, accepted by the candidate, confirmed by the superior, or not.

In all these cases the right of election does not, under the present law, devolve on the superior, but returns to the original electors, unless they had all approved the irregularities which rendered the election null, or the time allowed for it by the common law had elapsed.

334. 8. *Proclamation of the Election.* (Can. 174.) The presiding officer proclaims elected the candidate who has obtained the required number of suffrages. This ordinarily means, in accordance with the rule laid down in Canon 101, the candidate who in the first or second ballot has received the absolute majority of votes, *i.e.* one more than half of the votes validly cast; in the third ballot, when it is necessary, the relative majority suffices. Should then the votes be even and no relative majority obtained by any one, the president has the deciding vote; if he does not wish to use it, he declares elected the candidate who is senior in ordination, religious profession, or age.

335. 9. *Notification and Acceptance of Election.* (Can. 175, 176.) 1°. The result of the election should be communicated as soon as possible, morally speaking, to the person concerned, who has eight days after receiving the information directly and on reliable authority to decide whether he accepts or not. Should he fail, without legitimate excuse, to send his answer within the fixed time he forfeits the right acquired by election.

2°. If after receiving official notice of his election, he freely and deliberately refuses, whatever right had been conferred upon him by the action of the electors is irrevocably lost. He can not withdraw his refusal, at least not after it has reached the superior. The electors have to proceed to a new election, for which a month is given them by law, to be reckoned from the day the refusal becomes known to them. Nothing forbids them to elect the same candidate again.

3°. If the person elected accepts, he acquires at once a full right to the office in cases in which no confirmation is necessary; he may have to take possession before he can exercise its functions. When confirmation is required, he obtains a *jus ad rem*, the right to be appointed, but the appointment is not yet complete and he must meanwhile abstain from any interference in the spiritual or temporal administration of the office; his acts would be invalid and he would expose himself to severe punishments. (Can. 2394.)

336. 10. *Confirmation of Election.* When elections to secular ecclesiastical offices have to be confirmed this is usually done by the Pope, whom canonical laws can not strictly bind. In religious communities elections of local superiors often need confirmation, and it is to these that the following rules apply principally in practice under the present discipline.

1°. When required, confirmation is an essential

condition for the validity of the appointment. It must be asked for within eight days from the time the election was accepted under pain of losing all rights to the office, unless it be proved that there has been no negligence or malice.

2°. The confirmation must be given in writing and by the competent superior, which means the immediate superior, unless law or particular statute provides otherwise; thus the Pope, not the Metropolitan, confirms the elections of Bishops, wherever they exist, and of Prelates Nullius.

3°. Before ratifying the election the superior may and even should ascertain, in the manner he deems best, the fitness of the candidate for the office; if he finds in him the required qualifications he can not refuse confirmation. The decision should be announced without unnecessary delay.

4°. Once confirmed, the person elected has a full right to the office, unless some further formality be demanded by special law or statute.

If confirmation is refused, the right of electing returns to the electors, except when, on account of irregularities in the proceedings, it is taken from them and goes to the superior by devolution.

337. 11. *Devolution of Election.* Electors lose their right and it devolves on their superior chiefly in two cases: when the election has not been made within the allotted time through negligence or fraud, and when it has been made in an illegal manner, for example, if essential formalities were omitted or an unfit candidate chosen. The superior who would confirm the election or the one empowered to supply the negligence of the electors has then the free appointment to the office.

ARTICLE III

ON POSTULATION. (Can. 179-182.)

338. 1. *Nature.* Postulation in the strict canonical sense is a way of designating candidates for ecclesiastical offices which law permits in some cases as a substitute for election. It may happen that the candidate whom the electors consider as best qualified and whom therefore they wish to see appointed is afflicted with some impediment; they can not elect him but, if the impediment is one of those from which the Church can and does usually dispense, they are authorized to postulate him, that is, they may ask the competent superior to dispense and appoint him. This remains, however, an exceptional procedure and must be used exclusively in the cases here specified. For the same reason *compromissarii* can not have recourse to postulation unless explicitly empowered to do so.

2. *Rules for Postulation.* They are substantially the same as for election, and what has been said of one practically applies to the other with a few differences implied in the nature of the act or indicated here.

(*a*) The candidate is designated by the suffrages of the electors and the vote must have the same qualities as in elections. It may be by scrutiny or by compromise.

(*b*) When all the electors agree on proceeding by way of postulation and the contest is only about the candidate to be postulated, the usual majority, absolute or relative, decides. But when the question is between election and postulation, between candidates who can be elected and others who must be postulated, law naturally favors election, and the postulation to carry needs two-thirds of the votes.

(*c*) In the ballot the intention of postulating as distinct from electing must be clearly manifested, by using the word *postulo* or a similar one. Uncertainty as to the meaning of the vote would render it null. The Code admits the formula *eligo vel postulo,* which ancient canonists generally excluded; it may prudently be used in cases of doubt about the canonical freedom of the candidate and will serve for postulation or election according as the impediment really exists or not. *Postulo eligendo* or *eligo postulando* would express no definite intention and therefore have no effect.

339. 3. *Presentation of Postulation.* (*a*). The postulation must be presented within eight days to the competent superior, that is, to the one who should confirm the election, provided he possesses power to dispense from the impediment, otherwise it is sent to the Roman Pontiff or to another superior having this power, *v.g.* to an Apostolic Delegate. The superior who regularly should confirm the election loses his prerogative in such cases.

(*b*) If the postulation has not at least been sent to the superior within the eight days, it becomes null and void, and the electors are deprived of the right of electing or postulating for this time, unless they can prove that the delay was due to no negligence or malice on their part but to a just impediment.

(*c*) Once the postulation has come into the hands of the superior, out of regard for him the electors must not withdraw it; they could have done so before without injury to any one.

4. *Adoption or Rejection of Postulation.* (*a*) Postulation does not confer any right on the person who is postulated; on the part of the electors it is a petition for a favor. The superior is not bound

in justice to admit it, but accidentally he might have some obligation of doing so, if, *v.g.* regard for the reputation of the person concerned demanded it or the good of the community. As in the confirmation of election, he should give his decision without unnecessary delay, in writing, etc.

(*b*) When he rejects the postulation, the right of electing goes back to the college, unless the electors be guilty of knowingly asking for dispensation from an impediment over which the Church can not or does not exercise its authority, for, as a punishment, they then lose their prerogative and the superior makes the appointment without their intervention; not necessarily the superior who has rejected the postulation, but rather the one who regularly confirms the election or supplies the negligence of the electors, if he be not the same.

(*c*) If the superior admits the postulation, this should be made known to the postulated person, who must within eight days, as in the case of election, decide and declare whether he accepts or not.

The moment he accepts, the appointment is complete and he acquires full right to the office.

Chapter II

Loss of Ecclesiastical Offices

(Can. 183-195.)

340. Ecclesiastical offices become vacant by the death of the incumbent, which does not include what is at times considered as civil death, *v.g.* exile, imprisonment, perpetual infirmity, etc.

They are lost by lapse of time at the end of the period for which they were conferred when the appointment is a temporary one, as, for example, the office of diocesan consultor at the end of three (Can. 426), that of synodal examiner or parish priest consultor at the end of ten years. (Can. 387.)

In some cases loss of office may result from loss of authority by the superior who appointed to it. This occurs when the law so provides, as does the one which enacts that the powers of a Vicar-General cease with his Bishop's (Can. 371); or when the superior has made the appointment to depend on his own good pleasure by the clause *ad beneplacitum nostrum,* or an equivalent one. Canonists remark that the clause *ad beneplacitum Sanctae Sedis* does not have that effect, because the Holy See never dies. Regularly, however, the appointee retains his office independently of the appointing superior's continuation in authority.

More usual and more complicated is the loss of office by resignation, privation, removal, or transfer; of these, therefore, the Code treats with greater detail.

I. RESIGNATION. (Can. 185-191.)

341. The Church leaves every one free to accept or refuse ecclesiastical offices when offered and likewise to resign them after they have been accepted or held for some time, save in a few cases when, for special reasons, general or particular law forbids resignation. Thus a cleric in sacred Orders can not renounce the benefice he needs for his own support nor consequently the office connected with it. (Can. 1484, 1485.) In the absence of any such special provision the rule holds and applies to all offices, the lowest and the highest, not excepting the Supreme Pontificate. (Can. 221.) Some conditions are required and formalities prescribed.

1. *Conditions for Resignation.* (*a*) By the law of nature itself a person, in order to be capable of giving up one of his rights and resigning an office, must be in possession of his faculties and in a condition to perform a human act.

(*b*) Canonical law demands, besides, that he be free from unjust and grave fear as also from substantial error or deceit.

(*c*) He must have a just cause for resigning and one proportioned to the importance of the office and the closeness of the bond uniting him to it. The Decretals (10, X, I, 9) and Pius V (Const. *Quanta Ecclesia,* Ap. 1, 1568) give as valid reasons for resigning the episcopal office: old age, sickness, consciousness of a crime, hatred of the people, entrance into a Religious Order.

(*d*) Any simoniacal pact connected with a resignation would render it null and void.

342. 2. *Form.* To be valid, a resignation must be handed in by the person concerned personally or through a procurator specially commissioned to act in his name.

It must be presented in writing, or if presented verbally it must have two witnesses.

A record of the resignation should be preserved in the archives of the Curia for future reference, but evidently not as condition for the validity of the act.

3. *Presentation of the Resignation.* Ordinarily a resignation remains without effect till it has been submitted to the competent superior and accepted by him. General or particular law determines whether and by whom resignation from the various offices must be accepted.

Even when acceptance proper is not required, the

resignation must still be presented to the superior who conferred the office or to the one who holds his place, and this also under pain of nullity. Thus, when the appointment has been by election and confirmation or by postulation and admission or by nomination and institution, the resignation must be presented to the superior who possesses the ordinary right of confirming the election or admitting the postulation or giving the investiture, not to the one who might enjoy it in extraordinary cases, *v.g.* by devolution, still less to the electors, postulators, or patrons. Practically this means that in a diocese offices are resigned into the hands of the Bishop or of the Vicar Capitular (Can. 455), not of the Vicar-General unless he has a special mandate (Can. 455, 3), never in the hands of lay persons. (Can. 2400.)

Once legitimately handed in, resignation can not be withdrawn, but the same person may be appointed again. If acceptance is required and the superior refuses it this annuls the resignation.

343. 4. *Acceptance of Resignations.* (*a*) Superiors would act unlawfully, although validly, if they accepted resignations without just and proportionate causes.

(*b*) When it is the Ordinary of the place who has to pronounce on a resignation he must decide within a month whether he accepts it or not. This rule can not bind the Sovereign Pontiff and does not directly apply to religious superiors.

(*c*) As soon as the ecclesiastic who tendered his resignation has been duly informed that it is accepted, the office becomes vacant *ipso facto.* His responsibility ceases at that moment but not before; he should not give up the office until he is sure of the acceptance, either from an official document or at least from reliable testimony.

(*d*) Notice of the resignation must also be sent in due time to all persons who may have something to do with the filling of the vacancy, like the patrons, electors, etc.

344. 5. *Tacit or Equivalent Resignation.* (Can. 188.) By special disposition of the law, certain explicitly determined facts, of themselves and without the formalities of presentation, acceptance, or declaration, produce the same effects as resignation. They are the following:

(*a*) Religious profession, whether simple or solemn, temporary or perpetual; by it all the offices not connected with a benefice which the professed cleric possessed become vacant *ipso facto;* the beneficial offices which are parochial become vacant after a year, the others after three years.

(*b*) Failure to take possession of an office within the time determined by general law or, in the absence of such legal prescription, by the Ordinary. This negligence, when culpable, is punished with loss of the office to which one had been appointed, and the loss is incurred *ipso facto* as soon as the time elapses.

(*c*) Acceptance of an incompatible office. A cleric who accepts and obtains pacific, *i.e.* uncontested possession, of an office which the law considers as incompatible with one he has already loses the latter, and if he attempted to retain the old with the new one he would lose both. (Can. 156.)

(*d*) Public defection from the faith, by formal heresy or apostasy, with or without affiliation with another religious society. The offence must be public, that is, generally known or liable to become so before long. (Can. 2197.)

(*e*) Marriage, valid or invalid, even though it be a merely civil ceremony. A cleric in minor Orders can marry validly and even lawfully, but he forfeits thereby all ecclesiastical offices he may hold. *A fortiori*, marriage attempted by one in sacred Orders has the same effect.

(*f*) Enlisting in the army, in defiance of the law which forbids clerics to volunteer for military service, except in some special cases with the Ordinary's permission. (Can. 141.)

(*g*) Putting off the ecclesiastical dress, without authorization and without just cause, and continuing in this disobedience for a whole month after an admonition has been received from the Ordinary.

(*h*) Neglect of residence. An ecclesiastic who does not observe residence as prescribed by the canons and has received a warning from his Ordinary loses his office if he does not, when he could, return to his post or offer a satisfactory explanation within the time appointed by his superior.

II. PRIVATION. (Can. 192.)

345. 1. *Nature and Various Forms.* (*a*) Privation of office, in general, implies the taking away of that office from its holder, independently of his consent and, ordinarily, because of some fault or demerit.

In some cases the law itself decrees the privation, as, for example, against the *excommunicati vitandi* (Can. 2266; cf. Can. 1439, 2398, 188), or the competent ecclesiastical superior may pronounce it by condemnatory sentence or particular decision.

(*b*) Privation pronounced by the ecclesiastical superior may be judicial, administrative, or informal.

Judicial privation supposes a canonical offence, requires a regular trial, and has a strictly penal character.

Administrative or economic privation, more commonly called removal, does not necessarily presuppose any offence or guilt and is not in itself a punishment; jurisprudence had introduced it little by little and Pius X, in the decree *Maxima Cura* (Aug. 20, 1910), embodied afterwards in the Code, gave it full legal recognition and prescribed for it a special mode of procedure. (Can. 2147-2161.)

An ecclesiastical office may also, in some cases, be taken away without any other formalities than those demanded by natural equity.

346. 2. *Application.* (*a*) To deprive an ecclesiastic of an office to which is attached the privilege of permanency, judicial proceedings must be instituted against him, unless the office be a parochial one, in which case law permits administrative removal. (Can. 2147.) A trial is likewise required for all privations of a strictly penal character, whether the office be a removable or an irremovable one.

The economic or administrative form is prescribed for removals from parishes even when these are not irremovable, and may be used also when they are.

Deprivation of removable offices other than parishes may be pronounced in an informal manner, provided it be not in the nature of canonical punishment.

(*b*) Judicial privation can be pronounced only for some canonical offence, and when the office is an irremovable one the offence must be one of those specified by law. It may be pronounced also for other reasonable causes when the office is not irremovable. (Can. 2299.)

Although administrative removal does not presuppose guilt, it is permitted only for certain causes determined by law, at least in a general manner. (Can. 2147.)

Any cause which the Ordinary considers just and legitimate suffices for informal privation.

(*c*) From a decision imposing judicial or administrative privation appeal is allowed under the conditions defined by law (Can. 1879, 2146, 2153); against a decree of informal privation there is only recourse to the Holy See *in devolutivo.*

III. TRANSFER. (Can. 193-194.)

(Decretal., L. I, Tit. vii, De Translatione Episcopi; Wernz, II, n. 516-531; Thomassin, P. II, l. i, c. 15-21; l, ii, c. 60-64; Maroto, n. 688 ff.)

347. 1. *Nature and Kinds.* (*a*) Transfer may be defined as the change of an ecclesiastic from one office to another specifically or numerically different, by the competent authority. The Decretals treat *ex professo* only of transfers of Bishops; the Code deals here with the subject in general. It gives in other sections special rules for some transfers in particular. (Can. 430, 2162-2167.)

(*b*) A transfer may be voluntary and made with the consent of the ecclesiastic concerned, or compulsory and imposed on him by higher authority; the latter may be effected, like privation, in a judicial, administrative, or informal manner.

2. *Authority Required for It.* Transfer implying removal from, or resignation of, one office and appointment to another, it can be made only by the superior who has power to pronounce the privation or accept the resignation of the office to be relin-

quished and to confer the other one. Who this superior is in a given case depends on the nature of the office; the general principles on appointments, resignations, or privations, and more specifically the rules which govern the various offices, must decide. Regularly, transfers of Bishops are reserved to the Pope and those from minor offices to the Ordinary of the diocese.

3. *Causes.* (*a*) Any reasonable cause suffices for the lawfulness of voluntary transfers or also of compulsory but not penal transfers from removable offices other than parishes. The importance of the office should naturally be taken into account; authors mention the necessity or utility of the Church as justifying episcopal transfers. A less serious reason would no doubt suffice for the transfer of a pastor. Absence of just cause would not annul the act.

(*b*) Judicial or penal and administrative transfers presuppose an equally or almost equally grave cause as privations of the same kind, and the law permits them in about the same cases; it does not, however, specify any offence as liable to punishment by transfer nor does it allow the administrative transfer of an irremovable pastor against his will or that of a removable pastor to a parish of too inferior a rank. For this special faculties would have to be obtained from the Holy See. As a general reason for the administrative transfer of a removable pastor to a parish of about the same importance it gives the good of souls. (Can. 2162-2167.)

348. 4. *Procedure.* (*a*) No legal formalities are required for voluntary transfers, nor for compulsory transfers from removable offices other than parishes, unless they be imposed by way of punishment.

(*b*) For the administrative transfer of pastors the

Code prescribes a special mode of procedure. (Can. 2162-2167.)

(*c*) When transfer is imposed as punishment for some canonical offence, which the ecclesiastical superior may do for serious reasons although the law does not command it in any case, the ordinary form of judicial trial must be observed.

5. *Effect.* (*a*) In the transfer of an ecclesiastic from one office to another the first office becomes vacant when the second one has been taken possession of, unless otherwise provided by law or by the competent superior in an individual case. Thus, as soon as a Bishop is notified of his transfer his connection with his actual diocese changes and he becomes its Vicar Capitular or Administrator; still, the vacancy becomes complete only when he takes possession of the other diocese. (Can. 430, § 3, 1°.)

(*b*) In like manner the transferred ecclesiastic continues entitled to the revenues of the first office till he comes into possession of the second.

IV. EXCLUSIVE RIGHT OF ECCLESIASTICAL SUPERIORS IN THESE MATTERS. (Can. 195.)

349. The privilege granted to a person to cooperate in the appointment to an ecclesiastical office by election, postulation, or presentation does not give him any authority over the ecclesiastic thus appointed and does not carry with it the right of removing him, accepting his resignation, or transferring him. These last acts suppose jurisdiction; they represent an exercise of the power of ruling in the Church and must belong exclusively to canonically constituted superiors. This principle, implied very clearly in what precedes, the Code formally affirms here again, probably because of illegitimate claims occasionally put forth by electors or patrons.

TITLE V

ORDINARY AND DELEGATED POWER

(Can. 196-210.)

(Decretal., L. I, Tit. XXIX, XXXI; Wernz, II, n. 545 ff.; Blat, p. 130 ff.; Maroto, n. 694.)

With ecclesiastical offices are normally connected some powers of Order or of jurisdiction; clerics may, moreover, receive communication of the same powers independently of any office. Of these various powers which ecclesiastics may possess by reason of their office or otherwise, the Code treats here, laying down general rules for their acquisition, transmission, exercise, and extinction. It deals almost exclusively with jurisdiction, but it contains also some provisions regarding the power of Order, hence the wording of the heading: ordinary and delegated power.

350. 1. *Nature and Chief Divisions of Jurisdiction.* Jurisdiction, or the power of ruling given by Christ to His Church, may be ordinary or delegated, for the internal or the external forum, voluntary or judicial.

(*a*) Ordinary jurisdiction. (i) Nature. The ordinary jurisdiction is the one connected with an office in a permanent manner by the law itself, so that it regularly follows the office whoever may be the holder and does not exist without it; as, for example, the powers which make up the office of Bishop and those attached to it by common law, like the power granted Bishops by the Code to dispense in urgent cases from general obligations (Can. 81; cf. Can. 990, 1043, 506, § 2, 3, 4; 512, § 1; 603, § 1; 1491, 1492), but not the faculties given them by indult or as privileges, even though the concession be habitual.

(ii) Proper and vicarious jurisdiction. Ordinary jurisdiction may be proper or vicarious, that is, an ecclesiastic who possesses jurisdiction by reason of his office may exercise it in his own name or in the name of another. Ancient canonists more commonly considered vicarious as a form of delegated jurisdiction, others called it quasi-ordinary or mixed (Wernz, n. 545); the Code defines it as ordinary. There remains no doubt henceforth that Vicars-General, for example, have ordinary jurisdiction.

351. (iii) Ordinaries and Vicars. All ecclesiastics possessing ordinary jurisdiction might be termed Ordinaries, but the Code uses the title in a more limited sense and explicitly reserves it to the following: the Roman Pontiff, the Ordinary of Ordinaries, whose jurisdiction extends to all countries and all Christians, residential Bishops, Abbots or Prelates Nullius, and their Vicars-General; Administrators, Vicars and Prefects Apostolic. All these have ordinary jurisdiction in their respective territories over their own subjects, the *incolae,* the *advenae,* the *vagi* and also, in some measure, over the *peregrini* (Can. 14, 94); they are called local Ordinaries, *Ordinarii loci.* Major superiors of exempt clerical Orders have also ordinary jurisdiction over their subjects and come under the name of Ordinaries but not local Ordinaries. Moreover, any one who, by disposition of law or of approved constitution, takes the place of, or serves as substitute for, one of the Ordinaries here enumerated, acquires a right to the same title; thus the Vicar Capitular is the Ordinary of the diocese during the vacancy of the see.

Cardinals, Legates Apostolic, Patriarchs, Primates, and Metropolitans as such, Titular Bishops, Coadjutors and Auxiliary Bishops, Superiors of Missions not erected into Prefectures Apostolic, officials or vice-officials in diocesan courts, Vicars Forane, and pastors are not considered by law as Ordinaries although they possess ordinary jurisdiction.

The Code does not give the list of ecclesiastics who hold the canonical position of Vicars; it designates by that name: the Cardinal Vicar of Rome, Vicars Apostolic, Vicars Capitular, Vicars Forane, Vicars Parochial, Vicars of Superiors in Religious Orders. All these must, then, be considered as possessing some vicarious power even if it be only that of giving assistance in the form which remains to be determined by the superior who receives it. Legates Apostolic, Administrators, Prefects, and others exercise also vicarious jurisdiction.

352. (*b*) Delegated jurisdiction. (i) Nature. Delegated jurisdiction is one which a person possesses not by virtue of his office but by special commission. It is conferred upon him directly by the competent superior or even by law, but independently of his position. Thus delegation may be *a jure* or *ab homine.* Jurisdiction granted by law becomes *ipso facto* ordinary when it is connected with an office, but where no such connection exists it remains delegated. The powers granted to inferiors to dispense in certain matters from the laws of superiors, those given by law to all priests, even if they hold no office, to absolve from all sins and censures in danger of death (Can. 884), are examples of delegation *a jure.* These seem rarer under the present law, as several of the powers formerly exercised by Bishops as delegates of the Apostolic See have become attached to their office and, therefore, ordinary. (Can. 506, § 2, 4; 512, § 1; 603, § 1; Maroto, n. 699, 7°; 705.)

(ii) Particular and general delegation. Jurisdiction may be delegated for special, well-determined cases, *v.g.* for one confession, for ten marriages; or it may be general, *ad universitatem negotiorum,* including all the powers attached to a certain office, as in the case of a pastor absenting himself from his parish and leaving a substitute with full authority. Delegation for all that pertains, for example, to marriage or concerns the Religious of a diocese would also be general or universal as regards a certain kind of affairs. (Maroto, n. 705, 728.)

353. (*c*) Jurisdiction for the internal and for the external forum. (i) To the internal or private forum, called also *forum conscientiae,* belong all matters which, either of their own nature or because they have remained secret, concern directly man as an individual, his personal sanctification and salvation, his relations to God, although indirectly they may affect also the community and social order. Its jurisdiction is exercised in private, before God, not necessarily in secret, but without the Church authorities taking official cognizance of or giving any recognition to its acts. It may be exercised in connection with the administration of the sacrament of penance, *in foro sacramentali,* as in the absolution from sins, or outside of the sacred tribunal, as in dispensations from vows, from occult irregularities, marriage impediments or censures.

(ii) Jurisdiction of the external forum has for its object matters which directly affect the ecclesiastical society or the individual in his relations to the society. It is exercised *in facie Ecclesiae,* which does not necessarily mean in public, but in such manner that its acts may have juridical value and be capable of proof. To this forum belongs the legislative, judicial, coercive, administrative power strictly so called, also the concession of faculties for absolving, although absolution itself pertains to the internal forum.

354. (*d*) Voluntary and judicial jurisdiction. Voluntary jurisdiction, in the Code, is equivalent to non-judicial (Can. 201, § 3) and opposed to judicial, not as formerly in the teaching of many canonists, to contentious or non-voluntary; this distinction, therefore, is based not so much on the object of the jurisdiction as in the manner of proceeding in its exercise.

(i) Judicial jurisdiction ordinarily requires for its exercise the formalities described in the first part of the fourth book of the Code, which treats of Judgments. Contentious and criminal causes form its almost exclusive object. Absolution from sin in the tribunal of penance is, however, considered as a judicial act, although it belongs to the internal forum and does not presuppose all that a canonical trial implies.

(ii) Voluntary jurisdiction is exercised without strictly judicial, although not always without certain legal, forms. The administrative removal of pastors is an act of voluntary jurisdiction, as are also all acts of the legislative and administrative power, like the enactment of rules, concession of favors, dispensations from impediments, etc.

355. 2. *Delegation of Jurisdiction.* (Can. 199.) (*a*) Ordinary jurisdiction can be delegated wholly or in part, unless otherwise provided by law. Such provisions are met with in the Code; thus it explicitly forbids the Canon Penitentiarius (Can. 401) and implicitly parish priests (Can. 874, 875) to delegate their power to hear confessions or to absolve from reserved sins.

The delegation should not be both total and permanent, otherwise it would amount to resignation of office, which requires the competent superior's intervention.

(*b*) Jurisdiction delegated by the Holy See may be subdelegated either habitually or for a definite number of cases, unless this has been implicitly or explicitly prohibited, or unless the rescript or some other circumstance shows that the delegate was chosen because of his personal qualifications.

(*c*) Jurisdiction received from other superiors than the Sovereign Pontiff can be subdelegated only when it is general or *ad universitatem negotiorum,* and then only for particular specified cases, not habitually.

(*d*) Jurisdiction received by particular delegation from any other than the Supreme Authority can not be subdelegated except by special permission; it would require also an explicit permission to delegate again subdelegated jurisdiction. This rule does not apply to merely incidental, not strictly juridical, acts, and a delegated judge, for example, would not need a special authorization to commit to another person the translation of a document.

356. 3. *Interpretation of Jurisdiction and Proof of Delegation.* (Can. 200.) (*a*) The law permits the interpretation of ordinary jurisdiction and general delegations in a favorable, broad sense, supposing that the nature of the matter or other circumstances, like respect for the acquired rights of another person, do not demand a strict interpretation.

Particular delegations and all subdelegations must, on the contrary, be interpreted in a strict sense whenever any doubt arises as to their meaning or extent. They must, however, always be understood to include all the powers necessary for their exercise, *v.g.* the power of dispensing from censures, impediments, etc., if otherwise the delegation would be useless.

(*b*) Delegation being a fact, it should not be presumed but proved whenever a doubt arises about it or its existence is contested. The law supposes that it is granted in writing (Can. 206) without, however, making this a condition for the validity nor for the proof of authenticity; in the absence of a written document other evidence may suffice.

357. 4. *Exercise of Jurisdiction.* (Can. 201-206.) The Code here lays down the general condition for the exercise of jurisdiction and then gives special rules for its various kinds: judicial and voluntary, internal and external, and delegated.

(*a*) General condition. A person possessing jurisdiction can directly exercise it only over his subjects, that is, over persons or things placed under his authority. Indirectly he may exercise it over other people, because, for example, they entered into some contract or committed some offence within his territory. Which matters or persons come under the authority of a particular superior directly or indirectly must be gathered from various provisions of the law, such as those which define the extent of territorial jurisdiction (Can. 14), the relations of a Bishop to his clerics or of a superior to his subjects in a Religious Order, the competency of courts in judicial matters (Can. 1556-1568), etc.

358. (*b*) Special rules for judicial and non-judicial power. (i) Judicial power, whether ordinary or delegated, may not be exercised for one's own benefit, on the principle that one should not be at the same time judge and plaintiff or defendant; nor may it be used outside of one's own territory. A priest having ordinary jurisdiction may, however, absolve his subjects in any part of the world (Can. 881), and a judge expelled from his territory or prevented from discharging there the duties of his office may hold court elsewhere. (Can. 1637.)

Non-judicial or voluntary jurisdiction, on the contrary, unless the matter itself does not permit or the law forbids it in a special case, may be used for one's own benefit and outside of one's own territory, even when both the superior and the subject would be outside of the territory. Thus he who has the required faculties may dispense himself from fasting, from a vow. He could not, from the nature of the matter, absolve himself from censure, administer to himself a sacrament, or give to himself the blessing *in articulo mortis.* The Church forbids an elector to vote for himself or a superior to confer a benefice upon himself. Rescripts granting special faculties sometimes contain the explicit prohibition to use them outside of the territory.

(ii) In judicial matters, when a case is brought before a higher authority it passes entirely out of the hands of the lower judge, who ceases to have any jurisdiction over it; but in non-judicial ones recourse to a superior of higher rank does not suspend the powers, whether ordinary or delegated, of the inferior. The latter should, however, abstain from interfering in the case any longer, unless grave and urgent reasons compel him to do otherwise, and then he ought to notify the superior. Thus, if while a marriage is under investigation by the episcopal court the parties take it to the Apostolic Delegate, the Bishop, out of respect for the representative of the Holy See, ought to stop his own procedure; but should he go on even as far as the sentence his action would be valid.

359. (*c*) Exercise of jurisdiction of the internal and the external forum. (Can. 202.) (i) Jurisdiction, whether ordinary or delegated, must be exercised only in the forum for which it is intended; thus the power given to absolve a sinner can not be used where the Church demands an external reconciliation and reparation, nor will the faculties granted for this reconciliation suffice for the administration of the sacrament of penance. But an act of jurisdiction granted for and exercised in the external forum produces its effect also in the internal forum; for example, absolution which frees a man from censure externally, in the eyes of the Church, frees him also in conscience, before God; a dispensation from a public impediment secures the validity of marriage both in the internal and in the external forum. The same principle does not apply to acts of the internal jurisdiction; their effect does not regularly go beyond the forum of conscience. A dispensation granted in the internal forum does not remove a marriage impediment as far as the public and the ecclesiastical society are concerned, although it suffices for the validity of the contract in itself, and if the impediment becomes public afterwards the marriage will be null in the eyes of the Church till a new dispensation is applied. To simplify matters, however, the new Code permits, when such dispensations from occult impediments are granted, provided it be not in the tribunal of penance, that a record be kept of them in a special register, so that they may serve for the external forum also should the impediment become public. (Can. 1047.) It provides likewise that, whilst a person absolved from a censure only in the internal forum is not really absolved in the eyes of the public and of the Church, he may, nevertheless, act even externally as if he was, and claim again the privileges of which the censure had deprived him, provided all danger of scandal be avoided. Superiors may recognize his claims and allow him to receive the sacraments, perform the sacred functions, etc., but they are not bound to do so, and they retain the right of enforcing the censure till the reception of absolution be duly established or a new one be obtained. (Can. 2251.)

(ii) Jurisdiction of the internal forum is more ordinarily exercised in the tribunal of penance, *in foro sacramentali,* not necessarily so, however, and it may be exercised outside, as well as in, the sacred tribunal unless the latter mode of proceeding be demanded by the very nature of the case, the law, or the rescript. A person may receive dispensation from a vow, from an irregularity, an impediment, etc., without going to confession.

(iii) In the absence of any indication to the contrary, jurisdiction is supposed granted for both the internal and the external forum. Sometimes the object itself will show that it can be for only one; jurisdiction for the remission of sins is always for the internal and any other judicial power for the external forum.

360. (*d*) Exercise of delegated jurisdiction. (Can. 203, 205, 206.) (i) A delegate must not exceed the limits of his mandate but observe it at least in all its substantial injunctions and not extend it to persons or matters which it does not include, otherwise his act is null and void. Jurisdiction over non-exempt Religious, for example, does not imply authority over the exempt, and a judge in a matrimonial court is not competent to settle litigations about property.

The form of procedure does not, however, pertain to the substance of the mandate and departing in this from the method which has the preference of the delegating superior would not annul the act, unless the manner of proceeding had been specified and made a condition of validity.

(ii) Several delegates may be appointed for the same matter either simultaneously or successively. When appointed simultaneously they may receive the commission *in solidum,* so that each one has full, independent power, or collectively, as a body, the power being conferred not so much on the individuals as on the moral person. In case of doubt, or in the absence of any indication to the contrary, the law interprets a simultaneous appointment as a delegation *in solidum* in non-judicial, and as a collective delegation in judicial, matters. Jurisdiction for the tribunal of penance is, of course, never meant to be exercised *collegialiter.*

When several persons have been delegated *in solidum,* although each one has sufficient power, they can not all act at the same time, and the law provides that the first one who takes up the matter acquires an exclusive right over it. But if afterwards he can not or does not proceed to terminate the affair in due time, another one of the delegates may step in his place.

Collective delegation usually implies that, for the validity of the action, the delegates must all take part in it, the majority deciding in accordance with the rules laid down for collegiate bodies (Can. 1577), but the mandate might prescribe other formalities or dispense from some of the conditions regularly required, permitting, for example, the case to go on provided two of the delegates be present. (21, X, I, 29.)

When several persons have been delegated in succession for the same matter, priority of time carries with it priority of right, unless the first mandate be explicitly abrogated by a subsequent one. Priority of time is determined here, as when it is question of conflicting rescripts, by the date of the concession of delegation, even though the commission had been given verbally. (Can. 48; Maroto, n. 708.)

361. 5. *Cessation of Delegated and Ordinary Jurisdiction.* (207, 208.) (*a*) Delegated jurisdiction. The Code enumerates seven ways in which delegated jurisdiction may cease to exist:

(i) By fulfilment of the mandate. In judicial matters the mandate is fulfilled when the judge has pronounced the final sentence and ordered its execution. Should he discover after this some error or injustice he could not correct it without a new delegation. The normal remedy then would be an appeal.

In non-judicial matters the execution of the decree or the completion of the work assigned to the delegate puts an end to his mandate, but the present law would still allow him to correct a mistake without referring to the superior.

(ii) By lapse of time or completion of the number of cases. This occurs when a term has been fixed for the conduct of the matter, when faculties, for example, are granted for five years or for twenty cases.

For the good of souls, however, the legislator explicitly declares that, in matters of the internal forum, should the delegate, through oversight, continue to use his powers after the time has elapsed or the number of cases is exhausted, his acts would still be valid. This holds only in matters pertaining to the forum of conscience, whether sacramental or nonsacramental, and in cases of error due to inadvertence.

(iii) By cessation of the motive cause of the delegation. The cause must cease to exist entirely and not partially only, and if the delegation had been granted for several reasons, each one sufficient in itself, all of them must have ceased to exist.

(iv) By revocation of the delegation. A superior can at any time withdraw the jurisdiction he has freely granted, even after the case has already begun; he needs a sufficient reason for the lawfulness of his action, not for its validity. The revocation takes effect only when made known to the delegate directly.

This rule applies to subdelegation as well as to delegation, except that when a person has subdelegated all his powers he can not take them back after the case has begun, *re non integra.*

(v) By resignation of the delegate made known to the delegating superior directly and accepted by him. This notification is necessary for the efficacy of the act, and also acceptance by the superior even when the latter can not refuse, because, for example, he would have no authority to force the other party to act as his delegate.

(vi) By loss of the delegating power. Loss of power by the delegating superior does not, as a rule, affect the delegation, but in two cases it causes it to cease: when the delegation depends on the will of the superior, as if granted *ad beneplacitum nostrum,* unless the case has already begun, and when the rescript contains simply a *gratia facienda* and nothing has yet been done in the matter, *re integra. Gratia facienda* implies only power of granting a favor to certain expressly designated persons. (Can. 61; Maroto, n. 289, 712.)

(vii) When several delegates have been appointed to act collectively, if one of them, for whatever cause, loses his power all the others lose it also, unless provided otherwise in the delegation, as when it is stipulated that in the absence of the other delegates two or three shall have authority to decide the question. Ordinarily, the cooperation of all is necessary and full jurisdiction resides only in the complete body.

362. (*b*) Ordinary jurisdiction. It ceases with the loss of the office to which it was attached and the office itself, as said before (Can. 183), is not lost by the mere fact of the superior who conferred it going out of power, except in a few cases, like that of Vicars-General (Can. 371), or when the appointment was made *ad beneplacitum superioris.* But if not lost as long as the office is retained, ordinary jurisdiction may be limited in various ways both as to persons and matters by exemptions (Can. 464, 615) and reservations (Can. 893, 1435, 2245, etc.); it may also be temporarily suspended by censures (Can. 2264, 2284) and by appeals *in suspensivo,* not merely *in devolutivo,* to higher authority.

6. *Supplied Jurisdiction.* (Can. 209.) To secure the validity of acts which otherwise would be invalid the Church supplies the needed jurisdiction in cases of common error and of doubt.

363. (*a*) In the ancient Roman law it was a

recognized principle that juridical acts of a person commonly believed to have the necessary power although he has not must be sustained for the sake of the common good. A certain slave by the name of Barbarius Philippus had come to Rome, and giving himself out as a free man and Roman citizen, succeeded in rising to the pretorian dignity. When the fraud became known the question arose whether the nullity of his election vitiated all the acts of his administration. The negative answer, based on the demands of the general good and on the power of the Roman people to give value to those acts, obtained the force of a law known as the *lex Barbarius.*

Canonists admitted that the Church had accepted the principle involved in it; they concluded this from the close relations existing between civil and ecclesiastical law and from various texts in the *Corpus Juris,* particularly the chapter *Infamis* in Gratian's Decree (c.1. C. III, q. 7) and the chapter *Ad probandum* in the Decretals (c. 24, X, II, 27), but they did not agree as to the conditions required for the Church to supply the jurisdiction. Besides the common error, about which there could be no controversy, many demanded what they called a *titulus coloratus,* an apparent title, as existed in the case of Barbarius, who had been elected pretor but did not really obtain the office because he suffered from a disability. (Reiffenstuel, II, i, n. 198; Santi, II, 14.) Some, whose opinion tended to prevail in modern times, argued that the chief reason for the Church to supply jurisdiction in such cases being to protect the interests of souls, and as this reason exists independently of the *titulus coloratus,* of which the faithful know very little, its presence or absence should make no real difference. (D'Annibale, o.c., n. 79; Lega, I, n. 352.)

The Code adopts this second view and declares that the Church supplies the jurisdiction, both for the internal and the external forum, in cases of common error, without any mention of *titulus coloratus.*

The error must be shared in by all the people with the possible exception of only a few, at the time and in the place where the jurisdiction is exercised, but these few are not prevented by their knowledge from taking advantage of the concession made in favor of the community. The Church supplies the jurisdiction for the sake of the faithful exclusively, it does not supply the title; the superior remains really without power and, if conscious of it, acts unlawfully although validly.

364. (*b*) It had been likewise the teaching of canonists for a long time that the Church supplied the jurisdiction as far as needed when it was doubtful, but commonly they admitted this only for the doubt of law, *dubium juris.* Some, however, made no difference between the doubt of law and that of fact as long as it was not merely negative but rested on some evidence sufficient to give, if not certainty, at least real probability to the opinion in favor of the existence of jurisdiction. (D'Annibale, o.c., I, n. 80.)

Here again the Code officially confirms the more liberal view. The Church certainly supplies now jurisdiction for both the internal and the external forum, whether the doubt is one of right or of fact, as long as it is a positive and truly probable one.

A person, then, who is not sure whether a certain matter comes under his authority, whether such a sin, for example is reserved, whether faculties he obtained formerly have expired, should first inquire if he can, and if the investigation shows that probably, although not certainly, he possesses the necessary powers, he may act on this probability, at least whenever he has a reasonable cause for doing so. (Noldin, De Poenitentia, n. 355; Maroto, n. 731, 5a.)

365. 7. *Powers of Order.* (Can. 210.) As said before, the powers of Order in the Church are some of divine and some of ecclesiastical institutions. Those of divine institution, *v.g.* the power of offering the Holy Sacrifice, of administering the sacraments, are transmitted exclusively through the sacramental rites; there can be no question of delegating them or committing them to others in any different manner.

The powers of ecclesiastical institution are usually also connected with a sacred rite, but they may be communicated in any way chosen by the Church. Sometimes they are attached to certain offices, those for example, which go with the office of Prefect Apostolic (Can. 294, § 2), the consecrations regularly performed by Cardinals (Can. 239, § 1, n. 20) or by Bishops (Can. 323, § 2); at other times they may be committed to individual ecclesiastics by special indult, *v.g.* the power of confirming granted to a priest. They thus partake of the nature of ordinary and delegated powers.

Here the Code enacts that, whether attached to an office or committed to a person, power of Order can not be delegated or communicated to others unless expressly permitted by law or by indult. Formerly Ordinaries in the United States were authorized to depute priests for the consecration of chalices, patens, and altar stones. (Formula T, n. 26.)

TITLE VI

RETURN OF CLERICS TO THE LAY STATE

(Can. 211-214.)

366. 1. *Nature.* Sacred ordination once received can not be annulled; the character imprinted in the soul by the sacrament of Orders is indelible and the powers conferred through it inamissible. They can always be exercised validly and a deposed or degraded cleric does not have to go through the ceremony of ordination again when he is reinstated. This applies even to tonsure and to the Orders commonly considered as of ecclesiastical institution.

A clergyman, then, can never, strictly speaking, become a layman again, but he may return to the lay state, that is, lose the rights and privileges of clerics, so that, in this respect, he will be in the same condition as a layman. The change is juridical, not theological. Ecclesiastical history and legislation offer us numerous examples of ecclesiastics deprived of their clerical status by way of punishment or allowed to return to the lay state even after promotion to sacred Orders.

367. 2. *Modes.* The law makes a clear distinction here between clerics in major and those in minor Orders.

(*a*) Clerics in major Orders may return or be reduced to the lay state chiefly in three ways: (i) By rescript of the Holy See, freeing them from the obligations but also taking away from them the privileges of the clerical state. Dispensation from the law of celibacy or permission to marry is ordinarily conditioned explicitly on return to the lay state, and even if not expressed this condition would always have to be understood, according to canonists, on account of the incompatibility, more strongly affirmed in the present Code than in the former discipline, between the clerical and the married state. (Can. 132; Maroto, n. 734.)

(ii) By degradation, which entails loss of all ecclesiastical rights and privileges. (Can. 2305; Penal Legislation, n. 172 ff.)

(iii) By special decree or sentence, in cases of ordination received under the influence of grave fear. (Can. 214.)

Lack of consent on the part of the subject would render an ordination invalid, but it might happen that a person would give sufficient consent to receive Orders validly and yet do so under moral coercion, yielding to grave fear. An injustice is thereby done him, and to remedy it the Church provides that such a person does not contract the obligations regularly imposed by the ordination until he freely accepts them. He must do so explicitly or at least implicitly by exercising, once the coercion has ceased, the functions of these Orders, with the intention of ratifying what had been done irregularly. If he does not accept the obligations he must return to the lay state, provided the coercion and absence of subsequent ratification be duly proved.

The Code lays down rules for treating these causes in the fourth book, Can. 1993-1998.

Similar provisions existed in the former legislation in favor of persons ordained before the age of puberty or even before the canonical age. They have not been retained in the final text of the Code as at first intended, probably because, in the Latin Church, ordinations of children occur very seldom, if ever, and if a case presented itself it would suffice to refer it to the Congregation of the Sacraments, which would, no doubt, settle it on the old principles as set forth by Benedict XIV in the Constitution *Eo quamvis tempore.* (May 4, 1745.)

(*b*) Clerics in minor Orders. (i) They return to the lay state *ipso facto* by fulfilment of certain conditions determined by law as having that consequence, for example, when they fail to wear the clerical dress (Can. 136, § 3), when they contract marriage (Can. 132), when they spontaneously enlist in the army. (Can. 141.)

(ii) They may give up the ecclesiastical state if they choose; the law demands only that they notify their Ordinary, without having to wait for his consent.

(iii) The Ordinary may, on his side, for a just cause, decree the return of one of his clerics to the lay state. This just cause exists when in his prudent judgment said cleric does not, everything considered, possess the qualifications which would justify his promotion to sacred Orders. In the present discipline of the Church unfitness for sacred Orders practically implies unfitness for the clerical state. The Bishop pronounces on this in accordance with the rules of prudence and equity, but without being bound by any special legal form; there is no appeal from his decision, but recourse to the Holy See remains always possible.

368. 3. *Effect.* (*a*) By returning to the lay state, clerics, whether in major or in minor Orders, lose *ipso facto,* without any further formality, sentence, or declaration, all the ecclesiastical offices or benefices they may possess and all the clerical rights and privileges. They may not wear any longer the ecclesiastical garb and tonsure.

(*b*) They become free from all the obligations of the ecclesiastical state with the exception of one, *viz.* the obligation of celibacy for clerics in major Orders, and even this one ceases for clerics reduced to the lay state by special decree in cases of forced ordinations.

By explicitly mentioning only celibacy the legislator implicitly teaches that the recitation of the Breviary does not continue obligatory; under the former discipline canonists generally held that degradation did not take away the burden of the Divine Office (Wernz, VI, n. 138); still, in several practical cases, the Congregation of the Council and Clement XI, who was consulted on the subject, refused to give official sanction to this doctrine. (Aug. 13, 1707, Aug. 18, 1708, Dec. 15, 1719; Ferraris, Bibliotheca Canonica, v. Degradatio, n. 9.)

Rescripts of the Holy See reducing clerics in major Orders to the lay state ordinarily include also dispensation from the obligation of celibacy.

369. 4. *Readmission to the Clerical State.* (*a*) Under the present law to readmit to the ranks of the clergy an ecclesiastic in major Orders who had returned or been reduced to the lay state requires the permission of the Holy See.

(*b*) The Ordinary of the diocese has authority to reinstate a cleric in minor Orders, but the legislator directs him to examine the case carefully, to see whether the reasons for the first decision may not still exist, whether the life and character of the petitioner warrant a favorable answer and, if deemed advisable, to submit him to a suitable test. Readmission is granted by the Ordinary of the diocese to which the cleric had been incardinated by ordination, not, for example, by the Ordinary of the place in which the cleric may have his domicile at present.

INDEX

D

E

F

G

H

I

J

L

M

O

PRINTED BY BLASE BENZIGER & CO., INC., NEW YORK